STUDIES IN WEL

Edito

RALPH A. GRIFFITHS

GLANMOR WILLIAMS

———

14

AFTERMATH

REMEMBERING THE GREAT WAR IN WALES

AFTERMATH

REMEMBERING THE GREAT WAR IN WALES

by

ANGELA GAFFNEY

*Published on behalf of the
History and Law Committee
of the Board of Celtic Studies*

**CARDIFF
UNIVERSITY OF WALES PRESS
1998**

First published 1998
Paperback edition 2000

British Library Cataloguing-in-Publication Data
A catalogue record for this book is available from the British Library.

ISBN 0-7083-1680-8

Cover design by Chris Neale
Cover photograph by Kevin Thomas: a detail from the Merthyr Tydfil Borough War Memorial, designed by L. S. Merrifield

Typeset at the University of Wales Press
Printed in Great Britain by Dinefwr Press, Llandybïe, Dyfed

EDITORS' FOREWORD

Since the Second World War, Welsh history has attracted considerable scholarly attention and enjoyed a vigorous popularity. Not only have the approaches, both traditional and new, to the study of history in general been successfully applied to Wales's past, but the number of scholars engaged in this enterprise has multiplied during these years. These advances have been especially marked in the University of Wales.

In order to make more widely available the conclusions of recent research, much of it of limited accessibility in postgraduate dissertations and theses, in 1977 the History and Law Committee of the Board of Celtic Studies inaugurated a new series of monographs, *Studies in Welsh History*. It was anticipated that many of the volumes would originate in research conducted in the University of Wales or under the auspices of the Board of Celtic Studies. But the series does not exclude significant contributions made by researchers in other universities and elsewhere. Its primary aim is to serve historical scholarship and to encourage the study of Welsh history. Each volume so far published has fulfilled that aim in ample measure, and it is a pleasure to welcome the most recent addition to the list.

CONTENTS

LIST OF ILLUSTRATIONS

Between pages 86 and 87

Photographs by Kevin Thomas unless otherwise stated.

PREFACE

I took war memorials very much for granted as I grew up. I did not have to think about them because they were always part of my environment, enduring and unchanging. Their presence in the community was heightened on one Sunday in November but otherwise they blended into the urban and rural landscape and became meeting-places or a useful marker for giving local directions. The inscribed names were often faded and illegible and I accepted, and often ignored, memorials and gave little thought to the reasons why so many communities chose to build their own, local memorial. During my undergraduate studies at Cardiff, I became aware of the National Inventory of War Memorials, based at the Imperial War Museum, and offered my services as a volunteer in the nation-wide recording project. My interest in memorials was thus registered and it seemed a natural progression to research the commemoration of the Great War in Wales as a doctoral thesis. This study is based on the results of that research, but it is not a guide to every obelisk, cross, cenotaph, hall or other site of memory in Wales nor does it document the artistic design or architectural style of Welsh war memorials. It is a study of how the people of Wales remembered their fallen and came to terms with their losses in the aftermath of war. The numerous war memorials in villages, towns and cities throughout Wales remain as testament to their grief and suffering and to the human cost of war.

I am indebted to many people for assistance both during the research for the thesis and in preparing the manuscript for publication. I am grateful for the financial assistance provided by the School of History and Archaeology, Cardiff University; le Centre de Recherche de l'Historial de la Grande Guerre, Péronne, and the Glamorgan County History Trust. The help and information provided by libraries and record offices throughout Wales has been invaluable but particular thanks are due to staff at the Arts and Social Studies Library, Cardiff

University; the National Library of Wales, Aberystwyth; the Department of Manuscripts, University of Wales, Bangor; the Glamorgan Record Office, Cardiff; and the Local Studies Department, Cardiff Central Library. I am most grateful to the officials of town and community councils as well as members of the Royal British Legion and individuals throughout Wales who have responded to my numerous enquiries about local war memorials. My thanks to friends and colleagues at the National Museum & Gallery, Cardiff, and the Centre for Advanced Welsh and Celtic Studies, Aberystwyth, who have followed the progress from thesis to book with much interest and, I think, great forbearance at times. I am particularly grateful to Professor Geraint H. Jenkins for his support. Many people have listened, advised and encouraged along the way including Professor David Bates, Andy Croll, Sue Johns, Bill Jones and Stephanie Jones. I am grateful to the editors of the Studies in Welsh History series for their comments on the original manuscript and to Ceinwen Jones and Liz Powell at the University of Wales Press for their help in preparing the manuscript for publication. Particular thanks are due to Catherine Moriarty both for her professional expertise and for her support from the inception of this work. Her successor at the National Inventory of War Memorials, Nick Hewitt, has been equally helpful and interested in my work. Special thanks to Kevin Thomas for the photographs which have so enhanced the text and I am grateful to him for his skill and enthusiasm for the project.

My family in England and Canada has always supported my return to education and subsequent progress with an enthusiasm and interest far beyond the call of familial obligations. My husband Chris has witnessed and supported the transformation of an initial research idea through to the publication of this book with infinite patience and understanding and he probably now knows more about war memorials than he can ever have thought possible. I remain indebted to my doctoral supervisor, Dr Chris Williams, who guided and inspired my work with consummate professionalism and friendship and gave me the confidence to undertake and complete the thesis. Lastly, this book is dedicated to the memory of my parents who always believed in me and I hope would have been proud.

INTRODUCTION

By the time the guns finally fell silent in November 1918, an estimated nine million men had lost their lives in the Great War; over seven hundred thousand of these were British servicemen.[1] The loss of life on this scale ensured that bereavement became a shared experience throughout Britain as individuals and communities attempted to come to terms with their grief.[2] Memorials to the dead, often in the form of street shrines, had been erected during the course of the war, but the years after the Armistice witnessed a determination to provide a lasting tribute to those who had died. War memorials in virtually every town and village in Britain provide testimony to the need felt by society in the post-war years to commemorate the dead. Wales is no exception, with a prominent 'national' memorial at Cardiff and many local monuments throughout the country, and it is clear that the Great War marked a turning-point in the way society commemorated those killed in battle.

Eighty years after the end of hostilities, public and academic interest in the war and its aftermath has shown no sign of waning and, more recently, studies on Great War memorials have become as widespread and diverse as the memorials themselves.[3] James Mayo's work on American war memorials investigates the relationship between politics and design by demonstrating how war has been expressed symbolically as a political act.[4] A political consensus on the meaning of war could alleviate differences about memorials but Mayo suggests that wars which

[1] J. Winter, *The Great War and the British People* (London, 1986), p. 71.
[2] Adrian Gregory suggests that an estimated three million Britons lost a close relative in the Great War although, as he points out, 'This figure represents only the "primary bereaved" (parents, siblings, widows and orphans). In addition, the "secondary bereaved" ought to be considered, those who lost a cousin, uncle, son-in-law, a colleague, a friend or a neighbour.' *The Silence of Memory* (Oxford, 1994), p. 19.
[3] The National Inventory of War Memorials was set up in 1989 by the Imperial War Museum and the Royal Commission on the Historic Monuments of England. The aim is to establish an archive holding information on the estimated 50,000–60,000 war memorials throughout the British Isles.
[4] J. M. Mayo, *War Memorials as Political Landscape: The American Experience and Beyond* (New York, 1988).

the United States is perceived not to have won, such as Korea and Vietnam, aroused contention and controversy about the most appropriate manner to remember those who had died.[5] War memorials as repositories of diverse political messages have also proved to be a useful historical source. For example, George Mosse's work has shown how the memory of war in Germany was 'reshaped' into a virtually sacred experience and thus strengthened the nationalist cause.[6] Antoine Prost's comprehensive work on French memorials established a typology and suggested that the 'commemorations around these memorials illustrated the deep unity of French national sentiment and the strength of the adhesion to the republican State'.[7] In Australia, the frequent naming of all who served, combined with the absence of conscription, imbued war memorials with a very different meaning and acted as a reminder to those who had not volunteered: 'the missing names were those of the "eligibles", the shirkers, their absence a subtextual *dis*-honouring'.[8]

Alex King's recent detailed work on commemoration in Britain in the inter-war years suggests that commemoration was concerned with far more than mourning those who had died and became essentially a political act. His work seeks to reconstruct the meaning of commemoration for contemporaries by an analysis of the creative process involved in remembering the dead:

---

[5] Ibid., pp. 169–209.

[6] George L. Mosse, *Fallen Soldiers: Reshaping the Memory of the World Wars* (New York, 1990). In an earlier work, Mosse discussed the utilization of monuments by the Nazis: 'National monuments continued to be viewed as sacred places, as secular, national shrines, frameworks for acts of national worship.' *The Nationalization of the Masses* (New York, 1975), see esp. pp. 47–72. The ambiguities inherent in Soviet memorials erected after the Second World War have been discussed in an article by Michael Ignatieff, 'Soviet war memorials', *History Workshop Journal*, XVII (1984), pp. 157–63.

[7] Antoine Prost, 'Mémoires locales et mémoires nationales: les monuments de 1914–1918 en France', *Guerres mondiales et conflits contemporains*, CLXVII (Paris, 1992), pp. 41–50 (English summary, p. 174).

[8] K. S. Inglis and Jock Phillips, 'War memorials in Australia and New Zealand: a comparative survey', in J. Rickard and P. Spearritt (eds.), *Packaging the Past? Public Histories*, special issue of *Australian Historical Studies*, XXIV, No. 96 (1991), pp. 179–91 (p. 186, italics in text). See also K. S. Inglis, 'World War One memorials in Australia', *Guerres mondiales et conflits contemporains*, CLXVII (Paris, 1992), pp. 51–8, and K. S. Inglis, 'Memorials of the Great War', *Australian Cultural History*, VI (1987), pp. 5–17; C. Maclean and J. Phillips, *The Sorrow and the Pride: New Zealand War Memorials* (Wellington, NZ, 1990). For Canada, see R. Shipley, *To Mark Our Place: A History of Canadian War Memorials* (Toronto, 1987).

This process was fundamentally political, because it relied for its organisation on the institutions of local politics, on the press, and on other forms of association whose activities, if not overtly political, had political implications . . . Personal feelings and needs were deeply involved in the practice of commemoration, but political organisation played an essential part in giving it form.[9]

There is no doubt that the commemoration process, whether in an urban or a rural environment, was essentially a business arrangement and was as open to attempted physical or psychological manipulation by interested parties as any other local enterprise. Remembering the dead afforded many opportunities for competing factions to emerge, whether motivated by civic, commercial, political, secular or spiritual concerns, and a degree of flexibility is necessary in interpreting the role of political motivation which would allow acknowledgement of other significant influences within local commemorative schemes. The potential 'propaganda' opportunities offered by the commemoration process to those seeking to disseminate political or moral values are clear, but caution is necessary in interpreting the scale and success of such attempts, as a plurality of approaches and responses to memorials and the commemoration process is apparent.

The study of war memorials from an art-historical standpoint has, until recently, been less prominent in the historiography. Arnold Whittick's book published in 1946 placed emphasis on aesthetic qualities, with the intention of influencing the new spate of memorials being planned after the Second World War, and it was not until 1991 that Alan Borg undertook the ambitious task of examining war memorials as a distinctive art form 'from antiquity to the present'.[10] The most notable contribution to this

---

[9] Alexander M. King, 'The politics of meaning in the commemoration of the First World War in Britain, 1914–1939' (unpublished Ph.D. thesis, University of London, 1993), p. 11. Bob Bushaway has argued for the importance of war commemoration in understanding inter-war politics in the United Kingdom. He suggests that war memorials were 'emblems of remembrance for the post-war world, in which the dominant theme was that of sacrifice for the greater good. This interpretation of Britain's war losses constrained the development of popular socio-political criticisms of post-war conditions.' 'Name upon name: the Great War and remembrance', in Roy Porter (ed.), *Myths of the English* (Cambridge, 1992), pp. 136–67.
[10] Arnold Whittick, *War Memorials* (London, 1946); Alan Borg, *War Memorials from Antiquity to the Present* (London, 1991).

field of research is Catherine Moriarty's comprehensive work on figurative First World War memorials.[11] There can be no doubt that different approaches have contributed to our knowledge and understanding of war memorials, but little work has been undertaken on the social history of commemoration, focusing on the importance of memorials to the generations who lived through the conflict and struggled to come to terms with the emotional impact of the Great War.[12] Similarly, local responses and reactions to the war as embodied in the commemoration process have attracted little attention. Ken Inglis has noted that:

> In most studies so far, whether by art historians, war buffs, or students of *mentalités*, the memorial itself, the material object, has been the only or the principal source read, and the scrutiny has yielded some rich insights. It may now be time for scholars to look behind the memorials to the stories of their making.[13]

The Second World War and subsequent conflicts prompted a new era of commemoration although names of the fallen were often added to existing memorials. For example, the figurative Boer War memorial at Rhyl in north Wales was amended to

---

[11] Catherine Moriarty, 'Narrative and the absent body: mechanisms of meaning in First World War memorials' (unpublished Ph.D. thesis, University of Sussex, 1995). See also Catherine Moriarty, 'The absent dead and figurative First World War memorials', *Transactions of the Ancient Monuments Society*, XXXIX (1995), pp. 7–40.

[12] 'From the Acropolis to the Arc de Triomphe, war memorials have been central to the history of European architecture and public sculpture. They have been important symbols of national pride. But however powerful the aesthetic or political message they carried or attracted, these monuments had another meaning for the generation that passed through the trauma of the war. That meaning was as much existential as artistic or political, as much concerned with the facts of individual loss and bereavement as with art forms or with collective representations, national aspirations, and destinies.' Jay Winter, *Sites of Memory, Sites of Mourning: The Great War in European Cultural History* (Cambridge, 1995), p. 79. See also J. M. Winter, 'Communities in mourning' in Frans Coetzee and Marilyn Shevin-Coetzee (eds.), *Authority, Identity and the Social History of the Great War* (Oxford, 1995), pp. 325–55.

[13] K. S. Inglis, 'The homecoming: the war memorial movement in Cambridge, England', *Journal of Contemporary History*, XXVII, No. 4 (1992), pp. 583–605 (p. 585, italics in text). See also M. L. Connelly, 'The commemoration of the Great War in the City and East London, 1916–1939' (unpublished Ph.D. thesis, University of London, 1995). Recent examples of work on war and remembrance include Martin Evans and Ken Lunn (eds.), *War and Memory in the Twentieth Century* (Oxford, 1997) and Alex Bruce, *Monuments, Memorials and the Local Historian* (London, Historical Association, 1997). For general guides to British war memorials, see Derek Boorman, *At the Going Down of the Sun: British First World War Memorials* (York, 1988); and Colin McIntyre, *Monuments of War: How to Read a War Memorial* (London, 1990).

include the names of the fallen from the Great War.[14] This was repeated after the Second World War but the town also sought a separate yet complementary act of remembrance for this conflict. A garden of remembrance was built from reclaimed sandhills by local labour and subscription, and in August 1948 the memorial was moved from the promenade to the nearby garden; it remains an oasis of peace and quiet amidst the noise of a busy seaside resort. The names of those who died in the Falklands War and in Northern Ireland have subsequently been added to the memorial.[15] Memorials to such later conflicts have been described as 'little more than obligatory gestures to the memorial tradition' and it has been said that they do not

> spring from a genuine response to the tragedy of war. It is this that distinguishes the First World War memorials, for they were designed and built out of authentic feelings of pride and sorrow. In examining the various forms they took it is important to remember that they were envisaged as 'living' memorials, to recall for current and future generations the sacrifice of war.[16]

There is no doubt that it is the memory of the Great War that remains etched on the landscape in the tangible form of war memorials, and detailed study of the means by which communities argued, co-operated and compromised over their building reveals how the experience and memory of the war pervaded society in the inter-war years.

War memorials throughout Wales provide stark testimony to the price paid by Welsh participation in the conflict but also yield unique insights into the attitudes of the population towards the war and towards post-war society. By 1914 Wales was a diverse but divided society. The country was still ostensibly united in politics and religion but rapid industrialization in the late nineteenth century had created a different, vibrant Wales

---

[14] A new hospital had also been built as part of Rhyl's war memorial. This is discussed in more detail in ch. 4.

[15] The Great War memorial at Connah's Quay in north-east Wales also includes the names of those who died in Korea, Cyprus and the Falklands and this appears to be a general pattern throughout Wales. On occasions there may simply be insufficient room on the existing memorial and an additional form of commemoration is necessary, for example, an inscribed plaque situated adjacent to the memorial as at Pontarddulais in west Glamorgan.

[16] Borg, *War Memorials*, p. 84.

concentrated in the valleys of the south where pre-war episodes of industrial conflict gave notice of the future shape of coalfield politics. By 1919 the causes held dear by the pre-war Welsh Liberal élite seemed to belong to another age, along with the politicians who espoused such policies.[17]

Disestablishment of the Church in 1920 gained little popular attention and even less enthusiasm whilst the landowning class all but disappeared along with their land as the great estates were broken up and sold.[18] The advent of film, popular papers and radio added some much-needed levity to Welsh life in the inter-war years but as this was conducted primarily in English it created new problems, still to be resolved, over the place of the Welsh language in an increasingly anglicized population.[19] Developments in energy, transport and leisure held implications for labour and social mobility within Wales, but technological advances could not overcome the psychological barriers that remained in certain areas both to industrialization and anglicization. It was in the political and industrial sphere, however, that post-war changes appeared most marked. The presence of Lloyd George in Downing Street until 1922 cannot be equated with the realities of post-war Welsh politics. The 'coupon' election of December 1918 and the success of Lloyd George's coalition were unrepresentative of wider, long-term political changes in Wales and were more an expression of relief that the war was over.[20]

The massive changes in industrialization and population that had marked out south Wales in the Edwardian years reached their zenith in the immediate post-war years with over a quarter of a million workers employed in the coal industry. The experience of war itself had highlighted the immense economic power of the mineworkers.[21] The economic prosperity of the immediate post-war years ensured a confident work-force imbued with a

[17] For this argument see Kenneth O. Morgan, *Wales in British Politics, 1868–1922* (Cardiff, 1991). For an overview of the period 1918–22, see pp. 286–97.

[18] John Davies, 'The end of the great estates and the rise of freehold farming in Wales', *Welsh History Review*, VII, No. 2 (1974), pp. 186–212.

[19] See Aled Jones, *Press, Politics and Society: A History of Journalism in Wales* (Cardiff, 1993), pp. 228–38.

[20] See Kenneth O. Morgan, 'Post-war reconstruction in Wales, 1918 and 1945', in J. M. Winter (ed.), *The Working Class in Modern British History: Essays in Honour of Henry Pelling* (Cambridge, 1983), pp. 82–98.

[21] Edward Charles May, 'A question of control: social and industrial relations in the South Wales coalfield and the crisis of post-war reconstruction, 1914–1922' (unpublished Ph.D. thesis, University of Wales, 1995).

militant optimism as local negotiations over pay and conditions took place within a wider debate over the future ownership and control of the mines. Within a few years the mood had changed; the 1921 lock-out heralded a new era of industrial relations in which the work-force was increasingly on the defensive and relationships between employer and worker were marked by bitterness and antagonism. Class conflict and economic deprivation became political realities in the decade after the war. Kenneth Morgan has written that 'in Wales, the 1920s brought disillusion, despair and the crushing weight of mass unemployment and stagnation as the legacy of wartime'.[22] The legacy of war was also unprecedented loss and emotional trauma for thousands of individuals and communities in Britain, epitomized today by the many thousands of crosses, cenotaphs, obelisks, figurative sculpture and other forms of war memorial.[23]

By placing the commemoration process in the wider context of Welsh history in the decade after the war, it is possible to examine how the nature of remembrance was influenced by factors of language, cultural diversity and economic decline and whether the commemoration process can help to clarify the complex topic of national and local identity.[24] Detailed newspaper reports of the process of planning, building and unveiling a war memorial and minutes of war memorial committees provide clear evidence of the importance of memorials to communities throughout Wales and demonstrate how memorials as distinct artefacts helped people come to terms with individual and collective loss. Existing studies which use Welsh examples as an illustrative rather than an analytical tool can relegate Wales, albeit unwittingly, to the footnotes of debates on war and remembrance. Examining and analysing the ways in which the people of Wales remembered those who had fallen in the Great

---

[22] Morgan, 'Post-war reconstruction', p. 86.

[23] The style of war memorials in Wales is very similar to memorials throughout Britain. The majority of memorials were constructed in the decade after the war when public and private grief was intense and the resulting memorials were usually fairly 'traditional' in design. An exception in Wales can be found at Chirk with Eric Gill's memorial which was unveiled in 1920. It was commissioned by his friend and patron, Lord Howard de Walden. For details of the unveiling ceremony, see *Wrexham Advertiser*, 23 October 1920.

[24] Recent work on Scottish war memorials does not address these issues or the impact of war on Scottish identity. See Gilbert T. Bell, 'Monuments to the fallen: Scottish war memorials of the Great War' (unpublished Ph.D. thesis, University of Strathclyde, 1993).

War has the potential of adding a new dimension to our knowledge of post-war Wales and contributes to the wider historiographical debate on war and remembrance in its social setting.

I

'GOD KNOWS BETTER THAN WE': THE WELSH AT WAR

The concept of the Great War as a watershed in modern Welsh history has elicited an unusual degree of consensus amongst Welsh historians. For example, Dai Smith has commented: 'After the First World War all changed and, more importantly, is seen to change', whilst Kenneth Morgan has written that 'the war marked an immense break with the past, in social and ultimately in political terms. In no part of the British Isles was the contrast between pre- and post-war conditions more pronounced.'[1] The work of Gwynfor Evans also supports the importance of the war in Welsh history: the 'war years saw the deepest cleft in the history of the nation; the Wales of 1919 was very different from that of 1914'.[2] In view of these comments and increasing interest in the conflict, it is perhaps surprising that no substantial work has been undertaken on the themes of war and remembrance in Wales although this may in part be explained by the historiographical tendency to observe rather than to explain the war.[3]

Very few works with direct reference to Wales appeared during the war of 1914–18 and published works in recent years

---

[1] David Smith in Trevor Herbert and Gareth Elwyn Jones (eds.), *Wales between the Wars* (Cardiff, 1990), p. 4; Dai Smith, *Aneurin Bevan and the World of South Wales* (Cardiff, 1993), p. 56, and K. O. Morgan, *Rebirth of a Nation: Wales, 1880–1980* (Oxford, 1990), p. 177. See also Prys Morgan and David Thomas, *Wales: The Shaping of a Nation* (Newton Abbot, 1984), esp. p. 170 and pp. 144–5.

[2] Gwynfor Evans, *Land of my Fathers* (Swansea, 1974), p. 429.

[3] Herbert and Jones (eds.), *Wales between the Wars*. This places economic decline as the central feature of these years, whilst an earlier volume with the same editors finished its investigations in 1914: *Wales, 1880–1914* (Cardiff, 1988). See also Morgan, *Rebirth of a Nation*, and John Davies, *A History of Wales* (London, 1994), for the most comprehensive accounts of the impact of the war on Wales. Examples of work published on Wales and the war other than military histories include Tecwyn Lloyd, 'Welsh public opinion and the First World War', *Planet*, X (February/March 1972), pp. 25–37, although this is confined to intellectual opinion; Tecwyn Lloyd, 'Welsh literature and the First World War', *Planet*, XI (May 1972), pp. 17–23. For more recent writing, see Gerwyn Williams, *Tir neb: Rhyddiaith Gymraeg a'r Rhyfel Byd Cyntaf* (Cardiff, 1996). See also Keith Strange, *Wales and the First World War* (Mid Glamorgan County Supplies Department, n.d.), and Keith Strange, 'Welsh images of the Great War: a documentary history of the Great War' (unpublished: I am grateful to Dr Strange for allowing me access to his work).

have concentrated on political and economic problems during the war.[4] Commentators may agree that the Great War inexorably changed Wales but a crucial point about the nature of war has been ignored: war was about death and dying. Men from Wales enlisted, fought and died in their thousands whilst at home families waited, grieved and consoled each other. A glimpse behind the casualty statistics reveals the trauma endured by those who waited but their full story – the human experience of the Great War in Wales – remains to be told.

It was a different world in August 1914. Appeals to fight for King and Country were well received throughout the principality. In seeking to arouse popular sentiment behind the war effort, Lloyd George drew on his Welsh roots with great effect. This can be heard clearly in the famous speech he made at the Queen's Hall, London, in September 1914:

> I should like to see a Welsh Army in the Field. I should like to see the race who faced the Normans for hundreds of years in a struggle for freedom, the race that helped to win Crecy, the race that fought for a generation under Glendower, against the greatest captain in Europe - I should like to see that race go and give a taste of its quality in this great struggle in Europe. And they are going to do it.[5]

The speech apparently evoked an immediate response amongst members of the audience: 'Amid great enthusiasm a number of young Welshmen at once left the hall for the special recruiting station prepared in the precincts of the hall, where they enrolled themselves'.[6] Indeed, it was suggested that 'Had the message been given by Glyndwr himself it could not have fired the

---

[4] Revd J. Vyrnwy Morgan, *The War and Wales* (London, 1916). See also *The Land of my Fathers: A Welsh Gift Book* (London, 1915). This anthology of prose and verse relating to Wales was organized by Mrs Lloyd George in aid of the National Fund for Welsh Troops. Recent published work is largely confined to articles, including Deian Hopkin, 'Patriots and pacifists in Wales, 1914–1918: the case of Capt. Lionel Lindsay and the Rev. T. E. Nicholas', *Llafur*, I, No. 3 (1974), pp. 132–46; David Egan, 'The Swansea Conference of the British Council of Soldiers' and Workers' Delegates, July 1917', *Llafur*, I, No. 4 (1975), pp. 162–87; Aled Eurig, 'Agweddau ar y Gwrthwynebiad i'r Rhyfel Byd Cyntaf yng Nghymru' (Aspects of the opposition to the First World War in Wales), *Llafur*, IV, No. 4 (1987), pp. 58–68.

[5] *The Times*, 21 September 1914. The number of men from Wales who served in the armed forces was estimated to be 280,000. These figures are discussed in more detail in ch. 8.

[6] Ibid.

Cymric imagination more effectively'.[7] The same month the *Welsh Outlook* spoke of 'our conviction that we are bound to fight this war, and that we shall fight it to the end with all the strength we have got'.[8]

Men joined the colours for a variety of public and private reasons, but the opportunity to join up with friends and colleagues helped to boost recruitment levels. The 'Pals' battalions emerged throughout Britain, generally raised by prominent local individuals or local authorities and usually 'composed of men who lived in a particular city or district or who shared a common social and occupational background'.[9] Recruitment for the 11th (Cardiff Commercial) Battalion, Welch Regiment, started in late August 1914 and was brisk and successful.[10]

> In each platoon were men who worked together in civilian life like the batch from James Howells store or the Cardiff Gas Company. Teachers like James Griffiths and Oswald Sturdy were together in No. 4 Platoon of 'A' Company along with two solicitors named Coak and Lillington . . . A clutch of clerks joined from Spillers, the flour millers . . . four journalists came from the Western Mail . . . Brother enlisted with brother. Like Will and Oscar Hubbard, sons of a well-known Splott dentist. Or Gwynne and Lewis Prosser, whose young brother David . . . joined the Army later in the war.[11]

Those left behind settled into new routines and new anxieties as it soon became clear that the war would not be over by Christmas. The burden on those at home was carried primarily by women, who took over traditionally male-dominated jobs or

---

[7] *Welsh Army Corps, Report of the Executive Committee, 1914–1919* (Newport, Ray Westlake, 1989; originally published, Cardiff, *Western Mail*, 1921), p. 4. Lloyd George's hopes of raising a Welsh Army Corps were not fulfilled and ultimately only one division was formed.

[8] *Welsh Outlook*, I (September 1914), pp. 378–9.

[9] Peter Simkins, *Kitchener's Army: The Raising of the New Armies, 1914–16* (Manchester, 1988), pp. 79–103 (p. 79).

[10] 'The 11th Welch was known as the Battalion of Specialists, for there were in its ranks, civil, mechanical, mining and marine engineers, doctors, solicitors, schoolmasters, chemists and dentists, as well as journalists and linguists.' Major-General Sir Thomas Marden, *The History of the Welch Regiment*, vol. 2: *1914–1918* (Cardiff, 1932), p. 284.

[11] Gareth Bowen, 'To death and glory', *South Wales Echo*, 14 September 1964. Gwynne and Lewis Prosser died in Salonika in 1916. William Hubbard also died of wounds in Salonika in 1917. *Soldiers Died in the Great War, 1914–1919: The Welch Regiment* (Polsted, 1988), p. 47.

sought employment in the new industries spawned by the war. In 1915, the East Denbighshire Parliamentary Recruiting Committee received a request from a mother with two sons on active service. She had written to the chairman in an effort to get work on 'munitions or ammunition, as I have two sons in France fighting for their King and Country and I want to go and help them'.[12] The opportunities offered by the war did allow women a new sense of freedom and independence but this must often have been peripheral to the main experience of waiting and hoping for the safe return of husbands, fathers, sons and brothers.[13] Letters from the front were eagerly awaited but when news did arrive it was likely to be censored both by the armed forces and by the soldiers themselves. This was no doubt to avoid alarming, or inflicting further worry on, those waiting at home, but it also seems that for many servicemen there existed a chasm between themselves and non-combatants. The experiences of men such as Private W. D. Jones of the 10th Battalion, Royal Welch Fusiliers, who witnessed many of his friends being killed around him in Delville Wood, remained intensely personal and could never be fully understood except by those who endured the same conditions.[14] Perceptions of an uncaring and uninterested home front could also lead servicemen to feel that their greatest loyalty was to each other. Henry Williamson served throughout the war and wrote that:

> Those at home, sitting in arm-chairs and talking proudly of Patriotism and Heroism, will never realise the bitter contempt and scorn the soldiers have

[12] Report of the Executive of the East Denbighshire Parliamentary Recruiting committee, August 1915. A month after the formation of the committee in April 1915, a meeting of the Recruiting Executive reported the sad news of the death in action of the chairman's eldest son 'while serving his King and Country in Flanders'.

[13] Published work on women in Wales has focused on the inter-war years. See Deidre Beddoe, 'Munitionettes, maids and mams: women in Wales, 1914–1939', in Angela V. John (ed.), *Our Mothers' Land: Chapters in Welsh Women's History, 1830–1939* (Cardiff, 1991), pp. 189–209. For an interpretation of the war experience which is not confined to issues of employment and rights, see Susan Kingsley Kent, 'Love and death: war and gender in Britain, 1914–1918', in Frans Coetzee and Marilyn Shevin-Coetzee (eds.), *Authority, Identity and the Social History of the Great War*, pp. 153–74. See also Susan Kingsley Kent, *Making Peace: The Reconstruction of Gender in Interwar Britain* (Princeton, 1993).

[14] Diary of Private W. D. Jones, 10th RWF, entry for 19 July 1916. See also diary of L/Cpl. D. G. Gregory, who was at Mametz Wood with the 13th RWF, entry for 10 July 1916: 'Entered Wood and were greeted with machine gun fire. Dense undergrowth made movement difficult . . . Casualties commenced very soon but we got to positions near centre of wood where we dug in.' Diaries are held in the Liddle Collection, Brotherton Library, University of Leeds.

for these and other abstractions; the soldiers feel they have been betrayed by the high-sounding phrases that heralded the War, for they know that the enemy soldiers are the same men as themselves, suffering and disillusioned in exactly the same way.[15]

Whilst on sick leave in England in October 1916, Vivian de Sola Pinto, an officer in the Royal Welch Fusiliers, was 'conscious of a great gulf' which separated him from his father and sister:

> They still used the clichés of 1914 when they spoke of the war, and, like most people of their class, they swallowed quite uncritically the floods of hypocritical, pseudo-patriotic cant and uplift that poured from the Press and the political platforms . . . on the whole I was quite glad when I was examined by a medical board at Caxton Hall and passed as fit for service again.[16]

Soldiers returning from the Front were greeted with enthusiasm by their local communities, but for many men the short break was spent trying to forget their experiences of war, and for some alcohol proved a convenient opiate. Rupert Rees recalled a member of his local choir who volunteered to join the navy and took part in escorting shipping convoys. He had witnessed ships being torpedoed and heard the screams of his friends in the water but was unable to stop and help them. The sailor spent his leave permanently drunk in a bar in Aberdare refusing pleas from his father to return home.[17] Yet periods of leave did allow serving men to experience, albeit for a limited time, the worry and stress of those waiting at home. An officer in the South Wales Borderers serving in Gallipoli wrote that:

[15] Henry Williamson, *The Wet Flanders Plain* (Norwich, 1987), p. 17. Freud made the distinction in 1915 between 'those who themselves risk their lives in battle, and those who have stayed at home and have only to wait for the loss of one of their dear ones by wounds, disease or infection'. 'Thoughts for the times on war and death' *The Standard Edition of the Complete Psychological Works of Sigmund Freud*, ed. J. Strachey and A. Freud, vol. 14: *1914–1916* (London, 1957), pp. 275–300 (p. 291).

[16] V. de Sola Pinto, *The City that Shone: An Autobiography (1895–1922)* (London, 1969), pp. 185–6.

[17] Interview with Rupert Rees. Taped interview from BBC Wales series 'All Our Lives', Museum of Welsh Life (MWL), Sound Archive. See also Captain J. C. Dunn, *The War the Infantry Knew, 1914–1919* (London, 1991): 'A senior N.C.O., who hailed from a Welsh mining valley, went on leave. He was asked, after his return, what it was like at home. "I don't know," he said, "I got drunk the night I arrived, and was back in France again before I got sober"'(p. 374).

I can quite realise what a terrible anxiety it is for those at home, waiting for news and then hearing the worst; we who are out there don't realise it a bit, it is only when you come home that you can see how much one's brothers and friends at home have to put up with.[18]

Captain Wyn Griffith served with the 15th (1st London Welsh) Battalion, Royal Welch Fusiliers and described the parting from his wife as he headed back to France in 1916:

Shortly before eight o'clock in the morning the boat train steamed out of Victoria station, leaving Wyn standing on the platform, one of many women fighting each a lonely battle against a distant peril. Some were to know defeat, others triumph, but none was to escape the rack of doubt and suspense.[19]

The trauma of waiting for news became just too much to endure on occasions, with cases of suicide noted amongst women in Carmarthenshire with sons and husbands at the front as they 'found the pressures of the war too great to bear'.[20]

Certain dates and places from the Great War have a particularly tragic resonance for Wales. The 38th (Welsh) Division endured a baptism of fire at Mametz Wood in July 1916. The wood was held by the Germans and on the morning of 7 July the attack was to be led by the 16th Welch (Cardiff City) and the 11th South Wales Borderers. Over the next few days the fighting was fierce and costly: 'The division's casualties for the period 7–12 July totalled nearly 4,000, including 600 killed and a like number missing. Some battalions were severely mauled, including the 16th Welch (Cardiff City) which suffered more than 350 casualties – almost half its fighting strength.'[21] Wyn Griffith survived the action and his description of entering the Wood illustrates the human tragedy beyond the statistics:

---

[18] Letter to Grace Addams-Williams, undated. Papers of 2nd Lt. D. A. Addams-Williams, 4th Battalion, South Wales Borderers. Held in the Liddle Collection, Brotherton Library, University of Leeds.

[19] Wyn Griffith, *Up to Mametz* (London, 1981), p. 108.

[20] Russell Davies, *Secret Sins: Sex, Violence and Society in Carmarthenshire, 1870–1920* (Cardiff, 1996), pp. 106–7.

[21] Colin Hughes, *Mametz: Lloyd George's 'Welsh Army' at the Battle of the Somme* (Norwich, 1990), p. 124. See also Chris McCarthy, *The Somme: The Day by Day Account* (London, 1993).

Men of my old battalion were lying dead on the ground in great profusion. They wore a yellow badge on their sleeves, and without this distinguishing mark, it would have been impossible to recognise the remains of many of them . . . Equipment, ammunition, rolls of barbed wire, tins of food, gas-helmets and rifles were lying about everywhere. There were more corpses than men, but there were worse sights than corpses. Limbs and mutilated trunks, here and there a detached head, forming splashes of red against the green leaves . . . one tree held in its branches a leg, with its torn flesh hanging down over a spray of leaf.[22]

For those waiting at home, newspapers remained the main source of information and soon started to print the grim legacy of the 'battle for the Wood', with the daily lists appearing as a sombre roll-call of the men who had marched away. Reading the lists became a ritual for some families. Agnes Greatorex had three brothers serving in France and had to read the lists aloud to her mother who prayed for each name in turn. After a major offensive the lists were so long that Agnes was allowed to go outside and play for a short time but then had to return to finish the reading.[23] In August 1916 the *Cardiff Times* reported the deaths in action of the brothers Henry and Charles Morgan. They had both worked at the Blaenavon Steel & Iron Company, joined the 16th (Cardiff City) Battalion on its formation in late 1914 and were allocated to the same company. On 7 July 1916, during the battle for Mametz Wood, they died together.[24] In the same edition, the paper reported the deaths of Tom and Henry Hardwidge. Both brothers were married, lived in Ferndale, worked at the local colliery and enlisted in the 15th Battalion, Welch Regiment. On 11 July 1916, during the battle for Mametz Wood, Tom Hardwidge was fatally wounded and as his brother, Henry, went to his assistance, he was killed by a sniper. The brothers now lie side by side in Flatiron Copse Cemetery in France.[25] The lack of detailed information for those at home is

[22] Griffith, *Up to Mametz*, pp. 209–10.
[23] Interview with Agnes Greatorex. Taped interview from BBC Wales series 'All Our Lives', MWL Sound Archive.
[24] *Cardiff Times*, 19 August 1916. See Marden, *History of the Welsh Regiment*, pp. 285–6. Lt.-Col. F. H. Gaskell commanded the battalion. He was killed in action in May 1916. Memorial tablets to Lt.-Col. Gaskell and to the 16th (Cardiff City) Battalion were erected in St John's Church, Cardiff, and at Mametz Ward in Cardiff Royal Infirmary.
[25] *Cardiff Times*, 19 August 1916. See also *Soldiers Died in the Great War, 1914–1919: The Welch Regiment*, p. 60. For details of the graves, see *The War Graves of the British Empire: France* (London, Imperial War Graves Commission, 1928), vol. 20, Cemetery Index No. 453.

reflected in a letter written to the father of Henry and Charles Morgan by Lieutenant Richards, who wrote of there being 'little doubt that, like others of their comrades, they fell a prey to the enemy's snipers'.[26] Like thousands of other casualties, however, there is no known grave for Henry and Charles Morgan and their names are recorded on the Thiepval Memorial dedicated to the missing of the Somme.[27] Newspapers during and after the war carried many pathetic messages asking for information on missing servicemen, for some families never gave up hope that their loved ones would return. Agnes Greatorex's brothers were with the 2nd Welch stationed at Pembroke Dock and she recalled going to Cardiff railway station to watch their troop-train pass through *en route* for Southampton and France. Agnes remembered a woman whose son was on that train and was subsequently killed in action. For years after the war his mother went to the station, waiting for her son to return.[28]

As war progressed, protracted battles and mounting casualty figures took their toll. Ideas of the glory and glamour of war disappeared with the sight of maimed and shell-shocked men returning to Wales, and the enthusiasm of 1914 was replaced by a desire for the war and the dying to end.[29] At the 1917 eisteddfod in Birkenhead, the chair was draped in black in honour of the winner of the chief award, Ellis Evans, who had been killed in action shortly before the ceremony.[30] The impact of the war was also brought home at the eisteddfod by another moving incident. At the Bangor eisteddfod two years previously, two male voice choirs from the Welsh Army Corps, in training at Llandudno, took part in the music festival. The prize was awarded to the choir from the 17th Battalion, Royal Welch Fusiliers, which shortly afterwards left for France. At the ceremony in July 1917 it was announced that the conductor was now the sole survivor from the choir, that he was present at the eisteddfod, and that relatives of those who had fallen had sent the committee a

[26] *South Wales Echo*, 15 August 1916.

[27] *The Register of the Names Inscribed on the Thiepval Memorial, France* (London, Imperial War Graves Commission, 1931), Memorial Register 21. See also *Soldiers Died in the Great War*, p. 66.

[28] Interview with Agnes Greatorex. MWL Sound Archive.

[29] For the impact of the Great War on attitudes to death, see David Cannadine, 'War and death, grief and mourning in modern Britain', in J. Whaley (ed.), *Mirrors of Mortality: Studies in the Social History of Death* (London, 1981), pp. 187–242.

[30] Ellis Evans (Hedd Wyn) is discussed in more detail in ch. 7.

specific decoration to be presented to him. This took the form of a black and white rosette: black representing the mourning of close relatives and of the nation, the white representing the 'untarnished honour' of those who had died. The *Welsh Outlook* reported the ceremony:

> General Sir Owen Thomas, who was in deep mourning after the two sons he has lost in the war, was called to the platform to invest him. Lance-Corporal Evans was invited to come forward. A bent and broken man arose with difficulty and walked forward slowly leaning heavily on a stick. The feeling of the vast audience was intense and tears were in many eyes.[31]

In the years before the advent of mass instantaneous communication, death became 'a series of verbal descriptions', and for many families in Wales the long wait for news ended with the arrival of a telegram from the War Office.[32] Myfanwy Thomas recalled the day in 1917 when news came of the death in action of her father, the poet Edward Thomas:

> But on that bright April day after Easter, when mother was sewing and I was awkwardly filling in the pricked dots on a postcard with coloured wool, embroidering a wild duck to send to France, I saw the telegraph boy lean his red bicycle against the fence. Mother stood reading the message with a face of stone. 'No answer' came like a croak, and the boy rode away. Mother fetched our coats and we went shivering out into the sunny April afternoon.[33]

O. M. Roberts grew up in Llanrug and recalled that the sight of the telegram boy with his red bicycle began to be feared amongst those in the village with relatives on active service.[34] After the official notification, letters were often received from battalion officers giving more information and many were published in local newspapers. In May 1915 Captain H. T. Edwards of the 1st Monmouthshire Regiment wrote to the father of Bugler Bray who had been killed in action, aged seventeen:

---

[31] *Welsh Outlook*, IV (October 1917), p. 331. See also *Western Mail*, 7 September 1917.

[32] Allyson Booth, *Postcards from the Trenches* (Oxford, 1996), p. 25.

[33] Myfanwy Thomas, *One of these Fine Days* (Manchester, 1982), p. 62. Edward Thomas was born in London to Welsh parents, joined the Artists' Rifles in 1915 and was commissioned in the Royal Artillery. He was killed in France in April 1917. See R. G. Thomas, *Edward Thomas: A Portrait* (Oxford, 1985).

[34] Interview with O. M. Roberts. Taped interview from BBC Wales series 'All Our Lives', MWL Sound Archive.

I deeply regret to have to inform you that your son, Bugler L. Bray, was killed in action on the 23rd of last month. For the past month he has been acting as my servant and I made a point of keeping him out of danger as much as possible on account of his age. Fate, however, was too strong for us, but you will be glad to hear that his death was instantaneous and painless. Your son was [a] great favourite of both officers and men, and will be sadly missed. We buried him with six of his comrades behind the trenches on the side of a small wood, and I have since placed a small wooden cross on the grave to mark the spot. Please accept the deepest sympathy of myself, the officers and men of D. Company, and be comforted that your son was killed whilst doing his duty to the King and country – a better end no one could have.[35]

The quick and painless nature of death is frequently emphasized, as is the bravery of the individual soldier. This sanitization of death was no doubt out of consideration for the feelings of families, for the reality at times may have been impossible to put into words. Writing such letters was a regular part of trench life for officers, who faced the challenge of maintaining some degree of individuality and sincerity. Violent death was common: it was 'ordinary' and responses and reaction were conditioned accordingly. Writing a letter about death became just another task to perform:

On the other side of Aubers Ridge a German gunner twirled a few wheels into a new position, moved a bar of iron, and sent death soaring into the air; he went to his dinner. While he was moving his wheels and dials, three Londoners were filling sandbags in a ditch on the plain, arguing about Tottenham Hotspur. A flash, a noise, and a cloud of smoke. 'Blast 'em, they've killed old Parkinson – blown 'is 'ead off, they 'ave, the bastard.' . . . Blast them, and back to the weary lifting of mud, this time passing a stretcher covered with a blanket hiding all but a thin trickle of blood. Four children, and his wife's name was 'Liz' . . . must write to her tonight.[36]

---

[35] *South Wales Argus*, 12 May 1915. The 1st Battalion The Monmouthshire Regiment was involved in heavy fighting around Ypres in April and May 1915. See Les Hughes and John Dixon, *'Surrender Be Damned': A History of the 1/1st Battalion the Monmouthshire Regiment, 1914–18* (Caerphilly, 1995). The book also contains an appendix of letters, including the letter from Captain Edwards, which were published in the *South Wales Argus* and the *Western Mail*.

[36] Griffith, *Up to Mametz*, pp. 58–9. Other accounts of the war with a strong Welsh element include Robert Graves, *Goodbye to All That: An Autobiography*, ed. Richard Perceval Graves (Oxford, 1995); W. G. Bowden, *Abercynon to Flanders – and Back* (Risca, 1984); Emlyn Davies, *Taffy Went to War* (Knutsford, 1976); Frank Richards, *Old Soldiers Never Die*

The 'official' notification of death was insufficient for many of the bereaved who sought to penetrate the bland details and find out more about the circumstances of death. This sad search for information was made more urgent since there was no corpse to grieve over, no funeral to arrange and no grave to visit. Talking to men who had experienced the front, and perhaps with personal knowledge of those who had died, seems to have helped the bereaved in their attempts to come to terms with their loss. Even if the information gained was incorrect, there was still comfort to be gained from talking about the war. After the family of Edward Thomas had received news of his death in action, they were visited by a Canadian soldier on leave from France:

> He said he had been at Vimy Ridge and remembered my father – how everyone loved him, and how he had been smoking his pipe round the camp fire in the evening after a battle when he was killed. My mother had long talks with him and was greatly comforted to meet someone who was actually there, and who remembered Edward. We only learned years later that this soldier could not have known my father as Canadian regiments were nowhere near Arras at that time.[37]

In August 1915 Grace Addams-Williams found no solace in the War Office telegram informing her of the death of her son. Second Lieutenant Donald Arthur Addams-Williams was the only son of the Revd Herbert Addams-Williams and his wife of Llangybi, Newport. He was commissioned into the 4th (Service) Battalion of the South Wales Borderers in October 1914. After training in England, the battalion boarded the SS *Megantic* at Avonmouth for the journey to Gallipoli, arriving in July 1915. His letters home describe life in the trenches in vivid detail:

> The enemy is good at two things, sniping and bombthrowing . . . It is frightfully hot all through the day and the flies are much worse than the

(Sleaford, 1994); David Wyn Davies, *A Welshman in Mesopotamia* (Aberystwyth, 1986); Bernard Adams, *Nothing of Importance: A Record of Eight Months at the Front with a Welsh Battalion* (Stevenage, 1988); Lord Silsoe, *Sixty Years a Welsh Territorial* (Llandysul, 1976); G. D. Roberts, *Witness these Letters* (Denbigh, 1983); C. P. Clayton, *The Hungry One* (Llandysul, 1978); Captain J. C. Dunn, *The War the Infantry Knew, 1914–1919* (London, 1991). Siegfried Sassoon was commissioned in the Royal Welch Fusiliers in 1915; in his 'Memoirs of an infantry officer' the regiment became the 'Flintshire Fusiliers'. See also John Richards (ed.), *Wales on the Western Front*, (Cardiff, 1994), an anthology of writings, prose and poetry devoted to the experience of Welsh soldiers on the Western Front.
[37] Thomas, *One of these Fine Days*, p. 66.

snipers . . . There are quite a lot of dead bodies and bits of bodies about, a Turk's foot with a boot on sticks out of the parapet of one of the main communication trenches, and legs occasionally appear from others.[38]

Two weeks later he wrote to his parents:

You cannot possibly imagine the number of flies and how absolutely irritating they are. A lot of bodies are lying about that it is impossible to get at to bury so that helps to bring multitudes more flies . . . I think that by the time you receive this letter we shall have helped to make history.[39]

Ten days later, Arthur Addams-Williams was killed in action at Suvla Bay. He was nineteen years old. The company commander, Major Sir Lennox Napier, was killed in the same offensive but his widow immediately wrote to other bereaved families in her husband's company to offer her condolences. The reply from Grace Addams-Williams expresses concern for another woman's grief but the desperate need for information is clear:

I tried to write to you yesterday, but broke down utterly . . . To think you could find time to write to me, in the midst of your own grief, makes me feel how selfish I have been . . . My heart bleeds for you for I know what you must be suffering . . . Our boy was the light of our life, and had been nothing but a pure joy from the day of his birth . . . Oh how grand and brave they all are. Might I ask you, if your boy should tell you anything, to let us know. We do so yearn for details'.[40]

By contacting the mother of another battalion officer, also killed in action, Grace Addams-Williams obtained the address of her son's platoon sergeant.[41] Sergeant Worthington had been with her son when he died and had made three attempts to retrieve her son's body from the battlefield. She wrote to his wife, sent the family a present and in November 1915 finally tracked

---

[38] Letter to Mr and Mrs H. Addams-Williams dated 18 July 1915.

[39] Ibid., 3 August 1915.

[40] Letter to Lady Lennox Napier dated 23 August 1915. Lt. J. W. Napier also served in the 4th Battalion SWB.

[41] Letter to Grace Addams-Williams dated 9 October 1915. The letter was from Mrs Bell, whose son had been killed in action the day before Addams-Williams. Her letter concluded that 'the anxiety and sorrow gets worse not better'.

down Sergeant Worthington in a convalescent hospital in Malta. He wrote that

> I hardly know how to answer your questions . . . I promise I will tell you all about your dear Boy, when I get home. I wish I could have died to save him. I would have done it willingly for you. We used to sit in the trenches and talk of what we were going to do when we returned home. I would have followed him to the ends of the earth, as he had the Pluck & Heart of a Lion, and so considerate in all things.[42]

The correspondence continued and Grace Addams-Williams wrote to other officers and members of her son's platoon asking for, and receiving, details about her son and his death. Her anguish was increased by the fact that she had not received any information from the regiment. A letter was finally sent in October 1915 expressing regret but also reflecting the heavy losses incurred by the battalion:

> First let me tell you how extremely sorry we all are that you should have received no letter from the Regiment. In the ordinary course of events Sir Lennox Napier commanding the company would have written to you, but he, unfortunately, was killed on the following day . . . I should like to express on behalf of his brother officers who are still serving with the Regiment (alas there are only 5 of us left now) our deep sympathy with you in the loss of your son who was a brave soldier and a true gentleman.[43]

Arthur Addams-Williams's personal property was returned to his family at the end of 1915. His mother wrote to thank the officer concerned but his reply may have unwittingly added to her pain: 'I am glad to have been able to render this service to you, and I wish I could have collected more of your son's property, but I am afraid that the pockets had been rifled by the enemy.'[44]

These letters provide an insight into the mutual support given by bereaved families as wives and mothers contacted each other in a quest for information and solace. The mother of Lieutenant Cooper, killed in the same action at Suvla Bay, wrote to Grace

[42] Letter to Grace Addams-Williams dated 4 November 1915.
[43] Ibid., 6 October 1915.
[44] Ibid., 3 January 1916.

Addams-Williams: 'I often wish I could join him. I feel most depressed and life has lost its zest. Let us know when you return home and we will motor over to have another talk about our loved ones.'[45] The commanding officer of the battalion, Lieutenant-Colonel Gillespie, was also killed, leaving a widow and three young children. His widow wrote to Grace Addams-Williams in December 1915: 'This cannot be a happy Xmas for you so I shall just wish you some happiness and comfort in 1916 . . . I have to try to be cheerful for the sake of the children but it's very hard and almost unbearable.'[46] Perhaps the most poignant lines came from Marjorie Marshall. Her brother, Bathurst, and Arthur Addams-Williams had been friends, visiting each other's homes, but by June 1918 both men were dead. Marjorie wrote of her loss:

> The only thing is to remember that God knows better than we. Bath was more than an ordinary brother to me. He was the being who gave meaning to life. Everything that occurred I judged in reference to him . . . I cannot yet believe that I shall see him no more in this life. The future seems a blank . . . I was very fond of Arthur . . . His perfect unselfishness, his cheerfulness and sound good sense made him a most helpful friend for Bath. They were so fond of each other. I wonder if they have met by now. Somebody told me the other day that they think the very best are taken because there is some even finer work for them to do elsewhere. I hope that may be so.[47]

Arthur Addams-Williams is buried in the 7th Field Ambulance Cemetery in Gallipoli.[48] His death was recorded in the local press and his name appears in official casualty lists.[49] The registers of those killed in the Great War run to many volumes and the pages of names can induce feelings of emotional numbness, in the same way perhaps as visiting the battlefield cemeteries in France and Flanders does. Row after row of

---

[45] Ibid., undated.
[46] Ibid., 21 December 1915.
[47] Ibid., 12 June 1918.
[48] *The War Graves of the British Empire: Gallipoli* (London, Imperial War Graves Commission, 1928), Cemetery Index No. G1.17.
[49] Notification of his death was published in the *Free Press of Monmouthshire*, 15 October 1915. *Officers Died in the Great War, 1914–1919* (Polsted, 1988), p. 99. The year of death is given as 1918 rather than 1915.

uniform white headstones and the imposing Memorials to the Missing at Thiepval on the Somme, or the Menin Gate at Ypres, leave an overwhelming sense of sadness but also incredulity at the sheer scale of death. Individual stories become part of a wider text as they are merged in the statistics of battle casualties. The danger is that death has become a collective experience. Men may have worked, enlisted, fought and died together and, ultimately, they are remembered together. Yet each death, each name on a local war memorial was an individual trauma for a family. Grace Addams-Williams and her desperate search for information and comfort provide an insight into the very real and protracted personal tragedy experienced by so many families in Wales and elsewhere during the Great War.

Remembering men as soldiers but also as individuals after the war was a priority; the question remained as to how to do so appropriately. Prior to 1914, commemoration of men killed in battle was primarily defined by personal wealth, position and influence. Usually none of these was applicable to the private soldier, whose enlistment was often regarded as a 'last resort' and whose subsequent death remained largely unmarked, although the Crimean war memorial at Carmarthen was erected in 1858 in memory of officers and men of the 23rd Royal Welch Fusiliers who died in that war. The involvement and death of an estimated three and a half thousand British volunteers in the Boer War led to changes in the act of commemoration as it became necessary to remember those who had died not only as soldiers but also as citizens.[50] The loss of life in that war could not prepare society for the scale of death less than twenty years later. Casualty lists published in British newspapers gave daily notice of the catastrophic impact on society and it became clear that new forms of mass public commemoration would be necessary. During the early years of war, street memorials or shrines were made, often in the form of rolls of honour, and some of these were later incorporated into local war memorials,

---

[50] Total casualties were around 38,000. See Catherine Moriarty, 'Narrative and the absent body: mechanisms of meaning in First World War memorials' (unpublished Ph.D. thesis, University of Sussex, 1995), pp. 27–34. For a guide to Boer War memorials in Britain, see James Gildea, *For Remembrance and in Honour of Those who Lost their Lives in the South African War, 1899–1902* (London, 1911).

but very few civic memorials were erected before the Armistice.[51]
Before the war was over, advice was offered by such learned
bodies as the Church Crafts League and the Civic Arts Association as to appropriate forms of commemoration. Some communities started to plan their memorials before the end of the
war. At Coedpoeth in north Wales the views of local men on
active service were sought. In August 1916 the parents of a
soldier serving in France wrote to their son asking for his
suggestions and he replied that the best memorial would be a
playground for the local children. The war memorial, a
recreation park and a monument, was unveiled in November
1921 but the soldier who had made the original suggestion was
not there to witness the ceremony. He had been killed in action
one month after writing the letter.[52]

War memorials remain as potent evidence both of the
catastrophe of the Great War and of the challenges faced by
those seeking to commemorate the fallen.[53] Exhibitions of war
memorial designs were held at the Victoria and Albert Museum
and the Royal Academy of Arts in 1919 but there was no
'official' central direction or funding for commemoration.[54] In
Wales, as in the rest of Britain, most war memorials were funded
by public subscription and organized by local committees chosen
to reflect the structure of society but which inevitably also
reflected the social hierarchy of a community.[55] The plethora of
Great War memorials in Wales provides a unique link between
the different facets of Welsh life and also yields a rich harvest for
those seeking to explain how and why society commemorated
those who had died.

---

[51] I am grateful to Nick Hewitt from the National Inventory of War Memorials for his
views on this point. See Alice Goodman, *The Street Memorials of St Albans Abbey Parish* (St
Albans, 1987).
[52] *Wrexham Advertiser*, 19 November 1921.
[53] For a concise overview of commemoration in Britain, see Moriarty, 'Private grief
and public remembrance: British First World War memorials', in Evans and Lunn (eds.),
War and Memory, pp. 125–42.
[54] See also C. Harcourt Smith, *Inscriptions Suggested for War Memorials* (London, 1919).
[55] Alex King has written in detail on the composition and power structures within local
memorial committees in Britain and notes that 'war memorials were normally erected by
local committees whose organisation varied according to the kind of community in which
they were formed'. See 'The politics of meaning in the commemoration of the First
World War in Britain, 1914–1939' (unpublished Ph.D. thesis, University of London,
1993), p. 40.

II

'HE IS NOT MISSING. HE IS HERE':[1]
MEMORIALS FOR THOSE LEFT BEHIND

The decision taken in 1915 to ban the repatriation of bodies would have far-reaching consequences in the memorialization process. The formalities of burial had been taken over by officialdom in the form of the Imperial War Graves Commission, whose policy was guided by the principle of equality of sacrifice and therefore equality of commemoration.[2] Whilst this was a laudable ambition, in reality it appeared a bureaucratic and remote process into which those most affected by the war had little input apart from choosing a personal inscription for the official headstone.[3] Pilgrimages were organized to the battlefields in the decade after the war to enable relatives of the dead to visit either an individual grave or a memorial.[4] Although the pilgrimages no doubt offered some degree of consolation, the opportunity to travel abroad, even at a low price, was open only to those with the financial means to make such a journey, and in the many areas of Wales afflicted by high unemployment, foreign

---

[1] Extract from Lord Plumer's speech at the opening of the Menin Gate Memorial, Ypres. *The Times*, 25 July 1927.

[2] The Imperial War Graves Commission stated its reasons in January 1918: 'The Commission feels that it would be inadvisable to leave the provision of memorials to private initiative. If memorials were allowed to be erected in the War Cemeteries according to the preference, taste and means of relatives and friends, the result would be that costly monuments put up by the well-to-do over their dead would contrast unkindly with those humbler ones which would be all that poorer folk could afford . . . Thus the governing consideration which has influenced the Commission's decision is that those who have given their lives are members of one family, and children of one mother who owes to all an equal tribute of gratitude and affection, and that, in death, all, from General to Private, of whatever race or creed, should receive equal honour under a memorial which should be the common symbol of their comradeship and of the cause for which they died.' Taken from P. Longworth, *The Unending Vigil: A History of the Commonwealth War Graves Commission, 1917–1984* (London, 1985), p. 33. For a full discussion of the debate and controversy over the decision not to repatriate bodies to Britain and the subsequent decision not to allow private memorials, see ibid., pp. 29–55.

[3] Catherine Moriarty, 'The absent dead and figurative First World War memorials', *Transactions of the Ancient Monuments Society*, XXXIX (1995), pp. 7–40.

[4] David Lloyd, 'Tourism, pilgrimage and the commemoration of the Great War in Great Britain, Australia and Canada, 1919–1939' (unpublished Ph.D. thesis, University of Cambridge, 1994). See also T. Walter, 'War grave pilgrimage', in I. Reader and T. Walter (eds.), *Pilgrimage in Popular Culture* (London, 1993), pp. 63–91.

travel was simply not an option.[5] The emotional reaction of the British public to the temporary Cenotaph built in London for the Peace Day Celebrations in July 1919 was testament to the overwhelming need for a visible representation of their grief, whilst the many thousands of local war memorials reflected the desire for an immediate and permanent reminder of the dead.[6] Erecting a war memorial, the ritual involved in the subsequent unveiling ceremonies and the position of the memorial, invariably at the centre of a community both literally and figuratively, acted as an emotional catharsis enabling the bereaved to begin to accept the death of a loved one and to contemplate moving life forward.[7] In this context, commemoration of the individual was an extremely important element in the process of mourning as the local war memorial became the surrogate grave providing an essential focus for individual and collective grief. Ironically it was those most affected by the war who were often marginalized by the commemorative process.

An important factor in the role of ex-servicemen in the commemoration process was that society had to be seen to pay

[5] 'This is demonstrated by the figures for Poppy Day 1927–28 . . . A Wales Area delegate explained at the 1928 Conference that "Last year in the Rhondda Valley they collected £414, the whole amount in coppers."' Niall J. A. Barr, 'Service not self: the British Legion, 1921–1939' (unpublished Ph.D. thesis, University of St Andrews, 1994), p. 116.

[6] See B. Huppauf, 'War and death: the experience of the First World War', in M. Crouch and B. Huppauf (eds.), *Essays on Mortality* (Sydney, 1985), pp. 65–87. The permanent cenotaph was unveiled on Armistice Day 1920. For further reading on the background to both temporary and permanent cenotaphs, see E. Homberger, 'The story of the Cenotaph', *Times Literary Supplement* (12 November 1976), pp. 1429–30; Allan Greenberg, 'Lutyens' Cenotaph', *Journal of the Society of Architectural Historians*, XLVIII, No. 1 (1989), pp. 5–23, and Penelope Curtis, 'The Whitehall Cenotaph: an accidental monument', *Imperial War Museum Review*, IX (1994), pp. 31–41.

[7] A contemporary example can be found in the reactions to the Vietnam War Memorial in Washington. Although the lack of a consensus view on the meaning of American involvement in Vietnam was a major factor in the problems surrounding the controversial sculpture, the role of the traditional war memorial in the healing process was acknowledged. See L. M. Capps, 'The memorial as symbol and agent of healing', in W. Capps (ed.), *The Vietnam Reader* (London, 1991), pp. 272–89 (p. 272). Literature on the Vietnam Memorial is extensive. For example, see R. Wagner-Pacifini and B. Schwartz, 'The Vietnam Veterans Memorial: commemorating a difficult past', *American Journal of Sociology*, XCVII (1991), pp. 376–420; also, 'The Vietnam Memorial in Washington, DC,' in D. MacCannell, *Empty Meeting Grounds* (London, 1992), pp. 280–2; 'The Vietnam Veterans Memorial', in John Bodnar, *Remaking America: Public Memory, Commemoration and Patriotism in the Twentieth Century* (Princeton, 1992), pp. 3–9. American participation in two world wars necessitated the building of memorials on foreign soil. See Ron Robin, '"Footholds in Europe": the aesthetics and politics of American war cemeteries in Western Europe', *Journal of American Studies*, XXIX, No. 1 (1995), pp. 55–72. Political debate also took place over commemoration on the British sector of the Western Front: see Michael Heffernan, 'For ever England: the Western Front and the politics of remembrance in Britain', *Ecumene*, II, No. 3 (1995), pp. 293–323.

its respects to those who had fallen, and ex-servicemen looked upon it as their duty to ensure that their comrades were remembered – and remembered appropriately. In part this was a reaction to their own experiences and feelings of guilt that they had survived the war whereas others had not, and to the perception of a society increasingly absorbed with returning to 'normal' and showing little interest in the physical and psychological needs of many ex-servicemen. Whether initiating local commemorative projects, taking over existing schemes or by insisting on a particular type of memorial, ex-servicemen in Wales ensured that their opinions on local commemorative plans were heard, even if not always heeded. Clubs or institutes were often the preferred choice of memorial for ex-servicemen, although on occasion their motives may not have been altogether altruistic. At Aberdare the debate over the form of memorial started almost as soon as the war was over. In December 1918 the *Aberdare Leader* published a letter from the honorary secretary of the Aberdare branch of the National Association of Discharged Sailors and Soldiers:

> Perhaps it would be interesting for your readers to know the opinion of the discharged men of Aberdare on this matter. They strongly deprecate the old method of erecting a monumental memorial to the men who have fought and died for their country, and maintain that something might be erected which would perpetuate the memory of their fallen comrades and at the same time be an appreciation of the efforts of our sailors and soldiers on behalf of humanity and civilisation. Such a memorial could be possible in the form of an ex-servicemen's club.[8]

This suggestion did not gain wide support and a series of public meetings, held under the forceful direction of the local MP, Charles Stanton, who was vociferous in his support for a monument, approved a cenotaph design for the memorial. The ex-servicemen were not intimidated by Stanton, however, and voiced their displeasure at a packed public meeting in February 1920. The aim of the ex-servicemen was simple:

> the establishment of a social centre as a suitable memorial to the fallen, and which would also be of service to the living. Sunday concerts were

[8] *Aberdare Leader*, 14 December 1918.

being held for the purpose and already they had a matter of £350 in hand.
They did not favour the spending of money on cold granite when there
was so much suffering in the country.

Stanton addressed the meeting and succeeded in pacifying the
ex-servicemen by suggesting that they should accept representation on the memorial committee. It was finally agreed that one
representative from each of the eight ex-servicemen's
organizations in the district should attend all future meetings of
the memorial committee.[9] In September 1920, the *Aberdare Leader*
reported that moves were under way to provide a club and
institute for the ex-servicemen of the town and district using
United Services funds as a base for fund-raising.[10] Aberdare
town committee was subsequently formed to organize both the
'United Services Club and Cenotaph', and public appeals were
made for both schemes. The formal opening of the ex-
servicemen's club took place in November 1922 without any
further public opposition by the ex-servicemen to a monument
being erected as the town's war memorial. Four months later the
cenotaph was unveiled.[11] The opening of such clubs was on
occasion regarded with trepidation by sections of the community. In north Wales, the Prestatyn branch of the Comrades
of the Great War Association decided to have drinking facilities
at their new club. A meeting of the Prestatyn Temperance
Women's Group learnt of this 'with deepest regret . . . The
Prime Minister stated during the War that we had three great
enemies to fight – Germany, Austria and drink. Our boys have
defeated Germany and Austria, and we must help them to defeat
Drink.'[12]
At the very least, ex-servicemen expected to be consulted
about, and involved in, ceremonies to unveil or open local war
memorials. At Rhymney, the local war memorial committee had
proposed a memorial park on land donated by the Rhymney
Iron Company. This was adopted at an open meeting of
townspeople in July 1919, although opposition was voiced by
representatives from the Discharged Soldiers' and Sailors'

[9] *Aberdare Leader*, 21 February 1920. See also *South Wales Daily News*, 18 February 1920.
[10] *Aberdare Leader*, 11 September 1920, and *South Wales Daily News*, 11 September 1920.
[11] *Aberdare Leader*, 18 November 1922 and 17 March 1923.
[12] *Prestatyn Weekly*, 29 November 1919.

Association. Their scheme was for the building of two terraces of houses to be let rent free to the widows and dependants of men killed in action, but the proposal for a public park gained approval.[13] The scheme continued despite opposition from the residents of Abertysswg, who sent a deputation to the council protesting that 'they were too far removed from Rhymney for the park to be of any use to the inhabitants of their district'.[14] The council ignored this and the park, which included a recreation ground, tennis court and bowling green, was opened in grand style in May 1925. The procession assembled at the council offices and, headed by the Rhymney Brass Band, marched through the streets to the war memorial park with the members and staff of the urban district council leading the proceedings. They were closely followed by the Rhymney, Abertysswg and Pontlottyn Fire Brigades, the Rhymney, Abertysswg and New Tredegar Ambulance Brigades, Rhymney Girl Guides, Rhymney Scouts and Church Lads' Brigades, with extra music being provided by the joint bands of the Scouts and Church Lads' Brigades. The park was declared open by the chairman of the council who later in the evening entertained the members of the council and others to a meal at the Royal Hotel.[15] The council could scarcely have anticipated the barrage of protest that was to greet their action. Meetings of the men's and women's sections of the local branch of the British Legion passed a resolution of protest at the action of the council 'in their unjust act to the widows, orphans and dependants of those who made the supreme sacrifice, and to the ex-servicemen in general, by not inviting them to attend the opening ceremony of the War Memorial Park'.[16] A small committee was appointed and instructed to forward a letter of protest to all daily and weekly newspapers. The letter was published in the *Merthyr Express*:

> The Rhymney Urban District Council have probably placed on record an event that stands unequalled in War Memorials throughout Great Britain. We refer to the opening ceremony of the War Memorial Park . . . The ex-servicemen and members of the local branch of the British Legion were

---

[13] *Merthyr Express*, 26 July 1919, and *Cardiff Times*, 26 July 1919. See also minutes of Rhymney Urban District Council, 13 August 1919.
[14] *Evening Express*, 11 September 1919.
[15] *Merthyr Express*, 9 May 1925.
[16] Ibid.

not invited to attend – the men who stood abreast with the heroes when they fell, who ministered to them in their last moments, and who laid them to rest in non-consecrated places in foreign lands. Whatever may be our conception of the Great War, we can scarcely conceive of a more despicable, mean and ungrateful action than that of the Rhymney Urban District Council in failing to recognise these men. This surely constitutes a record, especially when they failed to recognise the widows and orphans of the men whose great sacrifice they claim to have been commemorating. In fact, the orphans were amongst those who had to be kept back to make room for the elect. Could hypocrisy have sunk to a lower depth?[17]

Letters appeared from other correspondents on the same theme: 'The Kaiser called the British Army contemptible. The Rhymney Urban District Councillors have endorsed his remarks to the full by the manner in which they have treated the widows, orphans and ex-servicemen of Rhymney.'[18] The controversy was discussed at a meeting of the public works committee a week after the opening of the park, when it was explained that the omission to invite the ex-servicemen was a pure oversight which the council regretted and arose from the fact that those who organized the opening had lost sight of the fact that the park was a war memorial park. It was resolved, somewhat optimistically in the event, that the whole matter should be allowed to drop.[19] The responses to this explanation were fast and predictable, with correspondents to the local press giving vent to their anger that the council had admitted forgetting that the park was designated as the town's war memorial:

> What an excuse! The first bye-law of the park states that the park shall be known as the Rhymney War Memorial Park. Surely our Council considered the bye-laws when making arrangements for the opening ceremony? . . . The programmes and bills exhibited were all headed with the words 'Rhymney War Memorial Park'. Why do our councillors stoop so low? Had they been at Ypres, Armentieres, Arras, Somme, Bullicourt, Passchendaele, Hill 60, or any other engagement they would probably make the same excuse, but they were not there! . . . The Council admitted they made a bad mistake, but they have done nothing to cover the great

[17] *Merthyr Express*, 16 May 1925. The same letter was published in the *Western Mail*, 14 May 1925.
[18] *Merthyr Express*, 16 May 1925.
[19] Rhymney Urban District Council. Meeting of public works committee, 20 May 1925.

insult to those gallant men from Rhymney who gave their lives for their country and whose sacrifices the park is intended to commemorate.[20]

A Celtic cross with one hundred and fifty-five names inscribed upon it was eventually erected in the centre of the town and unveiled in October 1929. On this occasion the ex-servicemen were prominent in the procession to the memorial and in the ceremony itself.[21]

The actions of local bureaucrats similarly incensed ex-servicemen in Swansea in the weeks following the unveiling of the memorial in July 1923. The Swansea memorial took the form of a cenotaph enclosed by a court of memory, within which were tablets inscribed with the names of over two thousand men and a number of female munition workers who lost their lives in the war. However, it was the addition of a tablet bearing the names of those involved in the building of the memorial that prompted the actions of local ex-servicemen. The tablet listed the names of mayors of Swansea during whose terms of office the memorial was inaugurated and completed, the town clerk, the ex-borough treasurer and honorary secretary of the war memorial fund, the architect of the cenotaph and the builders. In reporting the dispute, the *Western Mail* noted that 'public indignation has been growing because the names of civilians have thus been placed on a monument sacred to the dead'.[22] A meeting of the local branch of the British Legion was convened in July 1923 to register their protest. It was the opinion of the Legion that 'those whose names were on that tablet were getting a cheap advertisement throughout the ages' and that the court of memory should be reserved solely for the names of those who had fallen.[23] The war memorial committee in response denied any knowledge of the tablet, and as the local branch of the British Legion had a representative on the committee, it would appear that the offending tablet may have been council-inspired. The Swansea Ex-Servicemens' Labour League discussed the problem over the following months and wrote to the mayor stating that, if the tablet was not removed speedily, 'the League is

[20] *Merthyr Express*, 20 June 1925.
[21] *Western Mail*, 28 October 1929.
[22] *Western Mail*, 30 July 1923.
[23] *South Wales Daily Post*, 30 July 1923.

prepared to co-operate with any other body to remove the same and cast it into the sea'.[24] It is apparent that some of the civilian names had been inscribed on the tablet unwittingly. Mr John Glasbrook of Sketty Court wrote to the town clerk to protest and sent a copy of his letter to the press:

> I have just been informed this evening that my name appears on the Tablet in the Court of Memory . . . I write to you to enquire by whose authority this was done and my name used without my permission? I request that it is removed at once, otherwise I must take necessary action. I am exceedingly grieved and annoyed at such a scandalous exhibition of bad taste.[25]

A special meeting of the Swansea war memorial subcommittee met a deputation from the British Legion in August 1923 when tempers flared, the chairman of the committee accusing the ex-servicemen of wanting 'to make a little kudos out of their dead friends'. Councillor Bert Cronin, representing the Ex-Servicemen's Labour League, was having none of this and made the chairman aware of his views which reflected ex-servicemen's anger at the activities of war-time profiteers: 'As far as that tablet is concerned, your name with the others on it is going to be shifted off. If those who made their pile during the war had helped, there would have been no need for that committee.'[26] It was eventually decided that all names, other than those of the dead and those who laid the foundation stone, unveiled the memorial and placed the 'King's Shilling' beneath the stone, should be removed or erased. The offending tablet was subsequently removed. Apart from the names of those who died, the court of memory now contains the names of Earl Haig and Mrs Fewings, representing the war widows, who took part in a ceremony to lay the foundation stone, and Admiral Doveton Sturdee, who unveiled the memorial. The names of officers of local war memorial committees and other local dignitaries are rarely found on memorials in Britain, although an example exists at Senghennydd in south Wales, where the committee was

---

[24] *South Wales Daily Post*, 1 August 1923.
[25] Ibid.
[26] *South Wales Daily Post*, 5 August 1923, and *Western Mail*, 15 August 1923.

composed largely of councillors and officials prominent in the management of the local colliery.[27]

Ex-servicemen felt that honouring their dead comrades was a 'debt of honour', and even though they may have been overlooked or neglected by the commemorative process, ultimately their presence could not be ignored. This did not apply, however, to the immediate families of the dead: they had a negligible input into the 'official' commemoration of the nation's dead. At a national level there were no women present at the first meeting of the Imperial War Graves Commissioners in November 1917; unsuccessful attempts were made by various women's organizations to gain representation.[28] It appears that this attitude was often reflected at a local level in Britain and, once again, Wales was no exception. The inhabitants of Aberdare could not decide where to site their memorial in the town. Correspondence on the subject appeared in the local paper virtually every day, and it was finally decided to put the matter to three separate public meetings. Two of these were open to the general public and one confined to those with 'special interests', which were defined as those of war widows, dependants and friends of the dead, but the bereaved as a group were not represented on the official war memorial committee.[29] The possibility of a utilitarian memorial led to 'An Officer's Widow' writing to the *Aberdare Leader* in December 1922 on behalf of the bereaved: 'We demand the Cenotaph where we can ourselves protect it from other desecration than that meted out by children'.[30] In March 1919 the *Western Mail* reported that the bereaved were to be consulted as to the form of Porthcawl's war memorial. The following month, a meeting was held for those residents who had lost relatives in the war and it was

---

[27] A panel on the memorial at Magor has the inscription: 'Remember also David Alfred Thomas 1st Viscount Rhondda Born Aberdare 1856 Died Llanwern 1918 for he too died serving the nation as Food Controller.' I am grateful to Peter Strong for drawing my attention to this memorial.

[28] Longworth, *Unending Vigil*, see p. 29. War widows were represented in the British War Graves Association but this organization appears not to have played an active role in debates over commemoration in Wales. The British Legion offered opportunities, via the women's sections, for women to participate in a predominantly male organization. By December 1924, 270 branches had been formed, with a membership of approximately 15,700. See Niall J. A. Barr, 'Service not self', pp. 59–65, and also G. Wootton, *The Official History of the British Legion* (London, 1956), pp. 59 and 76.

[29] *Aberdare Leader*, 18 November 1922.

[30] *Aberdare Leader*, 23 December 1922.

unanimously resolved that the memorial should take the form of a bronze monument.[31] Yet occasions where the wishes of the bereaved were taken into account were the exception rather than the rule. In November 1923, at the height of the debate over the form of the Merthyr Tydfil War Memorial, the *Merthyr Express* published a letter from a 'War Widow':

> We are all anxious to know what form the memorial will take, but why a children's ward in the General Hospital? With all due respect to the hospital I felt very indignant when I read that Mr Williams would like the suggestion carried. I am a war widow and feel very strongly on the matter. If we are to have a war memorial, let us have one that we can go and look at whenever we feel inclined and place our flowers on, as they do in every other town. What better memorial do we want than that in Troedyrhiw? We do not want a large useless column as Mr Williams says, but whatever it may be, let us have it in the form of a cenotaph, so that we may look at it as we pass by, and say to ourselves that it commemorates our loved ones.[32]

Such letters are demonstrably angry and bitter at an official system from which they felt excluded, with the intensity of feelings prompting letters to a local newspaper; this also suggests that there was no other official public outlet for their frustration. On occasions, however, the emotional force of the bereaved could be manipulated either for initiating a memorial or to inject a degree of momentum into an existing movement. The war memorial committee in Lampeter was faced with an awkward situation because its recommendation that a monument be erected as the town's war memorial was rejected by a public meeting in March 1919. At a subsequent committee meeting, held the following month to reconsider the question of a memorial, Mr Rees Davies addressed the meeting:

> It occurred to him to find the names of those from this town and parish who have given their lives for their country. 27 young men and one young lady have made that supreme sacrifice. I made it my duty to go round these bereaved families to tell them what this Committee is doing and to ask them what their wish is in this matter of a memorial. They all gave me

[31] *Western Mail*, 29 March 1919 and 8 April 1919.
[32] *Merthyr Express*, 24 November 1923.

to understand their desire was to see a monument erected, and I cannot conceive of our going contrary to their wishes.

Other members of the committee considered this to be 'the final word in this matter'.[33] A further public meeting was held the next day. The outcome of this meeting is not recorded in the minutes of the war memorial committee, but a statement to a public meeting that a monument was the wish of the bereaved families must have affected support for opposing schemes. In these circumstances, to argue against a monument would have been both difficult and controversial.[34]

At Lampeter the apparent desire of the bereaved families for a particular type of memorial became useful propaganda, but in Barry the grief of the bereaved was an important element in the prolonged dispute over the form of memorial. In July 1925, the *Barry Herald* published a letter from a 'Barryite' protesting against the idea of a memorial hall:

> I think and many others agree with me that the mere suggestion of a hall is wicked. It would be used mostly for dancing and the brave ones who shed their lives for us would be forgotten . . . Why should other towns like Bridgend etc outshine us? Mothers of Barry would like to put some flowers in remembrance the same as mothers of other towns. So mothers wake up and protest against a Memorial Hall.[35]

The lack of any form of memorial by 1928 brought about further hostile comments, again invoking the image of grieving women to emphasize the point. An editorial in the *Barry and District News* spoke of

> Two wreaths in memory of dead Barry soldiers [that] could find no better resting-place than the lamp-post in the centre of King Square. They were

---

[33] Minutes of Lampeter War Memorial Committee Meeting, 1 April 1919.

[34] Lampeter's monument, designed by Goscombe John, was unveiled in 1921 and the name of Nurse Ella Richards is prominent on the memorial. The court of memory at the Swansea memorial contains bronze tablets listing the names of those killed, including the names of female munition workers killed during the war. Further examples of women's names on war memorials can be found at Colwyn Bay, Cosheston, Holyhead, Pembroke, Penarth and Seven Sisters. On occasion the design of a memorial, or the sheer numbers involved, did not allow for the inscription of individual names and a roll of honour was usually composed and held elsewhere in the community.

[35] *Barry Herald*, 3 July 1925. Bridgend's war memorial had been unveiled in 1921.

placed there by women who had cause to remember the war and trussed
against the gaunt piece of metal they made a pathetic picture.[36]

Such images appeared frequently in the pages of the local
press in Wales and there is an implicit assumption in reports of
the commemoration process that the bereaved are women. In his
study of Armistice Day ceremonies between the wars, Adrian
Gregory suggests that this was in part shaped by women's ability
to exercise a greater degree of control over their movements
during the day: 'As a result, the public face of crowds on
Armistice Day was often predominantly female. This in turn
helped shape the picture of the bereaved as primarily women.'[37]
It was in their role as grieving mothers that women usually
participated in the commemoration process in Wales by
unveiling local war memorials.[38] However, their visual image
was usually deemed sufficient as on such occasions the women
rarely addressed the crowd; this privilege was accorded to
selected guests who were invariably male. Women rarely appear
as grieving wives or mothers in memorial sculpture in Wales.
L. S. Merrifield's fine memorial for the borough of Merthyr
Tydfil includes a miner's wife holding a baby, whilst in
Goscombe John's memorial at Llandaff a female figure is
symbolic of Llandaff itself. Nurses are depicted on memorials at
Mountain Ash and Colwyn Bay, but allegorical representations
of women on memorials, especially as Peace or Victory, are
much more common in Wales, with examples at Abercarn,

[36] *Barry and District News*, 16 November 1928. The lamp-posts re-emerged a year later at
the annual dinner of the Barry United Veterans Association in November 1929 when Dr
E. Owens, an independent councillor and holder of the Military Cross, railed against the
inactivity: 'I am supposed to be a member of the War Memorial Committee but I have
not attended the meetings of the Committee because I am disgusted. When you see
numbers of wreaths on lamp-posts in this town it makes your blood boil.' *Barry Herald*, 15
November 1929.
[37] Adrian Gregory, *The Silence of Memory* (Oxford, 1994), pp. 32–4.
[38] Memorials at Brecon, Dolgellau, Kidwelly, Llanfairpwllgwyngyll and Mumbles were
also unveiled by mothers who had lost sons in the war. For Brecon, see *Western Mail*, 30
October 1920; for Dolgellau see *Carnarvon and Denbigh Herald*, 7 October 1921; for
Kidwelly, see *Western Mail*, 21 July 1924; for Llanfairpwllgwyngyll, see *Holyhead Chronicle*,
16 November 1928; and for Mumbles, see *South Wales Daily Post*, 31 July 1939. In
November 1938 the Welsh National Temple of Peace and Health was opened in Cardiff
by Mrs Minnie James of Dowlais, who had lost two sons in the Great War. *Western Mail*,
24 November 1938. Memorials at Bala and Letterston were unveiled by bereaved fathers.
For Bala, see *Y Seren*, 8 April 1922; and for Letterston, see *Pembroke County Guardian*,10
December 1920.

Aberystwyth, Bangor-on-Dee, Denbigh, Port Talbot and Tonyrefail.[39]

Controversy could continue after the unveiling ceremony had taken place and it often centred on the perceived insensitive treatment and lack of respect accorded to the bereaved families. A month after the unveiling of the Aberdare war memorial, the *Aberdare Leader* published a letter from someone who signed himself as 'A Maimed Ex-Serviceman':

> It made my blood boil to see some on that platform, who were only togged up for a dress parade, and more fit for a flower show or a race meeting than a war memorial ceremony. I blame the people who were in charge of that platform. Who did they lose in the war? Did they have thoughts for our fallen heroes? No, only on their dresses. There were poor war widows and mothers and other relatives in that crowd who ought to have been up there instead of those who had lost nobody.[40]

Although space at the unveiling ceremony had been reserved in front of the memorial for the bereaved and ex-servicemen, the platform itself was reserved for the great and the good, along with members of the local council, representatives from local industry, education and local churches and chapels.[41] In November 1924 the Penarth war memorial was unveiled by two women who had each lost three sons in the war. In the same edition that covered the unveiling ceremony a letter appeared from 'Merely a War Widow':

> At the unveiling of the Penarth War Memorial, many relatives of the fallen were insulted – I use the word advisedly – grossly insulted by the invitation of the Council to be present in the enclosure to take part in the ceremony. Judge then the feelings of the relatives when, on arriving as they were requested to do, early and presenting their programme, they were informed they could not be admitted, not, as was obvious, because there was no room for them, but because they were not lucky enough to have a ticket, for in the enclosure were scores who had neither served in the war nor suffered loss. I heard dozens of relatives turned away, and one poor old

---

[39] The figurative depiction of women and children on war memorials is discussed by Catherine Moriarty in 'Narrative and the absent body: mechanisms of meaning in First World War memorials' (unpublished Ph.D. thesis, University of Sussex, 1995), pp. 197–206.

[40] *Aberdare Leader*, 2 September 1922.

[41] *Aberdare Leader*, 5 August 1922.

woman refused admission say bitterly, 'Did not my boy die as well as theirs
for his country, although I am poor and they are rich?' How much more
bitter would she have felt if she had known how many in the enclosure had
lost nothing more substantial than prewar food. Who is to blame? It can
hardly be that it was a deliberate attempt to insult the relatives of the
fallen. Someone apparently blundered; and what a blunder! Had anyone
thought of a plan to hurt more, he would have been hard put to do so. I
should add, however, that when the fortunate ones in the enclosure had
left, the relatives were allowed to approach the Memorial and leave the
wreaths and flowers which so many of them carried in memory of the
fallen. One consolation, thank God, their men could not know how their
relatives in Penarth were treated on the one day it was in the power of the
authorities to honour, however slightly, their men through them.[42]

At times the commemoration process itself may have served to
marginalize and alienate the bereaved. In June 1922 Earl Haig
visited Swansea to lay the foundation stone for the war memorial
and it was decided that a local war widow should accompany him
and place the 'King's Shilling' under the stone. The local pensions
officer submitted the names of 'a few of the most noteworthy of
war widows' to the mayor; the names were placed in a hat and
Mrs Gertrude Fewings was chosen in this way. Edward Fewings
served in the 14th (Swansea) Battalion, Royal Welch Regiment,
and had been killed in July 1916, leaving Gertrude and five
children. His body was never found and his name is recorded on
the Thiepval Memorial.[43] The local paper reported her
involvement in the ceremony with a distinct lack of tact: 'The *Daily
Post* reporter was the first to inform Mrs Fewings of the result;
"Well, you are the lucky one," said the reporter after he had
explained the circumstances. "Is it luck, I wonder?" Mrs Fewings
replied.'[44] The column describing the event was headed 'War
Widow, Part in Swansea Memorial Ceremony – A Happy Idea'.
In the programme printed to commemorate the visit of Earl Haig
to lay the foundation stone, the itinerary is listed in detail but no

---

[42] *Penarth Times*, 13 November 1924. A bereaved father, Mr G. Hoult, who had lost
three sons in the war, was due to share the unveiling but a few days before the ceremony
decided not to take part. The local paper reported that 'he preferred not to undergo the
trying ordeal'. Ibid.
[43] *Soldiers Died in the Great War, 1914–1919: The Welch Regiment* (Polsted, 1988), p. 55. See
also *The Register of the Names Inscribed on the Thiepval Memorial, France* (London, Imperial War
Graves Commission, 1931), Memorial Register 21.
[44] *South Wales Daily Post*, 30 June 1922.

mention is made of the participation of Mrs Fewings in the ceremony. Similarly insensitive treatment occurred at the opening of the Barry Memorial Hall in November 1932. The local press reported that relatives of the fallen had complained because they had not been invited to the unveiling of the roll of honour. This was attributed to the size of the hall foyer which would only hold one hundred people and therefore it was impossible to invite all the relatives, so they invited none at all. Prominent guests included councillors and committee members connected with the project. After the opening, guests attended a luncheon. Between 3 and 5 p.m. of the same day there was an inspection of the hall, which was open only to members of the various committees, sub-committees and subscribers who had donated large sums of money. A public meeting was scheduled for the evening and tickets were issued to the relatives of the fallen. The families of the bereaved, therefore, were finally allowed access to the town's war memorial in the evening, after the committee members and generous subscribers had been shown around.[45]

As a group, the bereaved families were rarely either considered or consulted in local commemorative schemes. Despite this exclusion, it is clear that the many small ceremonies held to unveil memorials in schools, churches and workplaces throughout Wales did provide some comfort for families of the dead. The emotional impact of local ceremonies was highlighted by the experience of Charles Stanton, who had fought and won the Merthyr by-election in November 1915 on a strongly pro-war platform. As a local MP Stanton was involved in many local commemorative ceremonies and often made speeches on these occasions, but it was a relatively small-scale ceremony that revealed his own experience of the war. In 1920 he unveiled a memorial tablet to past students of Aberdare Boys' County School. The local newspaper reported that:

> A very affecting incident occurred in the course of a speech. Mr Stanton whose son, the late Lieutenant Clifford Stanton, is among those whose names are inscribed on the Memorial Tablet, was so overcome with emotion that he was for a time unable to proceed with his speech.[46]

[45] *Barry and District News*, 18 November 1932.
[46] *Aberdare Leader*, 9 October 1920. For a more traditional view of Charles Stanton, see Edward May, 'Charles Stanton and the limits to "Patriotic" Labour', *Welsh History Review*, XVIII, No. 3 (June 1997), pp. 483–508.

The central cenotaph at Aberdare does not have names inscribed on it and the fact that he was able to see his son's name on the school memorial tablet may have allowed a more intimate and emotional response than occurred at more formal 'civic' ceremonies. In July 1921 a tablet was unveiled at Cadoxton Boys' School, Barry, in memory of the sixty-eight old boys who died in the Great War. It was unveiled by Councillor Dudley Howe, an old boy of the School, with the ceremony punctuated by 'the sobbing of grief-stricken mothers'.[47] Just over a year later, in November 1922, the bishop of Llandaff dedicated the renovated ancient parish cross at St Cadoc's church in Cadoxton as a war memorial to the 109 men from the parish who had lost their lives.[48] Many of the names found on the tablet in Cadoxton Boys' School can also be found engraved on the base of the cross. For the family of James Mote, the ceremony in St Cadoc's churchyard may have been the third commemoration of their family member. In October 1920 a memorial tablet had been unveiled to the twelve employees of the Barry General Post Office in Dock View Road who had been killed in the war.[49] Fifty employees had enlisted and twelve had died, including James Mote. A random example, therefore, reveals that one man was commemorated at his old school, his church and his workplace many years before the 'official' war memorials in Barry were unveiled, emphasizing both the importance and immediacy of local commemoration.

It was clearly unusual for women to have been represented as wives, mothers or sisters on local war memorial committees.[50] As with such committees throughout Britain, it appears that it was usually the 'active women of the parish' who were involved. At the first public meeting of the war memorial committee in Barry,

[47] *Barry Dock News*, 22 July 1921.

[48] *Barry Dock News*, 17 November 1922.

[49] *Barry Dock News*, 22 October 1920.

[50] A random selection of committees throughout Wales reveals that those for Bangor-on-Dee, Llwydcoed, Machen, Maesteg, Prestatyn and Senghennydd did not have any female members. The Lampeter War Memorial Committee's thirty-four members included three women. The committee at Llandrindod Wells had an impressive 102 members on its general committee, representing the urban district council, local clergy and ministers, the five wards as well as 'additional members'. Forty-eight of these were women. The original committee formed in 1921 to co-ordinate the Carmarthenshire County War Memorial had included twenty-four men and twelve women. By the time of the unveiling of the memorial in September 1924, the committee consisted of thirty-four men. *Carmarthen Journal*, 12 September 1924.

held in November 1921, one female councillor was elected but otherwise the women elected to serve on the committee belonged to organizations which may have been represented on any council committee. The council minutes specifically refer to co-opting on to the war memorial committee four representatives of 'Women's Organisations in the district'.[51] These included the Barry Twentieth Century Club, the Co-operative Women's Guild (Barry Dock Branch) and the Barry Unionist Association. Throughout the long tenure of the war memorial committee women participated in fund-raising events such as house-to-house collections but were always in a minority on the various subcommittees. Of course, with so many families in Wales affected either directly or indirectly by the war, the probability must be that a number of members of memorial committees would have a claim to be counted amongst the 'bereaved'. However, for most women, becoming involved in what was essentially a business arrangement may have been neither appropriate nor practical after the war. Many women in Britain with families to support had few options open to them. Eleanor Cain became a wife and widow within eleven months, losing her husband, baby and brother and 'felt like lying down and giving up altogether'. Kitty Eckersley heard the news of her husband's death whilst seven months pregnant and recalled that she did not want to live because 'the world had come to an end then for me because I'd lost all that I loved'.[52] Many of the bereaved, particularly women struggling to bring up young families, may have chosen voluntarily not to participate in memorial committees as they tried to come to terms with their loss and to cope with the realities of post-war life, yet their stories remain largely untold. In her study of widows of German soldiers after the Great War, Karin Hausen describes the families of soldiers who died in the war as:

---

[51] Barry Urban District Council, 12 December 1921; report of a meeting of Barry war memorial committee held on 24 November 1921. See also *Barry Herald*, 9 December 1921, and *Barry Dock News*, 2 December 1921. See *Rhondda Leader*, 26 September 1924, and the Coelbren Miners' Welfare and Memorial Hall Minute Books, December 1922–June 1929, for examples of this type of involvement at Trehafod and Coelbren. Press coverage of ceremonies would, on occasion, carry a separate column on the 'woman's view'. These usually appeared when larger memorials were unveiled, such as the Swansea memorial and the 'national' memorial in Cardiff. See *South Wales Daily Post*, 23 July 1923, and *Western Mail*, 13 June 1928.
[52] Interviews taken from the Imperial War Museum Sound Archive.

a social group whose history has been forgotten . . . Their story requires two narrative tracks: one tracing how they were discovered and dealt with as a 'problem group' in society, and another showing how, under conditions of public support and social control, they faced crises in their private lives.[53]

Behind each name on a war memorial lay a personal family tragedy, and an interpretative context of female experiences placed firmly around emancipation may overlook the emotional burden carried by many women during and after the war.[54] A rare reference to this pressure was made by Field-Marshal Allenby at the unveiling of the Merthyr Tydfil memorial in 1931, prompted no doubt by the sculpture of the memorial itself:

> And not only the men, the daughters of your country came forward, at the call, as bravely as their husbands, brothers and sons . . . Others, at home, gave as great proof of endurance and patient bravery – in hospitals, munition factories and war work. The strain suffered by the woman who had to work and wait, in torturing suspense, apart from him she held most dear, while aware of the dire possibilities, without news, unable to share his danger or give active help, cannot be even faintly imagined by us. Such courage was of even a finer type than the heroism so splendid in the clamour and clash of battle. Your Memorial has rightly recognised the share of women as well of men, in the war; and of children, too – for they also suffered.[55]

Bureaucratic mistakes may also have reinforced the decision of some to remain apart from official commemoration arrangements. In the small town of Crickhowell, a succession of parish council meetings in late 1918 and early 1919 was held to make arrangements for returning soldiers and prisoners of war. It was finally decided to present a silver medallion and ten-shilling note to each returning soldier and to the next of kin of deceased

---

[53] Karin Hausen, 'The German nation's obligations to the heroes' widows of World War 1', in Margaret Randolph Higonnet et al. (eds.), *Behind the Lines: Gender and the Two World Wars* (New Haven, 1987), p. 126.

[54] The role of women during the Great War has received much attention. For a recent exposition, see G. Braybon, 'Women and the war', in S. Constantine, M. W. Kirby and M. B. Rose (eds.), *The First World War in British History* (London, 1995), pp. 141–67.

[55] *Merthyr Express*, 14 November 1931. The inscription on the memorial refers to 'The men and women of Merthyr Tydfil who died and suffered in the Great War'.

officers and men. This took place at a church parade held in the town square in September 1919. A parish meeting later in September resolved to recall the medallions given to the next of kin of the deceased and that the words 'Welcome Home' be crossed off and 'For King and Country' inscribed in their place.[56]

[56] See minutes of Crickhowell Parish Council, especially 18 September 1919. See also report of ceremony, *Abergavenny Chronicle*, 12 September 1919.

III

'THE GLORIFICATION OF CARDIFF': NATIONAL AND LOCAL MEMORIALS IN WALES

The Cenotaph in London was unveiled on Armistice Day 1920 and has remained the focus of public remembrance in Britain.[1] The Welsh National War Memorial in Cathays Park, Cardiff, has provided a similar function in Wales since its unveiling by the prince of Wales in 1928.[2] Press reports of the unveiling ceremony repeatedly emphasized the national character of the memorial and described the occasion as 'the act of a whole race; reserved to that race; meaning more to that race than anything else'.[3] Yet the authorities in south Wales had chosen to ignore the North Wales Heroes' Memorial in Bangor whose very existence negated the idea of a 'national' memorial in Cardiff.[4] The background to the building of the memorial in Cardiff provides further evidence that the notion of national unity in the tangible form of the Welsh National War Memorial was an illusion and that the title 'National' was a misnomer. Studies of the movements to establish county and borough memorials as well as smaller parish memorials suggest that civic pride and a desire for local commemoration provided a stronger link in the commemoration of the Great War throughout Wales than a desire to display national or regional unity.

The movement to establish a national memorial in Cardiff, inaugurated by the *Western Mail* in October 1919, is well documented in city council minutes and, predictably, in the columns of the *Western Mail*. The fund was sanctioned by the council, which offered a site in Cathays Park for the memorial, but it was anxious to retain some degree of control over the scheme and remained officially associated with the organizing

---

[1] For further reading on both temporary and permanent cenotaphs, see ch. 2, n. 6.

[2] The Welsh National Book of Remembrance, currently housed in the Temple of Peace and Health in Cardiff, lists 35,000 names.

[3] *Western Mail*, 13 June 1928.

[4] The North Wales Heroes' Memorial has received scant attention in Welsh historiography; a notable exception is J. Gwynn Williams, *The University College of North Wales: Foundations, 1884–1927* (Cardiff, 1985), pp. 374–8.

committee. Approximately £25,700 was subscribed to the fund; this was invested in government securities and rose to £34,000 over the seven years that passed before the memorial was built in 1928. The original committee consisted of the earl of Plymouth, Lord Glanely, William Davies in his capacity as editor of the *Western Mail*, and G. F. Forsdike, lord mayor of Cardiff, with the advice of Sir Cecil Harcourt Smith. The commission was offered to Sir Thomas Brock, designer of the Victoria Memorial outside Buckingham Palace, but his original design proved to be financially unrealistic and Sir Thomas died before submitting a further proposal.[5] Certain architects were invited to submit designs in a limited competition, and in 1924 the committee chose that of J. Ninian Comper. Selection of the site proved to be more problematic. The preferred site was a circular plot of land in front of the south façade of the City Hall, but objections were raised by the National Museum and the city council that the proposed site would interfere with both the City Hall and the museum.[6] An alternative site in Priory Gardens was discussed but Lord Bute withheld his consent, and it was finally decided to erect the memorial in Alexandra Gardens in Cathays Park.[7] Work commenced in March 1926 and was completed by early 1928. Preparations for the unveiling of the memorial by the prince of Wales and the event itself were covered in great detail by the *Western Mail*.[8] In early June the paper wrote of the imminent ceremony: 'Every care has been taken to make the event truly national in character. The movement to perpetuate the memory of the men of Wales who died in the Great War has been organized on national lines from its inception.'[9]

Local histories of Cardiff confirm this impression of national unity and describe how, although the idea of a national war

[5] Sir Thomas Brock's model for the proposed Welsh War Memorial was donated to the National Museum after his death. *Sixteenth Annual Report (1922–23), National Museum of Wales.*

[6] A model of the memorial was constructed to scale on this plot in order to give the council and the public an opportunity to assess the effect on the surrounding buildings, but it was finally deemed to be unsatisfactory. For details of the dispute, see *Western Mail* and *South Wales Daily News*, 9 December 1924. Photographs of the model of the memorial on both sites are held in the library of the National Museum & Gallery, Cardiff.

[7] Consent was necessary as the late marquess of Bute had stipulated during the conveyance of Cathays Park to the corporation that no buildings should be erected on this site. See *Western Mail*, 21 August 1925.

[8] *Western Mail*, 10, 11, 12 June 1928.

[9] *Western Mail*, 11 June 1928.

memorial was first mooted in 1917 by a local councillor, the idea did not come to fruition until October 1919 when the *Western Mail* opened a fund for this purpose.[10] In July 1917 a local councillor, H. M. Thompson, circulated a leaflet in which he put forward various ideas regarding war memorials and gave his own preference for a fountain in the midst of Alexandra Gardens. He suggested a national competition amongst artists and sculptors but it is clear from the local press that he was speaking of a memorial for 'my own city of Cardiff' rather than a national scheme.[11] Consideration of a national war memorial first emerged at a meeting of the general purposes committee of Cardiff City Council in November 1918 when it was decided that the mayor should invite representatives of all local authorities in Wales and Monmouthshire to a conference in Cardiff to discuss the subject.[12] Councillor Thompson re-distributed his circular when he appeared before the council subcommittee in January 1919. He put forward the same suggestion for a memorial but on this occasion saw it as being suitable for a national peace memorial and was promptly invited to join the Peace Celebration Committee.[13] The idea of a national conference was not discussed again until May 1919, but press reports are clear that there was substantial doubt within the council even at this early stage that Wales would unite in a national movement. It was Councillor Thompson who appeared most sceptical and he again argued the case that he had put forward in 1917 for a local memorial. According to the *Cardiff Times* report of the meeting,

> Alderman Thompson expressed the view that they were on the wrong tack. He did not think it would be possible to secure agreement with North Wales for a National Memorial at Cardiff, as most likely they would prefer memorials to their fallen in their own localities. What was wanted was a great memorial for Cardiff itself, and not for the whole of Wales.[14]

[10] See Dennis Morgan, *The Cardiff Story* (Cowbridge, 1991), pp. 219–21; *Cardiff, 1889–1974: The Story of the County Borough* (Cardiff, 1974), p. 34. It appears that both these publications take as their source of information Edgar L. Chappell, *Cardiff's Civic Centre: A Historical Guide* (Cardiff, 1946), pp. 27–8.

[11] *South Wales Daily News*, 21 July 1917.

[12] Cardiff City Council, general purposes committee, 29 November 1918.

[13] Cardiff City Council, parliamentary committee, 20 January 1919. See also report of meeting in *Western Mail*, 30 January 1919.

[14] *Cardiff Times*, 24 May 1919. See also *Western Mail*, 23 May 1919.

The letter was finally sent from Cardiff on 30 May 1919 to 200 public bodies throughout Wales with the optimistic view that 'the proposal is one which it is confidently anticipated will appeal to all Welshmen and receive the unanimous support of the whole Principality'.[15]

This was not borne out by the response to the letter; newspapers reported that sixty-three replies had been received and of these only twenty-one expressed willingness to send representatives to a conference.[16] The extant records reveal seventeen such authorities, with a fairly even distribution across Wales; there was an interesting element of dissent even amongst the positive replies to Cardiff's invitation.[17] Members of Bedwas and Machen Urban District Council originally voted to take no action with regard to the invitation. An amendment was put forward to send two delegates 'without committing itself to the proposal', which was only carried by the casting vote of the chairman.[18] Similar views were expressed in north Wales at a meeting of Caernarfon Town Council: there was some doubt as to whether it was worth attending the conference but it was finally agreed to send representatives, primarily because Caernarfon 'ought to make it clear that it was determined to have its rights . . . If you allow things to go to Cardiff, we shall get nothing'.[19] Glamorgan County Council could only provide a lukewarm response to the proposal. Representatives were appointed 'but without power to commit the Council'.[20] Even the local council in Lloyd George's home village of Cricieth made no response to the invitation from Cardiff, although

---

[15] Letter from J. H. Wheatley, clerk to Cardiff City Council, to the clerk, Mynydd-islwyn Urban District Council, 30 May 1919. The letter was sent to county, borough, urban and rural district councils but not to parish councils.

[16] *Western Mail*, 1 July 1919. See also *South Wales Daily News*, 1 July 1919. The minute books for every local authority in Wales in mid-1919 were sought and 135 were found to be extant.

[17] Aberavon Town Council, Abergavenny Town Council, Barry Urban District Council, Bedwas and Machen Urban District Council, Caernarfon Town Council, Carmarthenshire County Council, Gelligaer Urban District Council, Glamorgan County Council, Lampeter Borough Council, Llandyssul Rural District Council, Llantarnam Urban District Council, Llantrisant and Llantwit Fardre Rural District Council, Narberth Rural District Council, Neyland Urban District Council, Ogmore and Garw Urban District Council, Penybont Rural District Council, Valley Rural District Council.

[18] Bedwas and Machen Urban District Council, minutes of monthly meeting, 7 June 1919.

[19] *Carnarvon and Denbigh Herald*, 4 July 1919.

[20] Glamorgan County Council, minutes of quarterly meeting, 19 June 1919.

preparations for a local war memorial had been in hand from the early date of October 1916, with Mrs Lloyd George being added to the local committee in May 1919.[21]

The records of those councils which did discuss the question of a Welsh national war memorial give a unique insight into local attitudes throughout Wales towards Cardiff in 1919. The sheer distance and expense prompted some councils to decline the invitation. At a meeting in June 1919, Overton Rural District Council resolved that 'owing to inconvenience and the long distance this Council are unable to send representatives to a Conference', although it agreed to consider a report of the proceedings in due course.[22] New Radnor Rural District Council was particularly blunt in its response. The letter from Cardiff was read at a meeting on 7 June 1919 and 'the Council while approving of the principle of a Conference did not consider the matter of such importance or interest to the locality as to justify the expense of sending delegates to attend it'.[23] Financial considerations governed Pembroke Borough Council's response to Cardiff. Although the council sympathized with the project, the town clerk wrote that 'they fear they will be unable to take any part in supporting the movement. War memorials will be erected both in Pembroke and Pembroke Dock and some difficulty is already being experienced in securing the necessary funds.'[24]

Many local authorities were involved not only in their own memorial schemes but also in collaborative commemorative schemes within their area. At the same time as local councils in Monmouthshire considered the letter from Cardiff, they were also considering supporting the erection of a memorial to men of the 3rd Battalion Monmouthshire Regiment. Abergavenny was chosen as it served as the headquarters of the regiment; appeals for finance were made to each town from which men were recruited. The borough council duly sent deputations to the

[21] Cricieth Urban District Council minute book. See monthly meetings, 30 October 1916 and 26 May 1919.

[22] Overton Rural District Council, ordinary council meeting, 14 June 1919.

[23] New Radnor Rural District Council, ordinary council meeting, 7 June 1919.

[24] Letter book of Pembroke Borough Council, letter to Cardiff town clerk, 12 June 1919. See also minute book of Rhayader Rural District Council. At a meeting on 4 June 1919: 'The Clerk was instructed to reply that, having regard to this District having proceeded with a scheme at a cost of about £2000, this Council do not feel disposed, at the present moment, to consider a further object.'

urban district councils of Ebbw Vale, Abertillery, Nantyglo, Blaina and Tredegar to gain support for the project. The deputation that waited upon Abertillery Urban District Council on 30 June 1919 hastened to assure the council that the proposed regimental memorial was not intended in any way to interfere with the erection of the local war memorial. The members of Abertillery council were not impressed by such arguments and voted against the proposal. The letter from Cardiff proposing a national war memorial was discussed immediately afterwards and, perhaps not surprisingly, the council resolved that no action should be taken in this matter.[25]

Certain councils made it clear that antagonism towards Cardiff contributed in no small measure to their decision not to support the proposed national memorial. The *North Wales Chronicle* reported on the monthly meeting of Penmaenmawr Urban District Council in June 1919, when the invitation from Cardiff was discussed. The newspaper reported Councillor W. J. Roberts as arguing that 'the danger was that Cardiff would claim whatever was done, whilst Cardiff would not claim to be a Welsh town. One could not hear a word of Welsh spoken in the streets of Cardiff.'[26] Yet this should not be seen as a simple example of hostility towards the south as local authorities in south Wales were equally capable of such sentiments. The monthly meeting of Swansea Borough Council in June 1919 decided that the council should take no part in the movement and should decline the invitation from Cardiff. The press report of the meeting gives a more illuminating account of the meeting: it quotes Alderman Owen as saying that the council 'knew from experience that whatever might be done would be done for the glorification of Cardiff. The people of Swansea were anxious to have their own memorial in their own town, and he voted that the invitation be not agreed to.' The paper reported that this met with an enthusiastic response.[27] Montgomeryshire County Council decided, at its quarterly meeting in June 1919, that no action be taken but the press report gave a more graphic account of the meeting:

---

[25] Abertillery Urban District Council, minutes of meeting, 30 June 1919. The memorial to the men of the 3rd Battalion Monmouthshire Regiment was unveiled in October 1921 in Abergavenny by Lord Treowen, the lord lieutenant of the county. See *Western Mail*, 31 October 1921.

[26] *North Wales Chronicle*, 6 June 1919.

[27] *South Wales Daily News*, 19 June 1919.

National Disunity . . . When the letter circulated by the Cardiff City
Council mooting the idea of a Welsh National War Memorial came before
the Montgomery County Council on Friday the Chairman . . . said that
when any proposal came from Cardiff for promoting any Welsh national
object, it was looked at with considerable suspicion . . . because Cardiff was
evidently out for spoils, and he thought they were all pretty well sick of the
way she was exploiting Welsh affairs.[28]

North Walians considered that they had good reason not to
support the idea of a national war memorial in Cardiff, as a
scheme for a 'Memorial to the Fallen Heroes of North Wales' had
been in existence since 1917 and seems to have been either
overlooked or ignored by Cardiff City Council. The movement in
north Wales was inaugurated by R. J. Thomas, a Holyhead ship-
owner, in January 1917 with a £20,000 donation.[29] The aim of
the fund was to erect a memorial to the dead, provide bursaries
for the children of the fallen and to build new science buildings in
connection with the University College of North Wales, Bangor.
Local authorities throughout north Wales were circulated and
invited to attend a meeting in Rhyl in February 1917. The
circular proposed a 'National Memorial to the Men of North
Wales who have fallen in the War' and indicated that the scheme
had the support of the King. Amongst its signatories were some of
the most powerful men in Wales at that time, including Lords
Boston, Kenyon, Mostyn and Penrhyn. Indeed, Lord Anglesey
was said to be 'somewhat sore' at not being asked to sign the
appeal.[30] At the meeting in Rhyl, Lord Kenyon was voted to the
chair and a representative executive committee was formed,
the only note of dissent being sounded by the bishop of St Asaph,
who thought it premature to decide upon the character of the
memorial before the war was over.[31] The initial meeting decided
to drop 'National' from the title and thereafter the movement
was referred to as the 'North Wales Heroes' Memorial'.

[28] *South Wales Daily News*, 23 June 1919.
[29] *North Wales Chronicle*, 26 January 1917. See also *Holyhead Chronicle*, 26 January 1917,
and *Western Mail*, 25 January 1917. Much of the material on the North Wales Heroes'
Memorial is taken from uncatalogued college records, University College of North Wales
(UCNW) Heroes' Memorial File, held at University of Wales, Bangor.
[30] Letter from Lord Boston to Professor J. E. Lloyd, 1 February 1917. UCNW Heroes'
Memorial File.
[31] Letter from bishop of St Asaph to R. J. Thomas, 3 April 1917. UCNW Heroes'
Memorial File.

The organizing committee took full advantage of their connections in powerful places, with meetings held at Downing Street to promote the fund and Mrs Lloyd George acting as president of the London committee.[32] The scheme would cost approximately £150,000 and, by as early as February 1918, £61,000 had been promised. North Wales was divided into administrative areas, consisting of Anglesey, Caernarfonshire, Denbighshire, Montgomeryshire, Flintshire and Merioneth, and subscriptions were also received from London, Liverpool, Manchester, Stockport, Shanghai and the Welsh Hospital, India.[33] The movement to commemorate the fallen heroes of north Wales was therefore well under way by the time the letter was sent out from Cardiff in May 1919. The memorial arch was the first part of the scheme to be completed, with the names of 8,500 servicemen inscribed on wooden panels in the upper chambers by county and parish rather than by regiment.[34] This was formally opened by the prince of Wales in November 1923 and on the same visit the prince laid the foundation stone of the new science buildings.[35]

It is clear that the invitation from Cardiff City Council to local authorities throughout Wales was treated with a mixture of indifference, suspicion and hostility. Even allowing for the existence of the North Wales Heroes' Memorial Fund, many towns

---

[32] *Western Mail*, 18 May 1917. This report mentions that a movement was underway to commemorate the south Wales heroes but there is no extant evidence of it. In April 1917 the *Western Mail* reported an attempt to establish a national war museum in connection with the National Museum of Wales. See also Hubert Hall, 'A National War Museum and a Public Record Office for Wales', *Y Cymmrodor: The Magazine of the Honourable Society of Cymmrodorion*, XXVII (1917), pp. 206–29. This is not borne out by the *Annual Reports* of the Museum; see especially *11th (1917–1918)* and *12th (1918–1919)* which refer to the proposed establishment of a Welsh Naval and Historical Section to commemorate the labours of Welsh men and women in times of war. No further mention is made in subsequent *Reports* and the project does not appear to have materialized. A fund to establish a Welsh Pictorial War Record was opened in 1919 with the consent of the museum's council and over the years it purchased three major works of art for the museum until the monies were subsumed into a general fund in 1933. See *11th, 12th, 13th, 14th, 15th*, and *25th Annual Reports of the National Museum of Wales*.

[33] UCNW Heroes' Memorial File.

[34] Henry Thomas Hare had designed the new university building at Bangor and was to design the North Wales Heroes' Memorial. When he died in 1920 it was decided not to commission his successor and the new architect was chosen by competition at the Caernarfon eisteddfod of 1921. The design by D. Wynne Thomas of Bolton was successful. See J. Gwynn Williams, *University College of North Wales*, p. 375.

[35] The science buildings were finally opened in 1926, although they were not fully clear of debt until 1930. *Western Mail*, 3 November 1926, for details of opening.

and communities within the principality evidently resented what they interpreted as Cardiff's pretensions to grandeur and designs on becoming the Welsh capital.[36] The *North Wales Chronicle* commented on Cardiff's failure to establish a conference to discuss the proposed national memorial. In an editorial comment, the paper could scarcely conceal its pleasure at the very public rebuke delivered to Cardiff City Council:

> We offer our condolences to Cardiff. The cosmopolitan self-appointed 'metropolis' of Wales has experienced yet another and very serious rebuff. Public authorities in Wales have actually had the temerity to refuse to pander to Cardiff ambitions, and declined to find the funds for erecting an imposing National War Memorial in Cardiff, intended partly for the commemoration of Welsh heroes in the war and largely for the glorification of Cardiff in Wales. Some 200 public bodies in Wales were circularised by the Lord Mayor of Cardiff and invited to assist Cardiff in erecting a National Memorial in a town which prides itself ten times more on its cosmopolitan than upon its national character. Only one authority out of every ten so circularised even expressed willingness to send representatives to another Cardiff 'national' conference to discuss the proposal. In a huff, the Cardiff City Council now declares it can do without Wales, and will forthwith erect its own Peace Memorial.[37]

The results of the letter were discussed at a meeting of a subcommittee of Cardiff City Council when the consensus was for Cardiff 'to put up a peace memorial of its own and one worthy of the Welsh Metropolis'.[38] The *Evening Express* appeared prominently in the campaign for a local memorial. Many letters were published and, according to the paper, many more were received than they were able to publish, from the parents and friends of soldiers who fell in the Great War, in support of the idea of a cenotaph being erected in Cardiff. A typical example appeared on 19 September 1919 from Mr George Jukes of Cathedral Road in Cardiff; he wrote that

> It is left to us who are here to mourn those who fought and fell for us and the least the citizens of Cardiff can do is to erect a monument or shrine in

---

[36] See Neil Evans, 'The Welsh Victorian city: the middle class and civic and national consciousness in Cardiff, 1850–1914', *Welsh History Review*, XII, No. 3 (1985), pp. 350–87.

[37] *North Wales Chronicle*, 4 July 1919.

[38] *Western Mail*, 1 July 1919.

Cathays Park in memory of the Cardiff boys who gave their precious young lives that we might live in safety . . . If the editor of the *Evening Express* will start a fund I shall be pleased to subscribe 25 guineas.[39]

The lord mayor of Cardiff gave an interview on 25 September to the *Western Mail* and stated that he was in sympathy with the idea of a city subscription fund for a Cardiff cenotaph as it was now out of the question to hope that a national fund could be raised in Wales for a central memorial in Cardiff.[40] Yet it had been almost two months since the council enthusiastically endorsed the idea of a local memorial. Exactly four weeks later, in an editorial entitled 'Welsh War Memorial', the *Western Mail* stepped into the apparent vacuum:

> A purely local interest has in most instances attached to the proposals to erect memorials of the Great War in this country; but we feel that the participation of Wales in that vast conflict contains so much of a national character and quality that Welsh sentiment will be satisfied with nothing less than a national Welsh memorial. Each county and each town in Wales will no doubt have its memorial, as is the case in the counties and towns of England, but we in Wales have an inveterate habit of looking at everything we do from the standpoint of the nation, and investing it, wherever possible, with a national character, and it is, therefore, almost inevitable that the memory of our war effort and sacrifice should be perpetuated on a similar footing. When, therefore, we propose that there should be a Welsh National War Memorial we are sure that we are interpreting the wishes of our constituency and we feel sure that the relationship of this newspaper to its readers, which has on many previous occasions sustained a national effort, will on this occasion also prove an adequate rallying ground. The proprietors of the *Western Mail* have started with a donation of one hundred pounds the fund for the creation of a National War Memorial, and they are confident that their readers will emulate and better this initial effort.[41]

The paper had faithfully reported the steps taken by the city council in its attempts to establish a conference at Cardiff and had equally reported on the failure of this endeavour and the

---

[39] *Evening Express*, 19 September 1919. Mr Jukes fulfilled his pledge by subscribing 25 guineas to the National War Memorial Fund. See *Western Mail*, 22 January 1920.
[40] *Western Mail*, 25 September 1919.
[41] *Western Mail*, 24 October 1919.

subsequent moves toward a city memorial. Yet in the space of four weeks, the proprietors of the *Western Mail* decided that this was not adequate and that it would take on the responsibility for organizing a national war memorial. The fact that a substantial movement with influential backing was already under way in north Wales was ignored, despite the paper having reported on its progress. Six weeks earlier, the paper had published an editorial which spoke of the importance of war memorials, particularly for future generations. The editorial also made it clear that their preference was against utilitarian memorials, which may well have influenced the decision to promote a national 'sacred' war memorial.[42]

A national appeal was not unprecedented, as a similar campaign had been launched by the *Western Mail* in 1905 for a national memorial to the fallen of the South African war; it raised approximately £2,000. The memorial was unveiled in 1909 by Sir John French and its siting in Cardiff was later used as a precedent to justify the council's appeal to the whole of the principality.[43] Yet in 1919 the *Western Mail*'s zeal for the national cause may have been less altruistic than it liked to portray. The paper had successfully maintained its dominant commercial position in an overwhelmingly Liberal Wales, but in 1919 the face of politics was changing, particularly in south Wales, as the potential threat of socialism became a reality in many local authorities. In addition, the paper faced commercial threats from new British national daily papers.[44] The proprietors of the *Western Mail*, backed by a small but powerful Conservative lobby in Cardiff, may have felt that direct appeal to the people of Wales would bypass the bureaucracy of local councils, which perhaps did not accurately represent the views or desires of 'the man in the street'. The *Western Mail* fund provided the people of Wales with the opportunity to express their support for a national war memorial, whilst the appeal for national unity

---

[42] *Western Mail*, 3 September 1919.
[43] *Western Mail*, 20 and 22 November 1909. The balance of the South African War Memorial Fund, approximately £174, was eventually subsumed into the Welsh National War Memorial Fund. *Western Mail*, 3 September 1929. See also the report of a meeting of Cardiff City Council's general purpose committee held on 22 May 1919. *Cardiff Times*, 24 May 1919.
[44] See J. M. Cayford, 'The Western Mail, 1869–1914: a study in the politics and management of a provincial newspaper' (unpublished Ph.D. thesis, University of Wales, 1992).

provided the paper with an opportunity to assert its position in Wales.[45]

The fund raised over £24,000 in just three months and in January 1920 the paper noted with satisfaction:

> In view of the many considerations that surrounded the *Western Mail* appeal the response has been very gratifying. Many towns and parishes throughout the Principality have purely local memorial schemes of their own, to which the public were asked to subscribe. It was also quite natural to expect that, in view of the declared intention to locate the National Memorial in the city of Cardiff, the bulk of the money should have come from subscribers in Cardiff and Glamorgan. But despite all this, a glance through the list will show that the great public companies throughout the whole of South Wales and Monmouthshire are well represented, whilst every county in the Principality has provided subscriptions for the national memorial.[46]

Although certain fund-raising events were still taking place, such as football matches and concerts, the paper made it clear that no further lists of subscriptions would be published and to all intents and purposes the fund was closed. In the same edition, the paper published a 'full and final list of the subscriptions'.[47] Detailed study of these lists confirms that the bulk of the money did indeed come from Cardiff and Glamorgan, and the *Western Mail*'s assertion that every county provided subscriptions is more an example of editorial zeal than an accurate description of the facts. A total of 1,751 individual donations were examined; of these, 1,158 gave a Cardiff address, leaving 593 from elsewhere. Analysis of these latter revealed thirty-four donations from outside Wales with eighty-six listed as anonymous.[48] The figure for Glamorgan (381) includes a number of companies which are listed by name only. However, a random selection from these

[45] As a political and commercial rival, the *South Wales Daily News* did not become involved in the fund. Although it reported on the deliberations over the proposed site for the memorial and printed a special supplement on the day of the unveiling in June 1928, it did not refer to the part played by the *Western Mail*. Two months after the unveiling ceremony the paper was taken over by the *Western Mail*.
[46] *Western Mail*, 22 January 1920.
[47] Ibid.
[48] Donations were received from Bath, Bristol, Dublin, Exmouth, Gloucester, Inverness, Leicester, London, Middlesex, New York, Weston super Mare, Wimborne and York. In the case of anonymous donations, names or initials would often be given, or the name of the person being commemorated, but not the location.

revealed their registered offices to be in the heart of Cardiff.[49] There are individual donations too from men such as Sir Edward Nicholl and Sir William Seager, whose business interests and wealth were intrinsically connected with Cardiff.[50] West Wales was represented by a total of twenty-five individual donations from Pembrokeshire, Cardiganshire and Carmarthenshire, while Breconshire, Montgomeryshire and Radnorshire are credited with nine individual donations. Subscriptions from north Wales are conspicuous by their absence, with one donation reported from Denbighshire and none at all recorded from Flintshire, Anglesey, Caernarfonshire or Merioneth.

The reaction of local authorities throughout Wales to the establishment of a national war memorial and the geographical location of subscribers to the memorial fund suggest that whilst the memorial in Cardiff encapsulated the emotions of many hundreds of individual private subscribers, it remained a potent political symbol of the powerful, anglicized, industrialized communities of Glamorgan. It may therefore be more appropriate to label the 'National War Memorial' as the 'Cardiff War Memorial', or perhaps the 'Glamorgan War Memorial'. Unlike so many towns and villages throughout the principality, Cardiff did not have its own memorial and before the 'National' memorial was unveiled in Cathays Park, Armistice Day services in Cardiff occurred at individual churches and chapels with the two-minute silence observed at places of work. The main public gathering took place outside the offices of the *Western Mail* newspaper. The lack of a central focus of mourning prompted the Cardiff and district branch of the British Legion to take action in 1927, when a 'temporary' cenotaph was erected in the centre of Cardiff on a site lent for the occasion by the marquess of Bute. A service was held on Armistice Day and the structure stayed in place for three days. It was known as the 'Poppy Cenotaph', with people being encouraged to buy a poppy and

[49] The Windsor Rope & Brattice Cloth Co. Ltd., Anglo-American Oil Co. Ltd., Siemens Bros. Ltd., Star Patent Fuel Co. Ltd., Aadnessen and Dahl, Furness, Withy & Co. Ltd., Lancaster Steam Coal Collieries Ltd., Lewis Merthyr Consolidated Collieries Ltd., J. & M. Gunn & Co., Albion Steam Coal Co. Ltd., Plisson Steam Navigation Co. Ltd., J. Rank Ltd., Watts, Watts & Co. Ltd., Instone S. & Co. Ltd., W. H. Seager & Co. Ltd. See *Cardiff Directory 1919* (Cardiff, 1919).
[50] E.g. Edward Nicholl & Co., Shipowners, Cardiff Hall Line, 125 Bute Street, Cardiff and W.H. Seager & Co. Ltd., Shipowners & Shipchandlers, 108 and 109 Bute Street, Cardiff. See *Cardiff Directory 1919*.

place it on the structure. Ten thousand people were said to be present at the Armistice Day service, with places of honour reserved for men of the British Legion, widows, widowed mothers and orphans. The spontaneous gathering outside the *Western Mail* offices also took place, the crowd attending described as 'bigger and more impressive than ever'.[51] The project to erect a memorial that was under consideration by the city council was a purely local one until the *Western Mail* became involved, but many private subscribers may well have viewed the structure in Cathays Park as their local memorial, particularly those subscribers who may not have had the financial means to join in other commemorative schemes.

It is clear that by June 1919 many public and private commemoration schemes were already well under way, and the majority of local authorities in the principality showed little interest in, or sympathy with, the idea of a national war memorial in Cardiff. This is particularly true in north Wales, where the movement to build the Heroes' Memorial had been inaugurated in 1917 and fund-raising had started by February 1918. The people of north Wales had therefore committed themselves financially before the war was over and well in advance of the Cardiff appeal. Although the decision to drop the word 'National' from the north Wales scheme had been taken at an early stage, a letter from the secretary of the council of the North Wales Heroes' Memorial in November 1924 stated that: 'As a matter of public interest it may be stated that the number of visitors to the Memorial has been very large and the Archway is now clearly regarded as the National Memorial.'[52] Even allowing for the existence of the North Wales Heroes' Memorial, the political and commercial manœuvrings of the south were regarded as largely an irrelevance to the rural communities of north and west Wales. Other communities in south Wales embraced their own schemes whilst rejecting what they interpreted as Cardiff's civic pretensions in attempting to establish a national war memorial.

In responding to the Cardiff City Council circular, Brecon Town Council resolved, at a meeting in June 1919, not to

[51] *Western Mail*, 11 November 1927.
[52] Open letter from Major Wynn Wheldon as honorary secretary in an apparent attempt to collect all the names of those who had fallen for inclusion on the panels in the archway, 24 November 1924. UCNW, Heroes' Memorial File.

support any war memorial scheme other than for the borough or county.[53] It is clear that a desire to establish local memorials was paramount, yet even plans to provide borough and county memorials were prone to outbursts of parochialism and jealousy similar to those that had plagued the national memorial movement. In May 1921 the mayor of Carmarthen held a public meeting to consider the question of a borough war memorial. This had been prompted by the knowledge that the lord lieutenant of the county had initiated a movement for a county war memorial, and the suggestion was made that the county and borough might co-operate in erecting a memorial in Carmarthen, the county town. Expressions of unity were not forthcoming, however, and the only advantage in the borough combining resources with the county movement was seen in practical terms: 'that they would be more likely to get a memorial more worthy of the object they had in view'. This view was overwhelmed by a desire to 'go it alone' and by indignation at the idea of approaching the county 'hat in hand'.[54]

At a public meeting in September 1921 convened by the mayor and the lord lieutenant, a borough movement was decided upon, as it appeared that 'there was no possibility of any county movement for a memorial being made at the present time'.[55] The following month, however, a further public meeting decided to go ahead with a county memorial but to postpone any decision on the type of memorial for twelve months. The dominant reason given for going ahead with a county memorial was that to do otherwise would reflect badly on the prestige of the county itself:

> it would be a slur upon the great county of Carmarthen if they, when every parish and little village had put up its memorial to the men who saved this country and the world from destruction in the war, should do nothing, and say that sufficient had been done . . . Was the county of Carmarthen going to be behind every other little hamlet?[56]

The borough movement was also deferred for a year 'owing to the inappropriate time caused by the industrial depression . . .

[53] Brecon Town Council, minutes of meeting, 10 June 1919.
[54] Carmarthen Journal, 6 May 1921. See also Western Mail, 30 April 1921.
[55] Carmarthen Journal, 2 September 1921.
[56] Carmarthen Journal, 7 October 1921.

and now the committee were waiting to see what the county intended doing in the matter. They hoped to work in conjunction with the county to get a worthy memorial.'[57]

It appears that economic exigency rather than a demonstration of civic unity lay behind the final decision to combine the two movements in a county memorial fund, and the borough memorial committee imposed the condition that the county war memorial should be erected at Carmarthen. The projected memorial was a scheme to extend the Carmarthenshire Infirmary and erect a monument outside the Infirmary in Priory Street, Carmarthen. Yet even this decision evoked critical comment from representatives of towns within the county:

> Mr Dan Williams, Llanelly . . . saw a difficulty with regard to the venue of the proposed county memorial. Past county memorials had been erected at Carmarthen, and there was a certain amount of jealousy as to where the county memorial for the Great War should be placed, if it came into being . . . If the county memorial was to take the form of an extension to the Carmarthenshire Infirmary, they in Llanelly would certainly object. They did not see why they, in debt in Llanelly in connection with their own Hospital, should contribute towards a wing at the Carmarthen Hospital. If Carmarthen people wanted an extension for their own Hospital they should pay for it.[58]

Reservations continued to be expressed within Carmarthen Town Council at the perceived loss of control by subsuming a local scheme into a county one.[59] Doubts were also being expressed at the likelihood of obtaining co-operation from all areas of the county. It was stated at a meeting of the Carmarthenshire County War Memorial Committee in March 1923 that great difficulty would be encountered in persuading Llanelli and the Amman Valley to do anything 'as they had their own war memorials. The outlook in North Carmarthenshire was also black because of the many memorials there. He (the clerk) had spoken to a number of people and there was a great indifference

---

[57] *Carmarthen Journal*, 6 October 1922.
[58] Ibid.
[59] Carmarthen Town Council meeting as reported in *Carmarthen Journal*, 16 February 1923.

which was increasing.'[60] A meeting in June 1924 made un-favourable comparisons with Pembrokeshire, and the hope was voiced that 'Carmarthenshire would not be willing to be so surpassed by its sister county in showing its appreciation of the men who had fought for their country'.[61] The Carmarthenshire County War Memorial, designed by Goscombe John, was unveiled in September 1924, and speeches at the ceremony extolled the unity displayed throughout the county. John Hinds, lord lieutenant of Carmarthenshire, said that: 'Although there were countless memorials and tablets throughout the county in memory of the brave lads who fell in the Great War, they felt that those sacrifices demanded a recognition of the county as a whole, symbolical of their sacrifice.' The mayor declared that 'the Great War monument indicated an expression of unity on the part of the whole county with them in the borough of Carmarthen'.[62] Such sentiments, however, belie the animosity and ill-feeling that accompanied its building and the many war memorials that were built throughout the county are testament to the strength of local commemoration.

The borough of Merthyr Tydfil in Glamorgan also experienced great difficulties in its prolonged endeavours to fund and build a substantial war memorial. A letter in the local paper in December 1919 bemoaned the lack of a movement for a memorial in Merthyr and compared the borough's inactivity unfavourably with other communities located just a few miles from Merthyr: 'Other towns have erected memorials and are doing so now. In Troedyrhiw and Cefn steps have been taken to do so. Shall we be accused of lack of honour and respect to our dead?'[63] A public meeting in December 1922 initiated the movement for a memorial with the formation of an executive committee and smaller ward committees, but it appeared to be

---

[60] *Carmarthen Journal*, 16 March 1923.

[61] *Carmarthen Journal*, 20 June 1924.

[62] *Carmarthen Journal*, 12 September 1924. See also *Western Mail*, 5 September 1924. At the unveiling ceremony, custody of the memorial was entrusted to the mayor and corporation of Carmarthen. A problem arose in 1951 when the local branch of the British Legion requested that an inscription relating to the 1939–45 war should be added to the memorial. Their request was passed to the county council because, as far as the Carmarthen town clerk was concerned, it was a county and not a borough memorial and therefore the county council should take responsibility for the new inscription. *Carmarthen Borough Council: Correspondence re County War Memorial*.

[63] *Merthyr Express*, 13 December 1919.

assumed that it would be a memorial for the entire borough of Merthyr Tydfil.[64] Disapproval of the scheme was immediately apparent. At a ward meeting held in Dowlais just a few weeks later, strong views were expressed in favour of a local memorial. The ex-servicemen's representative, Captain E. H. Musgrove, thought that

> the feeling of the Dowlais people was dead against a Borough Memorial but in favour of a local one. His idea was that each ward should have its own as at Troedyrhiw and Pant . . . Dowlais ex-servicemen wanted a cenotaph erected in Dowlais where relatives of the fallen could place wreaths on the anniversary of their sacrifice, and what was more, they were determined to get it.[65]

A further local meeting a week later decided to appoint six representatives to the central committee but with obvious reluctance. Alderman Davies 'thought there was overwhelming evidence that Dowlais wanted a memorial of their own. Merthyr seemed to have all the good things including the South African obelisk.'[66]

By 1927 there was still no movement on the borough memorial and the populace of the conurbations within the borough had taken matters into their own hands and initiated their own memorial committees. In January a public meeting was called at which the secretary of the Treharris Chamber of Trade recalled that: 'Some years ago a deputation came down from Merthyr and wanted Treharris people to subscribe to a central memorial at Merthyr but this proposition disgusted all who were at the meeting.'[67] The absence of a borough memorial by Armistice Day 1929 prompted the *Merthyr Express*'s gossip columnist, 'Polonius', to air his thoughts on the matter in the columns of the local paper, drawing attention to the fact that the smaller districts of the borough had built their own memorials:

> Merthyr Tydfil is still one of the few towns of any importance in the United Kingdom which is without a war memorial of any kind and the Armistice

[64] *Merthyr Express*, 2 December 1922.
[65] *Merthyr Express*, 13 January 1923.
[66] *Merthyr Express*, 20 January 1923.
[67] *Merthyr Express*, 15 January 1927.

Day celebrations served as a vivid reminder of that regrettable fact . . .
Even in the suburban districts of the Borough the residents can proudly
point to their own memorials, but in the town itself, the heart of the
Borough, there is nothing to be seen.[68]

The borough war memorial was finally unveiled in November
1931 by Field Marshal Allenby, but the importance of local
identity and commemoration was confirmed by the existence of
smaller memorials at Dowlais, Pant and Treharris, as well as the
impressive monument for Merthyr Vale and Aberfan.[69] The
dissent voiced from the areas within the Merthyr district was
redolent of earlier exchanges over the question of Merthyr's
incorporation in the late nineteenth century. The strongest
opposition on that occasion came from Merthyr Vale and
Treharris, where fears were expressed over the loss of local
identity as well as the political and economic implications of
incorporation. It is apparent that reluctance to be subsumed
within Merthyr's civic ambitions was as intense during the
protracted negotiations for a borough war memorial as it had
been twenty-five years earlier.[70]

By far the most common reason for declining the invitation to
attend the proposed conference in Cardiff to establish a national
war memorial was the existence of small schemes for local war
memorials. Pontypool Rural District Council opted to inform
Cardiff council that 'the people of this district will no doubt
favour local memorials', whilst a meeting of Dwyran Rural

[68] *Merthyr Express*, 16 November 1929.
[69] For details of the borough memorial unveiling ceremony, see *Merthyr Express,* 14
November 1931. For Pant, see 10 July 1926; Treharris, 1 April 1933; Merthyr Vale and
Aberfan, 26 November 1927. Although no central memorial was built, the inhabitants of
Dowlais still insisted on smaller memorials within local places of worship. Examples can
be found at St John's parish church, Hermon Calvinistic Methodist chapel and
Caersalem Welsh Baptist church. For unveiling details, see *Merthyr Express,* 5 June 1920,
28 May 1921 and 14 March 1922.
[70] Merthyr Tydfil received its charter of incorporation in 1905. See Margaret S.
Taylor, *County Borough of Merthyr Tydfil: Fifty Years a Borough, 1905–1955* (Merthyr Tydfil,
1956). See also John G. E. Astle, *Merthyr Tydfil Incorporation 1897 and 1903: Proceedings on
Inquiries* (Merthyr Tydfil, c. 1903). I am grateful to Andrew Croll for these references.
Merthyr Tydfil erected a 'new' war memorial, a granite Celtic cross, in 1986 situated
outside the law courts. The reason given for the new memorial was that the location on a
steep site of the 'official' memorial gave problems for ex-servicemen attending
Remembrance Day services.

District Council resolved to take no action over the invitation from Cardiff 'as each district is making its own arrangements as to a memorial for the fallen heroes'.[71] This reaction was replicated throughout Wales and it is clear that, however small the numbers involved, the importance of local commemoration was deemed more relevant, immediate and important than participation in a national or even a regional scheme.[72] This was equally true whether the community was based in an industrial or a rural environment. In May 1925 a public meeting was held at Penygraig in the Rhondda to consider the question of a local war memorial. The chairman spoke of there being

> a mistaken notion abroad that a large monument was the most fitting commemoration for the heroic sacrifices of those who fell in the war. In his opinion, it was more in keeping with the spirit of the age that each village and township should possess a small memorial of its own.[73]

In February 1919, at the inaugural meeting of the Ruthin and District Memorial Committee, the mayor spoke of the 'perpetuation of the memory of those who had fallen not only from the borough of Ruthin, but from the surrounding parishes as well'.[74] Yet less than four months later, a further public meeting heard that the memorial committee considered the movement

> should be confined to the borough. A communication was sent to the parishes comprised in the Ruthin police division enquiring whether any movement was being made for raising memorials which would be confined exclusively to the various parishes. The replies show that in almost every parish something is being done to raise a local memorial, and there appears to be no disposition to join in a larger scheme to include the borough and district.[75]

[71] Pontypool Rural District Council, meeting 23 June 1919; Dwyran Rural District Council, meeting 11 June 1919.

[72] See minute books: Caerleon Urban District Council meeting, 4 June 1919; Penarth Urban District Council meeting, 6 June 1919; Cowbridge Borough Council meeting, 5 June 1919; Neath Borough Council meeting, 5 June 1919; New Quay Urban District Council meeting, 3 June 1919; Builth Wells Urban District Council meeting, 14 June 1919; Brecknock Rural District Council meeting, 13 June 1919.

[73] *Rhondda Leader*, 29 May 1925. Penygraig's memorial to the 153 local men who died was funded by local subscription and unveiled in November 1927 by the earl of Dunraven. *Rhondda Leader*, 12 November 1927.

[74] *Denbighshire Free Press*, 15 February 1919.

[75] *Denbighshire Free Press*, 7 June 1919.

The replies from the various parishes reveal that the numbers of local men who lost their lives were in single figures but they display a determination to commemorate in the immediate locality even though located just a few miles from Ruthin. The small community of Clocaenog lost twelve men and withdrew from the central scheme in order to raise their own memorial. They succeeded and 'an imposing structure of rough granite, standing some 11 feet high, surrounded by granite kerbstones and enclosed by iron pillars and chains' was built in the churchyard and unveiled in August 1920.[76]

Close proximity could on occasions be a problem. Less than a mile separates Ystrad Mynach and Hengoed, and at an initial public meeting in April 1924 representatives from both villages were elected to serve on a memorial committee.[77] A month later, a well-attended meeting was held in Hengoed hall to consider erecting a memorial purely for the Hengoed community. The *Merthyr Express* reported that:

> Several members of the Ystrad Mynach War Memorial Committee attended and pleaded for joint action between the two places, but a few of the Hengoed people stuck to their guns and said that Hengoed could put a gravestone to its own sons without the help or interference of outsiders.[78]

Similar sentiments were expressed a few weeks later at a further meeting in Hengoed, when the Ystrad Mynach movement was described as 'being due more to the yearning for something to ornament the village than a desire to honour the men who died to save their country'. Tempers settled quickly however and less than a month later it was announced that Hengoed had abandoned its plans for a separate memorial.[79] Expressions of localism came from a variety of quarters. The parishioners of St David's church, Carmarthen, raised £5,000 for a memorial hall. At the opening ceremony in November

[76] *Denbighshire Free Press*, 14 August 1920, and *Wrexham Advertiser*, 7 August 1920. The war memorial at Ruthin was unveiled in December 1925. For details of the unveiling ceremony, see *Denbighshire Free Press*, 12 December 1925.

[77] *Merthyr Express*, 5 April 1924.

[78] *Merthyr Express*, 24 May 1924.

[79] *Merthyr Express*, 21 June 1924, 12 July 1924. The memorial to the forty-eight men of Ystrad Mynach and Hengoed was unveiled in July 1932 by Colonel Morgan Lindsay. *Merthyr Express*, 23 July 1932.

1921, the Venerable Archdeacon Robert Williams of Llandeilo said that the parishioners of St David's could feel proud of their achievement in having built such a splendid memorial hall: 'They in Llandilo had contemplated building a hall, but had not done so, although they had a considerable amount of money in hand. While discretion seemed to live in Llandilo, courage was the resident in the parish of St David's.'[80]

It is clear that the invocation of civic pride played a prominent role in the commemoration process as newspapers frequently sought to compare communities still without a memorial to those who had 'done the right thing' or were in the process of doing so. A newspaper report in Penarth in May 1922 lamented the lack of a local war memorial and combined this with an appeal to local pride: 'All who have the honour of Penarth at heart must hope that something will be done. Apart from the dignity of the town, which does not want to be compared unfavourably with other communities, it is generally felt that something definite should be done.'[81] Similar sentiments were expressed at Porth after a public meeting in February 1919 had decided on a war memorial, but silence reigned until September 1921. Under 'Porth Pickings', 'The Pedlar' wrote in the *Rhondda Leader*: 'By the way, when is Porth to have its war memorial? Surely we are not going to be the last to see to the matter. So far, the only one in the valley is at Blaenrhondda. Now Porth fall in.'[82] No further action was taken until October 1924, when the paper expressed great pleasure: 'that a definite start has been made with a war memorial is news almost too good to be true. The town spirit is certainly lacking in Porth as this blot would not have rested on our name so long.'[83] The appeal to civic pride was often combined with the implicit accusation that the absence of a

[80] *Carmarthen Journal*, 18 November 1921.

[81] *Penarth News*, 11 May 1922.

[82] *Rhondda Leader*,1 September 1921. The memorial at Blaenrhondda had been unveiled the previous month; for details see *Rhondda Leader*, 4 August 1921. In November 1932 the Armistice service was moved from the Blaenrhondda memorial to Treherbert Park and this caused an outcry amongst the inhabitants of Blaenrhondda. They expressed the worry that the memorial itself would be moved: 'No effort was made in Treherbert to erect a memorial. Blaenrhondda folk set about the task with might and main.' *Rhondda Leader*, 19 November 1932. The two communities are less than a mile apart; the memorial remains in Blaenrhondda.

[83] *Rhondda Leader*, 24 October 1924. The memorial at Porth to the 328 men who died in the Great War was finally unveiled by Lord Tredegar in November 1928. *Rhondda Leader*, 24 November 1928, and *Western Mail*, 19 November 1928.

memorial, or of a movement to build one, displayed a lack of honour and respect for the dead. Newspaper comments were acerbic in their condemnation of local indifference to sacrifices made in the Great War:

> At one time there was much talk of Aberdare going to do a lot for the survivors of the Great War and also for the memory of those who fell. We were going to erect a cenotaph and a new memorial hall and ever so many other monuments of gratitude and appreciation. But all those elaborate schemes have gone the way of the best laid schemes of mice and men and the abstract homes fit for heroes to live in. 'Lest we forget' indeed! We have forgotten already. Buying poppies is far cheaper than building halls and houses.[84]

Throughout the 1920s the construction of war memorials made an unprecedented visual impact on the urban and rural landscape of Wales, and it is clear that the movement to commemorate the Great War offered a unique opportunity to make a very public statement on civic pride and honour. Whilst the desire to pay tribute to the sacrifices made by local men and women was fundamental to memorial movements, the protagonists behind larger civic memorials may well have had specific ideas as to how their own areas of social jurisdiction could and should be perceived by the larger community. The early movement for a county memorial in Carmarthenshire was initiated by the lord lieutenant of the county, who informed the mayor that 'the gentry of the county' had been discussing the matter amongst themselves, and the first committee to be formed consisted of the chairman and members of the county council, together with chairmen of urban and rural district councils throughout the county.[85] The executive committee appointed to oversee the Merthyr Tydfil borough memorial in December 1922 included the mayor as president, with Captain William James as secretary. Captain James was a wounded ex-serviceman who also happened to be the son of F. T. James, a well-known solicitor in Merthyr whose obituary would describe the family as occupying a prominent position in the public life of Merthyr for

---

[84] *Aberdare Leader*, 19 November 1921.
[85] *Carmarthen Journal*, 6 May 1921 and 6 October 1922.

nearly a century.[86] Of course, the creation or re-creation of civic identity was nothing new and probably reached its zenith in the late nineteenth and early twentieth centuries. In his work on Merthyr Tydfil in this period, Andrew Croll has pointed out that: 'Civic Merthyr was a town image that had constantly to be maintained and defended', and the construction of larger war memorials in the 1920s can perhaps be viewed as a continuation of this tradition.[87] A note of caution needs to be sounded, however, in attempting to connect the widespread movement to erect war memorials with the construction of civic identity in Wales in the post-war years. Civic pride did have a role to play, but in the movements for many hundreds of smaller memorials in Wales it can only be regarded as a minor factor. In town and country, local commemoration provided those left behind with an immediate, daily reminder of the sacrifice made by husbands, fathers, lovers, sons and brothers. This is especially relevant in rural communities, where a county memorial, and particularly the national memorials, could be perceived as impersonal and remote, both psychologically and physically. The desire for local memorials may also explain why eminent sculptors such as Goscombe John did not play a major role in Welsh commemoration. John did undertake a number of commissions in Wales, with examples at Carmarthen, Lampeter, Llandaff, Llanelli, Penarth and Wrexham, but his reputation and prominence no doubt placed his services well outside the financial capacities of many communities.[88]

The 'national' war memorials in Cardiff and Bangor and the many hundreds of local memorials remain as emotive testaments to Welsh involvement in the Great War and also to divisions within the principality. The stories behind the building of such memorials peel away the façade of national unity and reveal a

---

[86] *Merthyr Express*, 2 December 1922. For the full obituary on Frank Treharne James, see *Merthyr Express*, 21 February 1942.

[87] Andrew J. Croll, 'Civilising the urban: popular culture, public space and urban meaning, Merthyr *c.*1870–1914' (unpublished Ph.D. thesis, University of Wales, 1997), p. 76.

[88] Clough Williams-Ellis effectively took over the movement to construct a memorial in his home village of Llanfrothen. His offer of financial assistance to allow for a 'distinctive and creditable monument' and his artistic reputation were a formidable combination which no memorial committee could reasonably ignore, even if the working relationship at times was extremely strained. University of Wales, Bangor, MS. 5056 (10–30). I am grateful to Professor Geraint H. Jenkins for drawing my attention to these papers.

society determined to place commemoration of the individual within local communities above the creation and consolidation of broader civic and national images. The need and desire experienced by society to remember the dead was never in question, yet the location of individual memorials, whether in an urban or a rural environment, was a matter for comment, conjecture and controversy.

IV

'THE SPIRIT OF THE TRIBUTE': MEMORIALS TO HONOUR THE DEAD OR SERVE THE LIVING?

It is clear that the location of war memorials was of prime importance, but there would also be heated debate in Wales over the type of memorial to be constructed. In November 1918 the people of Barry in Glamorgan sought to commemorate their fallen. Fifteen thousand Barrians had enlisted and seven hundred failed to return. It would be twelve years, however, before the cenotaph was unveiled and a further two years before the war memorial hall was finally opened in November 1932, a delay that caused much resentment and controversy amongst the people of Barry. The existence of both a cenotaph and public hall are tangible symbols of the well-documented controversy that marked the story of Barry's commemoration of those who lost their lives in the Great War. The two memorials epitomize the very different needs that existed within communities throughout Britain after the Great War and also the perennial arguments as to whether war memorials should serve the living or honour those who had died. The frequent disputes in Wales over the form of memorial, highlight the difficulties in achieving a consensus over the most appropriate way to commemorate the dead.

The advent of the railway and the building of the docks in the late nineteenth century to cope with the huge demand for Welsh steam coal had transformed the coastal town of Barry in Glamorgan from a rural backwater into a prosperous industrialized town with a correspondingly dramatic rise in population. Though situated some distance from the coalfield, Barry played an integral role in 'this great Victorian economic drama of coal'. The local urban district council was pivotal to the progress of the town and the council debates have been described as 'the key to modern Barry'.[1] The debates were meticulously recorded in

---

[1] Peter Stead, 'The town that had come of age: Barry, 1918–1939', in Donald Moore (ed.), *Barry: The Centenary Book* (Barry, 1984), pp. 367, 368.

minute books and reported on in great detail by two local newspapers, and such records also provide the key to understanding why Barry, a town with obvious pride in its prosperity, took twelve years to erect a war memorial and subjected the council to unprecedented public criticism.

The initial motivation to erect a memorial of some form originated on Barry Island as early as June 1918. Island residents formed their own war memorial committee and asked Barry Urban District Council for support. In reply the council suggested that the whole town should join in and requested the Island committee to defer any action. An open meeting was held in January 1919, when 'a gathering representative of the chief interests of the town' put forward suggestions for a possible memorial.[2] These included an arch of triumph, stained-glass windows, a maternity and child welfare centre, a victory hall, Lord Roberts's memorial workshops, a drinking fountain, a sailors' home, an institute and hall near the docks, an additional chapel at the cemetery, a memorial column on Barry Island, and houses and land for soldiers' and sailors' dependants. After much discussion, a committee of fifteen was formed to consider suggestions and place them before a public meeting, after which a vote of the townspeople would be taken. A subsequent meeting of the committee in February 1919 attracted only a sparse attendance but even at this early stage it appears that a hall was a high priority, as the council surveyor was asked to submit three estimates for erecting a public hall. Correspondence to the committee and the local press lamented the lack of trade union or friendly society representation either on the committee itself or among the six co-opted members. This may explain why the committee received several letters in early 1919 from groups such as the Barry Workers' Vigilance Committee and the Barry No. 5 branch of the National Union of Railwaymen, expressing their desire for a hall.[3] By March 1919 the two favoured suggestions were either a monumental column on Barry Island or a

---

[2] *Barry Herald*, 31 January 1919.

[3] The following groups also sent letters to the committee in February, March and May 1919, suggesting that the memorial should take the form of a hall: Barry Branch of the National Union of Railwaymen Women's Guild, Barry Branch of the Co-operative Women's Guild, Barry 2nd Branch of the Amalgamated Society of Engineers, Barry No. 1 Branch of the National Union of Railwaymen, Barry Dock Branch of the Iron Founders' Friendly Society, Barry Branch of the Postmen's Federation, Barry Socialist Society and Barry Branch No. 30 of the Amalgamated Society of Engineers.

public hall. However, two further committee meetings were inconclusive and even at this early stage members of the committee could unite only in their disagreement. One member went so far as to say that if the inhabitants of the town were going to be divided it would be better not to have a memorial, as it was essential that the memorial should take the form of something that met with the wishes of the great majority of the town's inhabitants. It was finally decided to disband the committee and to refer the matter to the council for consideration, no agreement on the form of memorial or a general vote of the townspeople having been taken. An indication of the problems ahead can be seen in the comments of Hiliard H. Rosser, a committee member and prospective Labour councillor, who pointed out that the Discharged Soldiers' and Sailors' Association (DSSA) had not even received an invitation to send a representative to the committee, despite having applied twice, and that it was 'one of the most important bodies in the town'.[4]

It should be noted that the DSSA was not the only ex-servicemen's organization in Barry. During and immediately after the Great War a number of general ex-service organizations emerged and, until the founding of the British Legion in 1921, such groups often acted in isolation rather than in unison. Even after the formation of the British Legion, Wales differed in that the South Wales and Monmouthshire Discharged and Demobilised Sailors and Soldiers had joined with the Welsh branch of the National Federation in 1918 to form the Welsh Legion. When the national association was formed in 1921, the Welsh Legion, the Comrades, the National Association and the Officers' Association became the Wales Area of the British Legion. It took a lot longer for many local branches to come into existence; for example, the Barry branch of the British Legion was not formed until October 1923.[5] By mid-1919 there were at least three ex-service societies in Barry and the potential problems were illustrated just two weeks after the inconclusive war memorial committee meeting.[6] The Comrades of the Great

---

[4] *Barry Herald*, 28 March 1919.
[5] See Niall J. A. Barr, 'Service not self: the British Legion, 1921–39' (unpublished Ph.D. thesis, University of St Andrews,1994), p. 32. See also G. Wootton, *The Official History of the British Legion* (London, 1956).
[6] The third ex-servicemen's organization was the Barry United Veterans' Association (BUVA). This Association had been formed in 1896 for the purpose of assisting elderly

War (CGW) held a meeting in Barry Dock when members of the Barry branch of the DSSA entered the building and took over the meeting. The Comrades were condemned as an autocratic organization run by politicians and capitalists. The DSSA then passed a resolution to resist all attempts to join forces with the Comrades and left the building waving the Union Jack and singing 'It's a Long Way to Tipperary'.[7] Such public displays may have swayed the war memorial committee into believing that there was not a truly representative body of ex-servicemen in the town.

The full council met at a special meeting in July 1919 to consider the question of a war memorial. Opinion favoured the erection of a war memorial hall which, in the words of Councillor J. A. Manaton, 'was the pressing need of the town'.[8] It appears, therefore, that by this early date the council had come to the conclusion that Barry needed a new public hall and that the emotive idea of a war memorial provided a suitable channel for achieving this objective. Moreover, the people of Barry were to pay for this since the council agreed to apply to the Ministry of Health to sanction the levying of a rate of 3d. in the pound for a period of three years for the purpose of erecting a war memorial. Four councillors, headed by Dudley T. Howe, voted against this, preferring to pass the question of obtaining money to the finance committee for consideration.[9] Dudley Howe would be at the forefront of the movement to gain a memorial hall for Barry, but in July 1919 he was primarily concerned with the prospect of an imposition on the rates. He believed in a voluntary scheme and 'did not believe in a man being told that he must pay towards the

ex-servicemen. It ceased functioning in 1914 but reconvened weekly meetings early in 1919. It was open to all members of the forces. Despite the existence of the British Legion from 1921 as the 'official' body representing the interests of ex-servicemen, the BUVA continued to exist in Barry and to play an active role in pressing the ex-servicemen's case over employment, pensions and housing and also maintained its representative on the war memorial executive committee.

[7] *Barry Herald*, 4 April 1919.

[8] *Barry Dock News*, 11 July 1919. This view had been voiced at an earlier council meeting in December 1918, when Howell Williams, before he assumed the chair of the council, had commented that a large hall was one of the greatest needs of the town. *Barry Herald*, 18 December 1918.

[9] Dudley Howe 'had first been elected to the Barry U.D.C. in 1913, and then, after being commissioned in France in the Great War, he returned to involve himself in nearly all the most important of the town's affairs in the 1920s and 1930s . . . he was a Liberal in politics and yet never strictly a party man for the town's interests always came first.' Stead, 'Town come of age', p. 420.

cost, but rather he believed that the patriotism of everyone would rise to the occasion, and the money would be subscribed voluntarily'.[10] However, this resolution was lost and the council applied to the Ministry of Health, despite the fact that questions had recently been asked in Parliament as to whether local authorities were allowed to pay for war memorials out of public rates. The Local Government Board had replied that it was 'desirable that the general opinion of the inhabitants of a district should be ascertained before the local authority commit themselves to any proposal involving large expenditure'.[11] The council must have been in possession of this information, as it had been reported during the last meeting of the original committee in May 1919 and had prompted the resolution to call a meeting of the townspeople, which was subsequently lost. Although the Ministry of Health rejected the council's request to impose a rate levy, it raised the question of voluntary contributions towards utilitarian memorials. The oft-cited argument against such memorials was that they offered a convenient opportunity to provide civic amenities which would normally have been funded by local or central government. A clear example of this occurred at Pontypool in August 1919, when the local urban district council decided to prepare provisional plans and estimates for the local war memorial. This would comprise public baths as well as offices for the government departments of the Post Office, Inland Revenue, Employment Exchange and County Court.[12] In the event, it was decided that the war memorial should take the form of an entrance to the town's Italian Gardens. The memorial gates, flanked by bronze panels bearing the names of the fallen, were unveiled in December 1924.[13]

---

[10] *Barry Dock News*, 11 July 1919.

[11] *Hansard*, 114 H C Deb. 5s., written answers, 25 March 1919. The War Memorials (Local Authorities' Powers) Act, 1923, enabled local authorities under certain circumstances to maintain, repair and protect war memorials vested in them.

[12] *Evening Express*, 28 August 1919.

[13] *Western Mail*, 19 December 1924. A similar heated debate took place in Prestatyn, where the local paper criticized a 'monument-or-nothing' section of the townspeople. The paper also revealed its own preference by commenting that if Prestatyn was to continue as a pleasure resort then it should provide better facilities for amusing visitors on wet days and this could be provided for by a memorial hall. This was not to be, and the monument in the parish churchyard was unveiled in October 1920. *Prestatyn Weekly*, 22 February 1919, 17 May 1919 and 30 October 1920.

The debate over the form of memorial in Barry was articulated in a letter to the *Barry Herald* from two ex-servicemen in July 1922:

> The old argument has been raised time and again in private discussions 'what is the use of a monument; surely it is better to have something useful.' This is a question on which we are all bound to have different opinions but to our minds it appears a far more fitting manner in which to show our gratitude and thanks to the boys and our love towards them. Is there not a tendency at the present time to make good our wants, under the guise of a war memorial? Surely, all monies towards a Memorial should be given freely and with a willing heart.[14]

A similar point had been made at the very first meeting to consider a memorial, held in January 1919, when a spokesman deplored the suggestion of workshops and cottages for the disabled, claiming that these should be provided by the government.[15] The members of Cricieth Town Council were well aware of the problems involved in this issue. The inhabitants of Cricieth had voted in favour of a memorial hall in memory of forty-four local men who died in the war. Funds were raised locally and the hall was scheduled to be opened in 1924. In October 1923 the council discussed whether part of the memorial hall should be utilized as a council chamber. One councillor disapproved of the 'blood of the boys' being associated with such a proposal, and although the need for better council accommodation was acknowledged there was a call for this to be done 'honourably'. It was suggested that Cricieth would 'rend from top to bottom' if a council chamber was attached to the memorial hall and it was finally decided to seek alternative accommodation. The council may have been particularly sensitive to public feeling because of Cricieth's close proximity to Llanystumdwy, Lloyd George's home village, and may have felt vulnerable to adverse publicity.[16]

The debate over the most suitable type of memorial was as heated in Wales as elsewhere in Britain, and in September 1919

---

[14] *Barry Herald*, 28 July 1922.
[15] *Barry Dock News*, 7 February 1919.
[16] *Western Mail*, 31 October 1923. The Cricieth war memorial hall was opened by Lloyd George in July 1924. For details of the opening ceremony, see *Western Mail*, 21 July 1924, and *Carnarvon and Denbigh Herald*, 25 July 1924.

the *Western Mail* published a lengthy editorial on the matter and firmly declared against utilitarian memorials:

> It is probable that every town and village, perhaps every church and chapel, will ere long have its memorial, on which will be inscribed the names of the local warriors who sacrificed their lives. Those memorials will become objects of affectionate pride to the bereaved; but their meaning will fail to reach the mind and imagination of the coming generation, and those which have yet to come, unless each memorial sets forth the occasion of the sacrifice . . . Much discussion is taking place as to the form which memorials should take . . . Each locality should have its memorial, and the memorial should be in every case a memorial, pure and simple, divorced from every other interest – sectarian, utilitarian, or recreational – in order that its appeal may never be smothered and concealed by adventitious dressings.[17]

The determination of Barry Urban District Council to build a hall, however, is evident in their decision, taken at the special meeting in July 1919, to ask the public works committee to report on a suitable site or sites for a public hall. Progress was slow until August 1920, when David Davies was approached by the chairman of the council, Howell Williams, and by Dudley Howe. Although a Liberal Member of Parliament for Montgomeryshire, David Davies and his family had strong links with Barry as his grandfather had been deputy-chairman of the Barry Docks and Railways Company and had played a pivotal role in ensuring that new docks were built at Barry in the face of strong opposition from Cardiff. As a noted philanthropic coalowner and industrialist, Davies was well known for his generosity, and the council may well have hoped for a substantial grant, bearing in mind the family's local connections. In the event, David Davies expressed his approval of the proposal and also his willingness to issue a challenge with a view to raising the necessary funds.[18] A committee of council members was formed to submit proposals

---

[17] *Western Mail*, 3 September 1919. For examples of the case supporting utilitarian memorials, see Albert S. Bard, 'What sort of war memorial?', *Community Buildings as War Memorials Bulletin*, No. 1, Bureau of Memorial Buildings and War Camp Community Service (New York, 1919), pp. 1–16, W. R. Lethaby, 'Memorials of the fallen: service or sacrifice?' *The Hibbert Journal*, XVII (1918–19), pp. 621–5. See also Arnold Whittick, *War Memorials* (London, 1946), and Bernard Barber, 'Place, symbol and utilitarian function in war memorials', *Social Forces*, XXVIII (1949), pp. 64–8.

[18] Barry Urban District Council, ordinary meeting, 9 August 1920.

for David Davies's consideration, with Dudley Howe as chairman, a position he was to hold until the opening of the hall in November 1932. At the first meeting in September 1920, plans were submitted for a public hall which it had originally been intended to erect in connection with the council offices, and it was agreed that these plans, albeit with considerable alteration, might form the basis of a scheme subject to the approval of David Davies. By November 1921 Davies and his two sisters were prepared to contribute one pound for every pound collected from other sources up to a maximum of £10,000 towards the cost of a memorial institute. It appears, however, that no options as to other forms of memorial were put either to David Davies or to the townspeople, and the pre-existence of architectural plans were an added boost to the council's case for a public hall.

The offer from David Davies acted as a green light to the council and the first public meeting of the war memorial committee was held on 24 November 1921, when long discussions resulted in detailed plans for the raising of the £10,000 needed to match Davies's offer. The council had obviously learnt from their experience of 1919 and on this occasion announced that twelve representatives of branches of trade union and friendly societies would be co-opted to the committee. Local teaching associations, 'professional' men and other trades, industries and organizations of the district put forward a total of fourteen representatives. As far as ex-servicemen's organizations were concerned, the DSSA and CGW had sunk their previous differences, but the sole representative of ex-servicemen on the war memorial committee was Thomas Rossiter, a coal-trimmer, who represented the Barry United Veterans' Association (BUVA). The task of electing representatives occupied the committee for another six months as many additional organizations requested representation. The committee first met formally in June 1922 with thirty-four people present, but an indication of the council's intentions can be seen in the minute book which reports that the committee was named the war memorial hall committee.[19]

[19] Barry Urban District Council, ordinary meeting, 10 July 1922. Report of meeting of war memorial hall committee, 22 June 1922.

New executive and subcommittees were formed and the fund-raising appeal swung into action. The war memorial committee now appeared to be just another of the well-run council committees that played such a crucial role in Barry's local government structure. This may provide a further clue to the problems that beset the war memorial hall project. Barry Urban District Council was both efficient and conscientious, but its work was conducted largely through committees, often dominated by the same small group of people. Although the committees concerned with the war memorial hall were large in number, the crucial decisions were taken by the executive committee, which consisted of thirteen members, at least seven of whom were councillors. Even the design of the hall itself was decided on within council walls. In many towns and villages there was either a competition for designs or an open letter in the local press inviting tenders, but in Barry the borough architect and surveyor was appointed honorary architect at a meeting of the building committee in November 1929. The war memorial committee, however diligently it operated, may have appeared to be just a part of local government and thus in danger of losing touch with the people of Barry over this emotive issue.

The question of inscribing the names of those who had fallen in the war was considered in 1923. The initial problem was the assembling of a complete list of names of the deceased. This was a process fraught with difficulty, yet it demonstrates another similarity between Wales and the rest of Britain in the com-memoration process.[20] The war memorial committee in Barry decided to place advertisements in both local newspapers, inviting relatives and friends to forward the names of Barry men who had lost their lives in the war, on forms which would be provided for the purpose. Advertisements appeared in October 1923 but with little response from the public. In order to overcome this indifference, the committee sent supplies of forms and explanatory circulars to post offices in the district, and head teachers were asked to announce that the forms were also available at local schools. Head teachers were asked to contact parents of old boys who were killed in the war. An editorial in

---

[20] I am grateful to Nick Hewitt of the National Inventory of War Memorials for advice on this point.

the *Barry Herald* speaks of 'astounding apathy' reflected in the fact that only four forms had been collected.[21] The problem with collecting names was widespread, since there was no official, centralized military or civilian source in Britain from which this information could be obtained. As with the organization of memorials, the collection of names was local and voluntary, unlike in France where 'the names of those officially deemed to have died for the nation were supplied from Paris'.[22] Communities throughout Wales and indeed throughout Britain obtained the names on an *ad hoc* basis, usually by placing advertisements in local papers in the first instance and asking friends and relatives to submit details to the local war memorial committee. In February 1924, the *Merthyr Express* published a list of the fallen, the names sent in by friends and family or extracted from War Office regimental casualty records.[23] Letters were written to the infantry record office of the Royal Welch Fusiliers at Wrexham by officers of the Ruthin War Memorial Committee in an attempt to ascertain the full Christian names of some of the soldiers to be honoured on the memorial. The committee also received an interesting letter from the Aberdeen company which was to undertake the inscription on the Ruthin memorial, commenting on the problems being encountered in the search for names:

> We have had a big experience of War Memorials, and know the difficulties there are in getting in the names. In fact, it is much more difficult than getting in the money in most cases, and it is not infrequent that memorials are delayed on account of this.[24]

In Llandrindod Wells the usual advertisements were placed in local newspapers and a list of the fallen was placed in the local

---

[21] *Barry Herald*, 26 October 1923. Almost identical problems were encountered in other communities in Britain. See, e.g., the experiences of the war memorial committee in Walsall where, despite their best efforts, a number of names were received too late to be placed in the appropriate order on the Memorial Tablets. *Official Programme and Souvenir for unveiling of Walsall Memorials, February 1920.*

[22] K. S. Inglis, 'War memorials: ten questions for historians', *Guerres Mondiales et Conflits Contemporains*, CLXVII (1992), pp. 5–21 (p. 9).

[23] *Merthyr Express*, 23 February 1924.

[24] Letter to Baldwin Griffith from Garden & Co, Victoria Granite Works, Aberdeen, 23 May 1925, Ruthin Town Clerk's Papers. The unveiling of the memorial at Treboeth in Swansea had to be postponed because the list of names to be inscribed had been lost. *Western Mail*, 2 April 1924.

library with requests for relatives and friends to amend it if necessary. In January 1922 the organizing committee received a letter from the Revd Father Cook of The Presbytery, Llandrindod Wells, who had the fortunate and, sadly, rare task of being able to report 'that each man of this little flock returned safe'.[25] Lack of a formal system of notification could result in names being received months or sometimes years later. The secretary of the Tonyrefail and Coedely War Memorial Committee complained to the *Rhondda Leader* that 'owing to the apathy of the relatives of the fallen heroes' in failing to return circulars, eighteen names had been omitted from the inscription, whilst in Barry sixteen additional names were received for inclusion in the roll of honour over a year after the opening of the memorial hall.[26]

The collection of names would be yet one more problem in Barry, but the raising of funds presented a more immediate task for the war memorial committee. By September 1923 the committee had raised approximately £3,400 by a variety of methods, including a flag day, silver band concert, flower day, house-to-house collections and a trade and friendly society carnival and demonstration. The Barry Chamber of Trade set up their own committee, representing five associations, with a view to making collections from the tradespeople in the town. Representatives were also appointed to approach brewers, colliery proprietors, ship-owners and ship-repairers for donations. The Barry Choral Union and Barry Temperance Choir arranged concerts; Barry Women's Conservative Association arranged a whist drive and dance, as did the dock mechanical engineer's department of the Great Western Railway. Signs that all was not going entirely to plan are evident from the meetings of the executive committee in November and December 1923. Two subcommittees were merged to intensify fund-raising efforts, and public meetings were to be held in various wards and on Barry Island 'to arouse enthusiasm for the memorial'.[27] One hundred and twenty-one appeals issued to banks and multiple

[25] File on Llandrindod Wells war memorial.

[26] *Rhondda Leader*, 23 January 1925; Barry Urban District Council, report of meeting of memorial hall management committee, 15 March 1934.

[27] Barry Urban District Council, report of meeting of war memorial executive committee, 12 December 1923.

shops had yielded only £24 and further efforts were urged to obtain donations. The Coal Trimmers' Union was to be asked whether they could contribute by means of either a grant from their funds or a levy upon their members, but their commitment to a memorial hall may have lessened with the opening of a new Labour Hall in Broad Street, Barry, in June 1923. The majority of the £3,000 cost had been contributed by individual trade-union members. The building, named Unity Hall, was officially opened by John Marchbank, president of the National Union of Railwaymen, who noted 'that this beautiful building indicated that it had long been necessary for the workers of Barry to have a suitable place to meet in, free from the domination of landlord-ism, and relieved from the pernicious influence of licensed premises'.[28] The chairman of the hall committee stated that the venture was largely carried into effect by the Labour women of the town, principally the Railwaymen Women's Guild. It was the Barry branch of the National Union of Railwaymen Women's Guild who had been amongst the first to send letters to the original war memorial committee back in 1919, supporting the idea of a public hall as a suitable memorial. In fact, all the letters received in February, March and May 1919 advocating a public hall came from trade union and friendly societies. The opening of a new Labour Hall primarily designed to meet the particular needs of these groups may well have assuaged their desire to have a public hall as the town's war memorial, and even if it is not possible to tell whether or not such groups now actively opposed the town's memorial hall, it is probable that at the very least they were neutral in the matter.

The year 1924 saw a distinct lack of activity by the war memorial committee. Opinion in the town, however, was becoming more vocal in its opposition to the hall. The tone of newspaper reporting also changed. The *Barry Dock News*, which to date had been supportive, headed an unsigned letter: 'Barry's Elusive War Memorial. Discussed, broadcasted, and now apparently forgotten. Will it ever materialise?' The 'correspondent' wrote of the six years since the end of hostilities with still no sign of a town memorial. The article commented on the plethora of small memorials within the town itself:

---

[28] *Barry Dock News*, 22 June 1923.

Our schools have realised the debt they owe to those men, and have performed what was expected of them by unveiling some form of commemoration at those institutions. Private concerns, the Post Office, Works and Clubs in the town have also shown their feeling of reverence and gratitude in some form or other. Probably, when the local Council have completed the Cold Knapp Lake and Barry Island Development Scheme, they will be prepared to once more 'exchange opinions' on this public demonstration of thanksgiving and memory . . . There is hardly a city, town, or village in the country which has not honoured the men from its area who fell for a great cause. Barry is one of the few, and its people are forced to admit the humiliating position . . . The matter has been delayed or forgotten for so many years that it has now become almost a public scandal.[29]

These sentiments were echoed by both the BUVA and the Barry Fragments, an ex-service social group founded in 1919 which held an annual dinner to celebrate the signing of the Armistice and to commemorate fallen comrades. Both organizations deplored the lack of a memorial and suggested that Barry had neglected its duty to those who had died. The general tone of discontent was summed up in a letter to the *Barry Herald* in November 1924 from 'One Who Fought', commenting that:

In Barry a large and unwieldy War Memorial Committee has been functioning for a long time. We find spasmodic bursts of enthusiasm on their part to make money trickle into their coffers. What can be the cause of the slowness in achieving the required sum of £10,000? Let those responsible look the facts squarely in the face. There is a sum in hand now large enough to provide a most perfect example of a War Memorial, but let it be of the plain unpretentious type as typified by the Cenotaph, and not a large vainglorious building, which shall become the habitation of jazzers, card players and political wranglers.[30]

The criticism from ex-service organizations appears to have influenced the executive committee, as a resolution was passed at their meeting in February 1925 that the Barry war memorial scheme should include a memorial monument in addition to a public hall. Thomas Rossiter of the BUVA expressed surprise at

[29] *Barry Dock News*, 6 June 1924.
[30] *Barry Herald*, 21 November 1924.

this, as he had been under the impression that there was a definite minute stating that a monument would be built. His surprise was well-founded as the BUVA had written to the council in January 1921 initiating the question of erecting a cenotaph in the town as a memorial.[31] It is unlikely that the BUVA saw this as an alternative memorial at this time or that they were acting in opposition, as the idea of a hall in January 1921 was not yet fully in the public arena. It is more likely that they felt that it was time Barry had a permanent memorial to the 700 fallen from the town to bring them in line with many other communities throughout Glamorgan, Wales and Britain. Barry Council, however, referred the BUVA's request to the sub-committee which was considering the question of a memorial, and it appears to have been forgotten except by the ex-servicemen. Pressure for a monument continued but the reluctance to build one was evident at a meeting of the war memorial committee in September 1923, when

> several rate payers had expressed the opinion that a monument should be erected in addition to the hall. The Chairman observed that at public meetings, he, with other members of the Executive, had been asked this question, and he had told enquirers that if there was sufficient money left after the establishment of the Hall, a monument would be erected.[32]

It appears that the BUVA's letter in 1919 was quietly shelved, and the reaction in 1923 to build a monument was an after-thought. It was only because of very public pressure in early 1925, particularly from ex-service organizations, that the executive committee finally relented and agreed to the construction of a monument as well as a hall.

Progress towards any form of memorial in Barry was slow, and by March 1925 there was still approximately £5,000 to raise in order to match David Davies's offer. Dudley Howe confessed disappointment and stated that the committee had not been as successful as they anticipated nor as successful as the movement deserved. In his opinion 'there was a profound spirit of gratitude in the hearts of the people of Barry for those who had served and

---

[31] Barry Urban District Council, monthly meeting, 17 January 1921.
[32] *Barry Dock News*, 7 September 1923.

sacrificed but that the Committee had failed to mobilise this spirit and focus it upon the memorial movement'.[33] The council decided to step up its efforts, and the BUVA, the Barry branch of the British Legion, the Barry Women's Section of the British Legion and the Barry Fragments were asked to nominate representatives on the subcommittees. This move may have been a further attempt to pacify these groups who were unhappy at the executive committee's actions to date and whose absence from the committees was the cause of disquiet in the town. In a separate development, however, the Barry branch of the British Legion wrote to the council in March 1925 stating that they had decided to obtain a building in which to hold meetings and social functions and asked for the council's support. The council reacted against this suggestion in no uncertain terms by informing the Legion that they had no power to expend money for this purpose and reminding them of the efforts being made by the war memorial committee to obtain funds for the erection of a hall. They also pointed out to the Legion that they were represented on this committee and their assistance was expected. The Legion subsequently withdrew their representatives from the war memorial committee on the grounds that they disagreed with the council's attitude over the war memorial and that they were in favour of a cenotaph and not a hall.[34] The branch also inaugurated a separate fund for a suitable building and made a public appeal for financial support. Yet again the sole representative of ex-servicemen on the war memorial committee was Thomas Rossiter of the BUVA.

Letters to local papers began to call for a plebiscite to ascertain the wishes of the local people, because to many Barrians there seemed to be an inordinate delay between giving money and any sign of a memorial of any description or any chance of their being allowed to express their opinion. The delay was also noted by David Davies, whose agent, Major J. Burdon Evans, wrote to the executive committee in June 1925 referring to the correspondence which had taken place in 1921 and asking to be informed of the present position.[35] Despite the original offer of £10,000, it appears that no information had been relayed to the

[33] Barry Dock News, 6 March 1925.
[34] Barry Urban District Council, meeting of public works committee, 26 March 1925.
[35] Barry Urban District Council, letter read at monthly meeting, 8 June 1925.

Davies family for at least four years as to the position of the war memorial appeal. Arguments over the form of memorial became more heated in the ensuing months, but calls for a plebiscite were turned down. An objection to calls for an alternative memorial was that the money had been given specifically for erecting a hall and if it was used for any other purpose then the council would be in duty bound to return it to the donors. Further evidence of the determination to go ahead with the plans can be seen with the appointment of yet another council subcommittee in October 1925 to consider possible sites for the hall, with detailed and complex negotiations continuing throughout 1926. The General Strike and the ensuing economic uncertainty necessitated the postponement of several fund-raising events, including a grand bazaar and prize draw, leading a rather disillusioned Dudley Howe to remark in October 1926 that 'for some unknown reason the War Memorial seemed to be under an everlasting cloud'.[36]

The year 1927 saw the selection of the site for the war memorial hall in the centre of Barry, but with almost £5,000 still to be raised to meet David Davies's challenge. At a meeting of the general committee in February, the council itself was blamed for the apathy and indifference towards the movement, as, although nearly all the council were on the various committees, very few actually attended the meetings; to this accusation the Labour councillor, E. C. Gough, retorted that his interest in the war memorial was nil, because there were sufficient war memorials in the human wrecks going about the land.[37] Dudley Howe may have felt that the luck of the war memorial committee was exemplified by the experience of the Barry Male Voice Choir, whose recent concert to raise funds for the memorial had proved to be the most unsuccessful event in the history of the choir.

By December 1927, £1,400 were still needed to meet David Davies's challenge and Dudley Howe acknowledged that opposition remained to the memorial hall and that gratitude was leaving the hearts of the people.[38] This was not altogether justified, for the generosity of the people of Barry had been

---

[36] *Barry Dock News*, 1 October 1926.
[37] *Barry Herald*, 18 February 1927.
[38] *Barry Herald*, 2 December 1927.

proved in the difficult post-war years. The importance of south Walian coal to the world economy in the years before the Great War had yielded years of prosperity and confidence in Barry, via its rail links to the valleys and the docks. However, such close ties with the coal industry meant that Barry had to endure the scourge of unemployment. Although the scale of suffering was not as marked as that of the valleys, many in Barry faced financial hardship throughout the 1920s, though the town continued to respond to these challenges. For example, during the industrial problems in 1921, a relief committee was set up by the council which raised over £1,000 in three months.[39] Contributions were also forthcoming for the *Western Mail*'s appeal for the Welsh National War Memorial. In Barry, the railwaymen donated £400 from their Christmas prize draw to the appeal and organized a successful concert at the Theatre Royal in January 1920.[40] These efforts cannot be seen as competing with the local memorial appeal, as official fund-raising did not start in Barry until June 1922. For a time in 1929, nearly 3,000 were unemployed and a town distress fund was set up which raised nearly £300 in three months.[41] On a lighter note, the same year saw the summer carnival raise nearly £1,000 for new X-ray equipment for the local accident hospital.[42] It is clear, therefore, that after the Great War the people of Barry had many calls upon their limited financial resources but responded willingly to causes they considered worthy of support.

It is also clear that the people of Barry and the surrounding areas were making their own arrangements to commemorate the fallen before any move was made towards a town memorial. Between August 1919 and December 1922, at least twenty-eight memorials were unveiled and dedicated in schools, churches and workplaces.[43] These ceremonies were often intensely moving and intimate occasions in small, tightly knit communities. In July 1920, in the tiny village of Michaelston-le-

---

[39] *Barry Herald*, 29 April 1921.
[40] *Barry Dock News*, 26 December 1919 and 16 January 1920.
[41] *Barry Dock News*, 10 February 1929.
[42] *Barry Dock News*, 23 August 1929.
[43] These included Hannah Street boys' council school, Bethel Baptist church, Pennel Welsh Calvinistic Methodist chapel, Bethel Presbyterian church, Trinity Presbyterian church, Bethesda Welsh Congregational church, a lich-gate and tablet at St Michael's church Michaelston-le-Pit, stones and hall at Wenvoe, Holton Road boys' council school, Wesleyan church, St Andrews Major parish church, Cadoxton boys' school, Llancarfan,

Pit, a lich-gate was dedicated as the parish war memorial, yet only nine months later in April 1921 a memorial tablet was unveiled inside the parish church itself. Inscribed in bronze on the black marble tablet are the names of the three men from the parish who died, including two brothers, and empanelled underneath are the names of the officers and men of the parish who served in the war.[44] In June 1920 a memorial was unveiled at Llancarfan to commemorate the sixteen men who had died from the rural parishes of Llanvithen and Llancarfan. A roll of honour was also unveiled containing the names of the eighty-three men who had enlisted from the two parishes, whose joint population was 400. The chairman of the memorial committee, the Revd W. E. Evans, said that it was a credit to the parishioners that they had contributed the sum of nearly £500 by July 1919 and that 'everyone helped and no-one hindered'.[45] The proliferation of such memorials may also point to why many people may not have given the war memorial hall project their whole-hearted support. The rituals re-enacted time after time at these local ceremonies played a vital role in the mediation of bereavement and to the families of such men, once commemoration had taken place locally, the prolonged campaign for a town memorial may have simply lost interest or momentum for them. Apathy may be too strong a word, but there was, perhaps, a reluctance to enter actively into raising funds for a project which did not command universal support and appeared to be very much a council-organized venture. It may also, of course, be true that to the families of local men who had died, the fourteen years between the end of hostilities and the opening of the war memorial hall may have appeared almost an insult to their memory and sacrifice. The families of the bereaved may well have agreed with the comments of a member of the original committee in 1919 that 'we did not have to scrape for the boys to go. It seems strange that bricks and mortar should be so dear, and life so cheap.'[46]

Clive Road boys' council school, Romilly Road boys' school, All Saints church, Rhoose Mission church, St Helen's Roman Catholic church, Barry Railway Company, St Cadoc's church, Barry boys' county school, a stained-glass window and lich-gate at Sully parish church, Barry general post office.

[44] *Barry Dock News*, 2 July 1920, and *Barry Herald*, 8 April 1921.

[45] *Barry Herald*, 25 June 1920. See also the minutes of Llancarfan Parish Council.

[46] *Barry Herald*, 28 March 1919.

The Welsh National War Memorial, Cathays Park, Cardiff, was designed by J. Ninian Comper and unveiled in June 1928 by the prince of Wales.

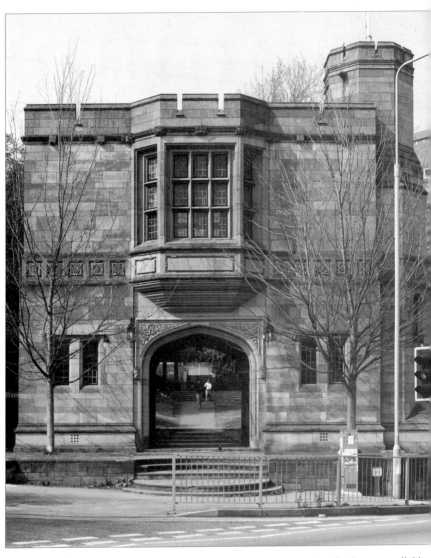

The North Wales Heroes' Memorial, Bangor. The memorial arch leading to the university was unveiled by the prince of Wales in November 1923. The names of 8,500 servicemen are inscribed on wooden panels in the upper chambers.

(above) The unveiling ceremony at Caernarfon. Both Welsh and Union flags can be seen on the memorial.

(left) A rare depiction of a dragon on a Welsh memorial. The memorial at Caernarfon was unveiled in November 1922.

The war memorial at Lampeter was unveiled in October 1921. It was the work of the distinguished sculptor Sir William Goscombe John, and other examples of his war memorial work in Wales are at Carmarthen, Llandaff, Llanelli, Penarth and Wrexham.

TO THE
IMMORTAL MEMORY
OF THE MEN OF
CARMARTHENSHIRE
WHO FELL
IN THE GREAT WAR

1914-1918

MEWN ANGOF NI CHÂNT FOD

Carmarthenshire County War Memorial by Goscombe John was unveiled in September 1924 after a prolonged dispute over its location.

Eric Gill's unusual war memorial at Chirk was commissioned by his friend and patron, Lord Howard de Walden, and unveiled in October 1920.

The clock tower in the centre of Senghennydd was unveiled in March 1921 by Percy Ward, general manager of the Lewis Merthyr Collieries.

The memorial at Mountain Ash was organized by a committee from Nixon's Navigation Colliery Workmen's Institute. It was designed by J. Havard Thomas and completed by his son George Thomas. The memorial was unveiled in May 1922.

Members of the Merthyr Vale and Aberfan War Memorial Committee in front of the memorial, designed by George Thomas. The memorial was unveiled by the earl of Plymouth in November 1927.

The existence of both a memorial hall and a cenotaph at Barry is testament to the difficulties faced by many communities in choosing the most appropriate form of memorial. The cenotaph was unveiled by the earl of Plymouth in November 1930, and the memorial hall was opened by David Davies in November 1932.

The war memorial at Swansea includes a court of memory listing over two thousand names including female munitions workers. The memorial was unveiled by Admiral Sir F. C. Doveton Sturdee in July 1923.

(top left) St George slaying the dragon was chosen by local ex-servicemen as the war memorial for Johnstown in north Wales. It was unveiled in March 1926.

(top right) The popular visual embodiment of the empire in the form of Britannia was chosen as the design for Bridgend's war memorial. The memorial was unveiled in April 1921.

(left) Loyalty to Britain and the empire is inscribed on Llanbradach's war memorial which was unveiled in February 1925.

"EU HENWAU'N PERAROGLI SYDD"

TO THE GLORY OF GOD
AND IN SACRED MEMORY OF
THE GALLANT BOYS OF THE
PARISH OF BERSHAM WHO GAVE
THEIR LIVES IN THE GREAT WAR
1914 - 1919.

CAPT. GODFREY FITZ HIGH, MONT.YEO.
2ND LIEUT. GWILYM JAMES, R.W.FUS.
C.S.M. ROBERT R.C.NEWMAN,
JOHN H.ROBERTS,
SGTS. ROBERT W.EVANS,
JOHN ROBERTS,
CPLS. HAROLD KING, M.M.
GEORGE MATTHEWS,
L/CPLS. CHARLES HOPE,
HAROLD HUGHES,
THOMAS JONES,
JOHN P.ROBERTS, M.M.
PTES. ARTHUR DAVIES,
THOMAS E. DAVIES,
WALTER DUNKLEY,
WILLIAM J. DUTTON,
ROBERT W. EDWARDS.

1939-1945.
FLYING OFFICER GWYNNE L. BLACKSHAW R.A.F.
FLIGHT SGTS. HUGH I. JONES,
GWILYM POWELL,
L.A.C. IVOR HUGHES,
A.C. ALEXANDER K. RICHARDS.

he figurative depiction of a mourning soldier can be found on many Welsh war memorials. The memorial
Coedpoeth for the parish of Bersham was unveiled in November 1921.

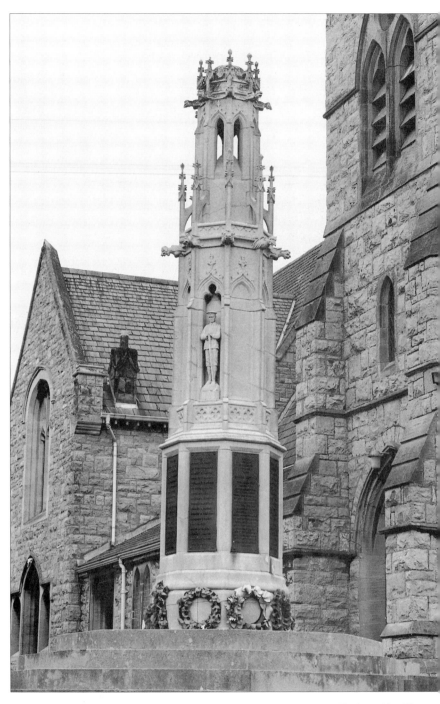

The memorial at Prestatyn is in the style of an Eleanor Cross with a mourning soldier in a niche. The memorial was unveiled in October 1920.

GLORIA
IN EXCELSIS DEO
✦ TO THE ✦
HONOURED MEMORY
OF THE MEN
OF THIS PARISH
WHO FELL
IN THE GREAT WAR
1914 —— 1918
PRO DEO PRO REGE
PRO PATRIA

WELE Y MAEN HWN FYDD YN DYSTIOLAETH INI

1939 —— 1945
IN REMEMBRANCE OF THOSE
WHO GAVE THEIR LIVES

Celtic crosses were often chosen as war memorials. The original inscription on the memorial at Llanbadarn Fawr was in English and Latin. After a public dispute, a Welsh-language inscription was added after the memorial was unveiled in January 1921.

The war memorial at Trelewis was unveiled in May 1925. Ceremonies to unveil war memorials were comprehensively reported in the local press and were often described as the highlight of the year.

The war memorial at Trawsfynydd includes the names of Ellis Evans (Hedd Wyn) and thirty-two other men who lost their lives in the war. It was unveiled in September 1921 by Lady Osmond Williams.

The Merthyr Tydfil Borough War Memorial was designed by L. S. Merrifield and unveiled in November 1931. Merrifield described the memorial as a shrine to the spirit of self-sacrifice in Merthyr Tydfil.

The scene after the unveiling of the war memorial at Abertillery in December 1926 encapsulates both the pride and sorrow of the local community as they remembered their fallen. The memorial was designed by George Thomas and unveiled by Field Marshal Allenby.

Many communities in Britain, particularly in rural areas, initially opted for a memorial hall, but the high costs involved often deterred committees. A monument could be a more economic option. The decade after the war was a flourishing time in Britain for monumental masons and commercial foundries. Catalogues of memorial designs were published and mass-produced memorials were often much cheaper to build and maintain. The proposed war memorial hall at Barry, however, was a far larger and more grandiose project than a small-scale village hall. It was envisaged as a way of promoting Barry by attracting national conferences and organizations to the town rather than meeting the specific needs of the local community. Smaller halls and buildings for communal involvement already existed in Barry, and this point was often made in the local press as the people of Barry attempted to understand why the need was so pressing for such a large hall. Another hall was added to this number in March 1927, when Major William Cope, MP, opened the new British Legion headquarters in Broad Street less than two years after the Legion had withdrawn from the war memorial committee.[47] The achievement of their objective enabled the Legion to campaign even more vigorously for the erection of a monument to their fallen comrades. A letter in the *Barry and District News* in September 1927 summed up this attitude:

> Since opinions seem far from unanimous as to the suitability of the proposed Memorial Hall for Barry, may I ask whether the general desire of the townspeople could be registered in some way, say by general vote? To carry out a scheme which does not meet with the approval of the public, especially the bereaved ones, would, perhaps, destroy the spirit of the tribute to their memory.[48]

By 1928 even the usually supportive chamber of trade spoke of the long silence on the question of Barry's war memorial. Its disquiet may have been heightened by the unveiling of the Welsh National War Memorial in Cardiff in June 1928. In December 1918 the chairman of Barry council, George Wareham,

---

[47] *Barry and District News*, 1 April 1927.
[48] *Barry and District News*, 23 September 1927.

mentioned that he had been hoping to put forward a scheme for a Welsh national monument to be erected on Barry Island which might be a landmark on the lines of the Statue of Liberty.[49] However, Barry was not destined to welcome a new influx of huddled masses and the scheme disappeared along with any thoughts of a separate memorial for the Island. This did provoke some irritation among Barry Island residents, particularly as it had been their original idea that had motivated the council back in June 1918.[50] Local papers published more letters voicing the widespread concern that the people of Barry had had no choice in the matter:

> I wonder how many people of our town want this Memorial Hall as a token of remembrance. I also noticed in the Chairman's remarks that they were bound to abide by the decision of the majority. Which does he mean, majority of the committee or majority in the town? If he means majority in town he is far out in his calculation. I have not heard of anyone voting individually to that effect or of anyone going from house to house asking one to vote for the kind of memorial one would like to have. How many relatives of our fallen soldiers are there upon this War Memorial Committee? Very few. How many ex-servicemen – fewer? I do not think our townspeople have had a proper voice in the matter.[51]

Despite mounting criticism, the war memorial committee was adamant that it could not go back on the form of memorial. It would be unfair to label the committee members as completely inflexible. The construction of a hall large enough to attract national conferences may have been seen as essential in Barry's struggle to cope with the economic problems of the 1920s. Other opportunities for generating income had to be found and the promotion of the war memorial hall as a national venue attracting hundreds of paying visitors must have appeared an attractive proposition. By adhering to the idea of a hall, committee members were acting in the long-term interests of the town but perhaps losing sight of the spirit behind the hall in the process. By November 1929, £465 remained to be raised but plans continued for the construction of the hall, with the cenotaph due

---

[49] *Barry Herald*, 18 December 1918.
[50] *Barry Dock News*, 14 June 1918, and *Barry Herald*, 21 June 1918.
[51] *Barry and District News*, 15 November 1929.

to be completed by November of the following year. Even at this late stage, arguments over the hall continued in the council chamber. At the monthly meeting in October 1930, Dr Owens argued that the feeling of the people of Barry was against the hall and that they would rather see a new wing for the accident hospital or houses built around the cenotaph, which was due to be unveiled the following month, for the families of some of the men who had fallen in the war, rather than a hall that was not required. He again called for a plebiscite, but this was turned down on the grounds that the council had insufficient money to undertake it.[52]

The cenotaph was completed on schedule; in a simple and moving ceremony on 11 November 1930, it was unveiled by the earl of Plymouth, watched by a crowd of approximately 15,000. Special accommodation was reserved for the bereaved families and more than a hundred floral tributes were laid at the foot of the monument.[53] The unveiling was described as having long been the desire of all ex-servicemen in the district, but it did not signal an end to controversy over the war memorial hall. Whilst the hall was being built, arguments continued over the possibility of its becoming a burden on the rates and over the question of dancing in it. At a particularly acrimonious meeting of the full council in February 1932, both subjects were discussed. Fears were voiced that the hall would become the biggest 'white elephant' that Barry had ever seen and that the burden of support would fall onto the rate-payers.[54] The question of dancing in the hall aroused highly emotive language, yet it was not a new problem nor was it exclusive to Barry. Dire consequences arising out of the potential misuse of memorial halls had been raised by the Revd Jubilee Young in an address to the Caernarfonshire Baptist Festival held at Pwllheli in 1928. During his speech, he noted that 'Wales erected hundreds of memorial halls to her gallant sons, but the use made of those halls was an insult to the memory of those heroes. On their polished floors young husbands and young wives danced

---

[52] *Barry and District News*, 24 October 1930, report of monthly meeting of Barry Urban District Council.

[53] For a full account of the unveiling ceremony, see *Barry and District News*, 14 November 1930.

[54] *Barry Herald*, 12 February 1932, and *Barry and District News*, 12 February 1932, reports of the monthly meeting of Barry Urban District Council, 8 February 1932.

themselves to divorce courts.'[55] In July 1930 at a public meeting of donors in Barry, Dudley Howe stated that he had been asked questions on this subject 'hundreds of times and had addressed scores of meetings on the matter'. His reply was always the same: 'the management of the hall will be in the hands of the people. It is for the people to decide what the hall should be used for.'[56] Dudley Howe's patience finally ran out as he was repeatedly pushed to say whether or not dancing would be allowed. He replied that people who said that they did not want a hall in which to dance on the graves of dead soldiers, but wanted a cenotaph, came forward with 11 guineas towards a total of £1,000 and that subscriptions were only £28 at the time of building, leaving a substantial debt to be cleared. This was not totally accurate, however, as it was not until October 1925 that subscribers were given the opportunity to earmark their subscriptions, or a portion of them, for the purpose of a cenotaph or other monument to be erected in front of the hall. At that time over £4,000 had already been raised but no mention is made of this nor of apportioning any of the Davies family's £10,000 towards a monument, and it was not until a meeting of the war memorial executive committee in September 1930 that a sum not exceeding £1,000 was voted for the purpose of erecting a cenotaph.[57]

The war memorial hall was finally opened on 11 November 1932 in a solemn and impressive ceremony witnessed by over 20,000 people. The official opening was performed by Miss Davies of Llandinam, after which David Davies unveiled the roll of honour in the Hall of Memory.[58] In December 1932 the council took over the hall and cenotaph from the trustees and a management committee was appointed to administer the daily running of the hall, whose final cost had been approximately £23,000. At the very first meeting of this committee in January 1933 it appears that the fears of some of the hall's critics were justified. Application was made to the local justices for a dancing licence, which was granted the following month, and it was also

[55] *Western Mail*, 16 June 1928. I am grateful to Mari Williams for this reference.

[56] *Barry Herald*, 1 August 1930.

[57] Barry Urban District Council, report of meeting of war memorial executive committee, 23 September 1930.

[58] For a full account of the unveiling ceremony, see *Barry and District News*, 18 November 1932, and *Barry Herald*, 18 November 1932.

decided that the word 'War' should be dropped and that Barry's commemoration of those who died in the Great War should be known simply as the Barry Memorial Hall.[59]

It cannot be denied that the various war memorial committees in Barry worked conscientiously and the memorial hall was a worthy tribute to the hard work and perseverance of men like Dudley Howe. Indeed, as David Davies commented on the day of the opening, 'had it not been for the untiring efforts of Dudley Howe they would not have been sitting in the hall that night. He was a man of whom Barry could be justly proud and had done much for the cause of peace.'[60] Whatever their political persuasion, the members of Barry Urban District Council worked assiduously for the good of the town, but as dedicated committee men and women it is possible that for them the memorial hall became yet another item on the council's busy agenda. The meaning and emotions behind the hall became blurred as economic realities had to be faced and members of the committees thought and acted as councillors rather than as relatives of the fallen or as ex-servicemen. As the architectural merits and the 'austere beauty' of the building are undoubted, the level of opposition within the town during the years leading up to its opening may appear difficult to comprehend. The memorial hall was truly a building of which Barry could be proud, but its prime function as providing material and physical benefit may have appeared to the bereaved families and ex-servicemen of the town to have taken precedence over its role in commemorating the fallen. The cenotaph provided an alternative focus of mourning, but it is apparent that it would not have been built without pressure from the ex-servicemen of the town who articulated these concerns.

Hospitals were another popular form of utilitarian memorial in Britain, through either new construction or extensions to existing buildings. In Wales, they were often chosen as the focus of larger

[59] Barry Urban District Council, meeting of memorial hall management committee, 23 January 1933. See also *Barry and District News*, 27 January 1933, and *Barry Herald*, 27 January 1933.

[60] *Barry and District News*, 18 November 1932.

memorial projects, such as the county war memorials in
Carmarthenshire, Merioneth, Pembrokeshire, Radnorshire and
east Denbighshire. The Breconshire War Memorial Hospital
replaced the Brecon Borough and County Infirmary and was
opened by Lord Glanusk in January 1928. Unfortunately, Lord
Glanusk suffered a heart attack during the opening ceremony and
his close proximity to the hospital was to no avail as he died within
the hour.[61] The city of Cardiff provides an interesting example of a
utilitarian memorial losing its commemorative meaning and
demonstrates what can be interpreted as an attempt to manipulate
the commemoration process in order to gain finance for a
favoured local project. Plans for extensions to the King Edward
VII Hospital had been approved as early as January 1916, with a
committee appointed specifically to consider building schemes, but
no mention was made of appealing to the public in terms of a war
memorial fund.[62] By 1917, however, the fund was being described
as the Cardiff War Memorial Fund. In July 1917 the *Western
Mail* published a letter from Oakley Williams, a soldier on active
service in France, supporting the idea in fulsome detail, and also
purporting to speak on behalf of the dead:

> The gallant dead themselves are pleading the hospital's cause. They, being
> dead, yet speaketh . . . These men who, in their lives, have borne witness to
> that 'greater love' plead in their death the cause of the hospital with an
> authority none can gainsay . . . By making its hospital its war memorial
> Cardiff is paying due honour to its heroes, and will complete a work of
> which its civic pride is justly and honourably jealous.[63]

The prime mover in the campaign was Colonel E. M. Bruce
Vaughan, vice-chairman of the hospital and chairman of the

[61] *Western Mail*, 12 January 1928. The county of Flint came up with an original idea for
a county war memorial. It was decided that the memorial should take the form of a
personal presentation of a specially designed Commemorative Address and the
compilation of a County Record of Service. The Commemorative Address was to be
presented to each man and woman who had served and to the relatives of the fallen by
the lord lieutenant of the county, Henry N. Gladstone, who played a prominent part in
the county movement. *County Herald*, 15 August 1919. The Flintshire Record Office at
Hawarden holds the card index, the County of Flint War Memorial, which gives details
of over 10,700 men from Flintshire who saw military service.
[62] Cardiff Royal Infirmary, Board of Management minute books. See especially a
meeting of the special committee (the emergency committee) on 17 January 1916.
[63] *Western Mail*, 2 July 1917. The paper subsequently published the full text as a
pamphlet. See Oakley Williams, *A War Memorial: Cardiff's Debt to Dead Heroes* (Cardiff, 1917).

house committee, whose letters on behalf of the fund appeared regularly in the columns of the local press. Yet when the emergency committee met in 1916, Colonel Bruce Vaughan had expressed the hope that sufficient money could be raised in six months. By 1919 it was clear that this was wildly optimistic and it is tempting, if uncharitable, to surmise that the idea of raising the necessary funds for the extensions under the guise of a war memorial fund was too attractive a proposition to be ignored. This was not unique to Cardiff, as many British charity hospitals were experiencing financial difficulties by the end of the Great War and 'war memorial funds offered an alternative to state aid which the charity hospitals grasped'.[64] A letter to the *Western Mail* in May 1919 illustrates Colonel Bruce Vaughan's approach to the public:

> I have made no direct appeal to you for the extension of our buildings since 1908, so that these appeals for capital sums do not come frequently, and when they do come they should be given preference over all other charities, for it includes them all . . . There is scarcely a family in our county which has not one 'empty chair' and those of us who wish to honour their dead or make a thanks offering for peace and for lives which have been mercifully spared to us could have no worthier or more lasting memorial to their loved ones than by contributing to the completion of this building.[65]

The inscription on the building, 'King Edward VII Hospital War Memorial', suggests that the appeal was ultimately successful, but there is no extant evidence of either an official opening ceremony or public involvement. The memorial element was, to all intents and purposes, lost in 1923 as the hospital gained its charter and became the Cardiff Royal Infirmary.[66]

Concern that utilitarian memorials such as hospitals were an inappropriate and insufficient tribute to those who had given their lives in the Great War prompted some communities to seek an additional 'sacred' memorial. In November 1923 the prince

[64] Alexander M. King, 'The politics of meaning in the commemoration of the First World War in Britain, 1914–1939' (unpublished Ph.D. thesis, University of London, 1993), p. 121. With reference to Cardiff Infirmary, see Neil Evans, 'The first charity in Wales': Cardiff Infirmary and South Wales Society, 1837–1914', *Welsh History Review*, IX, No. 3 (1979), pp. 319–46.

[65] *Western Mail*, 20 May 1919.

[66] For a general history of the hospital, see Arnold S. Aldis, *Cardiff Royal Infirmary, 1883–1983* (Cardiff, 1984).

of Wales opened the memorial hospital at Rhyl, which was soon renamed the Prince Edward War Memorial Hospital.[67] Less than eighteen months later, Councillor O. P. Jones, who also chaired the local branch of the Comrades of the Great War, raised the possibility of a memorial on the promenade. Discussion centred on the surplus from the Rhyl National Kitchen Committee and the best way to dispose of the money. Suggestions included a donation to the building fund of the Prince Edward War Memorial Hospital and the Rhyl Silver Band. Councillor Jones made his case:

> Some time back he was given what he regarded as an honourable undertaking that a certain portion of that money should be applied to the erection of a memorial on the 'front'. But now it seemed that somehow or other an endeavour was being made to defeat that object . . . He did not wish to chastise any member of the Hospital Committee, but he considered they had put the names of the fallen in the worst possible place. People entering a hospital did not want to be confronted with a list of the dead.[68]

Councillor Jones succeeded in gaining £65 for his cause and went on to chair the local memorial committee. Two granite cenotaphs bearing the names of the 200 local men who fell in the war, located on either side of the South African war memorial, were unveiled in November 1928.[69]

Many examples exist in Wales of successful combinations of memorial forms, such as Menai Bridge, where both utilitarian and sacred memorials were erected with the consent and approval of the local community. This decision had been made at the very beginning of the commemoration process in January 1919, when 'it was unanimously decided to prepare a scheme for the erection of a memorial cross to the dead at Llandysilio . . . and also a meeting place for the living in the form of a new institute'. The cross was unveiled in Llandysilio churchyard in April 1921 by Lieutenant-General Sir Philip Chetwode, whilst

---

[67] *Western Mail*, 3 and 12 November 1923.
[68] Report of meeting of the finance and general purposes committee, Rhyl Urban District Council. *Rhyl Journal*, 17 January 1925.
[69] *Western Mail*, 12 November 1928. The Prince Edward War Memorial Hospital was demolished approximately twelve years ago. After the closure of the Memorial Hospital, the services were divided between two existing hospitals, the Royal Alexandra and Glan Clwyd. The original memorial plaques were transferred to the Royal Alexandra.

the Menai Bridge War Memorial Club was opened in January 1927.[70] The passage of time and the elements have taken their toll on many original memorial halls. Some halls incorporated rolls of honour in their design and these would usually be transferred to a suitable site if the original hall was demolished 'intentionally'. Other communities opted for a memorial hall but placed the roll of honour in a local church, where it was less likely to suffer from neglect or vandalism. The lifespan of some halls was limited, particularly if they were wooden constructions or adapted from old army huts, and after the Second World War some communities chose to rebuild their memorial hall and dedicate it to the dead of both conflicts. If the memorial had been in the form of a monument, the additional names could either be inscribed or added to existing rolls of honour. A memorial in the form of a monument, however, occupied an almost 'sacred' space within the community, a space that was rarely challenged by inappropriate use or subsequent neglect, and it is clear that the potential loss of meaning attached to a utilitarian form of memorial was a major reason for opposing this form of commemoration.[71] The fear that the sacrifice made by those who had died, and ultimately perhaps the dead themselves, would be forgotten is an integral part of remembrance, as 'lest we forget' became almost an admonition to society. A purely utilitarian memorial was functional but its wider commemorative meaning could become submerged or even lost. By providing a visible and constant reminder of the dead, the meaning of a monument was both unambiguous and enduring.[72]

---

[70] File on Menai Bridge War Memorial. The community at Solva in west Wales erected a Celtic cross as their memorial and also opted to plant trees, shrubs and flowers on the approach to and at the site of the cross. MS Solva Roads of Remembrance. For commemorative planting on battle grounds and military cemeteries, see Paul Gough, 'Conifers and commemoration: the politics and protocol of planting', *Landscape Research*, XXI, No. 1 (1996), pp. 73–87.

[71] Overt vandalism to monuments is fairly unusual although they have been the targets for various political pressure groups over the years. An exception to this is Northern Ireland, where war memorials have been damaged or destroyed in sectarian attacks.

[72] 'A memorial is a memorial, not a social service. If the two functions are combined, the fact that a building or a fund may be a memorial will quickly be forgotten . . . A true memorial should simply *be*, and not be confused with good works. Its purpose is to cause people to remember, and to provide a reminder. Its *raison d'être* is to keep before the beholder what or who is being commemorated.' James Stevens Curl, *A Celebration of Death* (London, 1980), p. 316, italics in original. See also Gavin Stamp, *Silent Cities* (London, 1977), p. 18.

V

UNITED IN GRIEF: REMEMBERING THE WAR IN THE SOUTH WALES COALFIELD

The response in the coalfields of south Wales to the outbreak of war had been immediate and overwhelming.[1] By April 1915 Glamorgan had provided approximately 50,000 men for the New Army, with the Rhondda Valleys raising two battalions consisting largely of miners or mining officials.[2] At the unveiling of the Porth war memorial in 1928 local newspapers noted that the ceremony took place amidst scenes 'worthy of the splendid patriotism that so distinguished the Rhondda in the early days of the war'.[3] In November 1918 the Armistice signalled an end to hostilities, but new battle lines were about to be drawn in the British coalfield as political and economic positions were established. Nowhere in Britain was this more focused than in south Wales, where by 1919 the mining work-force was united, strong and ambitious.[4] New pits were opened, trade-union membership soared and commemoration of those killed in the Great War would take place in a coalfield where wages and expectations were high. Post-war industrial relations in south Wales were marked by bitterness and social unrest, but it appears that both the practical and emotional aspects of remembering those who had died overcame, albeit briefly, traditional enmities.

Certain colliery companies chose to mark the return of their employees who had served in the armed forces. In August 1919

---

[1] See Hywel Francis and David Smith, *The Fed: A History of the South Wales Miners in the Twentieth Century* (London, 1980), p. 22. By November 1914 fears over the production of coal led to limits being placed on the numbers of recruits from various collieries, *South Wales Daily News*, 17 November 1914.

[2] For a comprehensive account of recruitment in Glamorgan, see Desmond F. Quinn, 'Voluntary recruitment in Glamorgan, 1914–1916' (unpublished MA thesis, University of Wales, 1994). See also Clive Hughes, 'Army recruitment in Gwynedd, 1914–1916' (unpublished MA thesis, University of Wales, 1983), and Clive Hughes, 'The new armies', in Ian F. W. Beckett and Keith Simpson (eds.), *A Nation in Arms* (Manchester, 1985), pp. 99–125.

[3] *Rhondda Leader*, 24 November 1928, and *Western Mail*, 19 November 1928.

[4] See R. Page Arnot, *South Wales Miners: A History of the South Wales Miners' Federation*, vol. 2: *1914–1926* (Cardiff, 1975). See also Bernard Waites, *A Class Society at War: England, 1914–1918* (Oxford, 1987).

the directors of the Ocean Company entertained over 2,000 ex-servicemen employed at the company's pits at Treharris, Ynys-y-bwl, Nant-y-moel, Ogmore, Blaengarw, Blaengwynfi, Cwm-parc and Ton Pentre to lunch, tea, entertainment and games at the Ystradfechan Field, Treorchy.[5] On a somewhat smaller scale, the Cardiff Steam Coal Company hosted a victory banquet in September 1919 at Caerphilly Castle for the 500 workmen employed at their Llanbradach Colliery.[6] Five years later, the company paid the expenses of constructing a foundation for the Llanbradach war memorial and contributed £200 at the inauguration of the fund.[7] The commemoration process itself was often initiated by colliery companies with the placing in the workplace of memorial plaques to employees killed in the war. In July 1919 workmen and officials of Llwynhelyg Colliery met to commemorate seven of their fellow workmen who died in the war. Relatives of the deceased were each presented with a framed portrait of 'the brave lads'. The local miners' agent, Owen Powell, spoke of the workmen of Llwynhelyg giving a lead to the district in unveiling rolls of honour to the brave colliers who had fallen. He hoped that the amicable relationship existing between workmen and officials at Llwynhelyg would be emulated at other collieries.[8] In December 1921 the boards of directors of Guest, Keen and Nettlefolds Limited and Crawshay Brothers decided to erect an engraved and designed bronze tablet at each works or colliery bearing the names of workmen who died.[9] Individual commemoration of employees was unusual, although an exception to this occurred at Gelligaer. The *Merthyr Express* reported in August 1922 that a large congregation gathered at Gelligaer Parish Church for a memorial service to the memory of Major John McMurtrie, formerly manager of the Penallta Colliery belonging to the Powell Duffryn Company. John McMurtrie had won the Military Cross for action in Mametz Wood and was killed at Ypres in July 1917, aged thirty-two. During the course of the service, a memorial tablet was unveiled

[5] *Western Mail*, 1 September 1919, and *Merthyr Express*, 6 September 1919.
[6] *Merthyr Express*, 11 October 1919.
[7] *Merthyr Express*,, 27 September 1924.
[8] *Aberdare Leader*, 19 July 1919.
[9] *Merthyr Express*, 21 December 1921. Examples of these tablets are stored at the Cyfarthfa Castle Museum in Merthyr Tydfil and I am grateful to Derek Phillips for bringing them to my attention.

by Major J. R. N. Kirkwood, DSO, a fellow officer and manager of the Bargoed Colliery. A procession of ex-servicemen was headed by the Penallta Workmen's Band and the Aberbargoed Drum and Fife Band.[10] This was not a magnanimous gesture on the part of Powell Duffryn but was originally the idea of the rector of Gelligaer, Jesse Jones. He wrote to the Powell Duffryn management committee in January 1922 suggesting that the company should erect a memorial tablet in memory of their former manager. The company agreed to do so at an estimated cost of £30.[11] John McMurtrie's position as colliery manager no doubt influenced Powell Duffryn to fund the memorial, but in general workmen and officials tended to be commemorated together at the place of work. As the collieries have all but disappeared from south Wales, workplace memorials have tended to suffer the same fate. Yet the Great War has left an indelible mark on the local landscape, with elaborate memorials situated in communities which had already suffered tragedy, often on a far greater scale, than that inflicted by the Great War.

The pits of south Wales were notoriously difficult to mine and the accident statistics are a grim testament to the dangers faced on a daily basis by the workers.[12] A glance through local newspapers confirms the frequency of pit accidents. Reports of pit accidents and fatalities were usually relegated to a few lines at the bottom of a page, suggesting that such items appeared regularly and did not merit more attention. As in contemporary society, it was the major disasters that attracted wider attention and the long list of such tragedies provided the British press with many opportunities to visit the valleys of south Wales. An explosion in June 1894 at the Albion Colliery, Cilfynydd, killed 290 men and boys.[13] The Great War, by contrast, claimed the lives of sixty-two men from the village and in November 1925, a substantial

[10] *Merthyr Express*, 19 August 1922.

[11] Powell Duffryn managing committee minute books, meeting of management committee, 10 January 1922.

[12] 'On average, during the forty-six years before the First World War, one miner was killed every six hours, with a further twelve being seriously injured daily.' R. Williams and D. Jones, *The Cruel Inheritance: Life and Death in the Coalfields of Glamorgan* (Pontypool, 1990), p. 16. See also Trevor Boyns, 'Work and death in the South Wales Coalfield, 1874–1914', *Welsh History Review*, XII, No. 4 (1985), pp. 514–37.

[13] For details of the Albion Colliery disaster, see Williams and Jones, *Cruel Inheritance*, pp. 50–4. In July 1907 a memorial was unveiled in Llanfabon churchyard, Nelson, but this was dedicated to the eleven unidentified victims of the disaster: *Western Mail*, 2 July 1907. To commemorate the centenary of the Albion disaster, a memorial was unveiled in

memorial was unveiled in the centre of the village to those who lost their lives in the conflict.[14] In three years the local community collected over £400 and succeeded in raising an elaborate memorial designed by a local ex-serviceman who had been seriously wounded in the war. Three columns represented the Army, Navy and Air Force and the inscription recorded that 'This memorial was erected by the inhabitants of Cilfynydd in grateful appreciation of the sacrifice made by the men of the village in the Great War, 1914–1918'.[15] The Albion Colliery's unenviable record of the highest number of fatalities in a single explosion was maintained until October 1913, when the coalmining community of Senghennydd endured the worst accident in British mining history. An explosion underground at the Universal Colliery killed 439 men and boys.[16] This occurred just twelve years after a similar explosion claimed seventy-nine lives at the same pit. In the centre of the square in Senghennydd is an impressive clock tower in a prominent position at a road junction. The monument records, however, not the mining accident of 1913 but the sixty-three men from the village who were killed in the Great War. In July 1919 a public meeting, under the auspices of the local reception and memorial committee, was held to decide on the form of the war memorial. The original scheme had been to build a monument in the main square in Senghennydd. At the meeting, various alternative suggestions were put forward, including a memorial hall, swimming baths, a monument, gymnasium rooms and the offering of scholarships. After much discussion and an open vote, it was decided to continue with the original resolution and to erect a monument on the local square.[17] It was financed entirely by public subscription and unveiled in March 1921 by Percy Ward, general manager of the Lewis Merthyr Collieries which owned

June 1994 at Coedylan Comprehensive Upper School, Cilfynydd, although this was reported as being dedicated to all the men and boys who had died whilst working in the Albion Colliery. *South Wales Echo*, 23 June 1994.

[14] According to the *Rhondda Leader*, 6 November 1925, 37 per cent of the employees at the Albion Colliery had enlisted.

[15] Ibid. The original memorial committee at Cilfynydd consisted of sixty-six people, twenty-two of whom were workmen from the Albion Colliery. *Rhondda Leader*, 29 February 1924.

[16] For details of the Senghennydd explosion, see J. H. Brown, *The Valley of the Shadow* (Port Talbot, 1981); Williams and Jones, *Cruel Inheritance*, pp. 74–82; M. Lieven, *Senghennydd: The Universal Pit Village, 1890–1930* (Llandysul, 1994), especially pp. 215–68.

[17] *Caerphilly Journal*, 19 July 1919. See also *South Wales Daily News*, 17 July 1919.

the Universal Colliery. Local newspapers reported that several thousand people watched the procession and the unveiling ceremony.[18] The memorial was unveiled only eight years after the pit tragedy which had claimed so many more local lives than the war, yet until 1981 there was no official memorial to the 1913 disaster.[19]

The impact of a major mining accident on a community has been compared to the effect of war: cutting a swathe through the menfolk, leaving desolation and often deprivation in its wake.[20] Certainly both events witnessed collective grief and mourning, but it is evident that local communities were willing to subscribe to and finance a war memorial during times of economic hardship and emotional trauma. It may be that such communities were so hardened to the reality of death in the workplace that they were able to separate such tragedies from local involvement in a wider conflict. Death underground was undoubtedly viewed as a harsh but unavoidable fact of life in the valleys of south Wales, whilst participation in the war and death on the battlefield may well have been seen as a noble sacrifice for a higher cause. Although a contributory factor, the proliferation of war memorials in such communities, often just a few miles apart, cannot be attributed solely to pride in local sacrifice. Accounts of rescue operations following major pit explosions include stories of great courage and heroism and immense danger for those involved in the struggle to rescue survivors. A similar sense of urgency is apparent even when all hope of life has faded: it becomes no less important to retrieve bodies from the mine wherever possible. This was evident in the aftermath of the Senghennydd explosion, when the urgency was fuelled by

[18] For full details of the unveiling ceremony, see *Western Mail*, 2 March 1921, and *Caerphilly Journal*, 5 March 1921. The programme produced for the unveiling ceremony included a roll of honour listing sixty-two names with age, regiment, number, home address and place and date of death.

[19] A memorial to the victims of the 1901 and 1913 pit disasters was unveiled in October 1981 in Senghennydd. With the demolition of so many pits, there was a danger that all evidence of their existence was disappearing from the landscape. The memorials erected in more recent years, including those at Ferndale and Abertillery, served a dual purpose in providing both a permanent reminder of the industry that had shaped the local landscape and a tribute to those who had died working underground. For details on the Ferndale Miners' Memorial unveiled in 1988, see Coalfield Archive Special Collection 835. For details on the memorial to the victims of an accident at the Six Bells Colliery in 1960, see *Western Mail*, 24 August 1995.

[20] Helen and Baron Duckham, *Great Pit Disasters: Great Britain, 1700 to the Present Day* (Newton Abbot, 1973), p. 14.

'strongly held feelings about the significance of a proper burial and of a horror, common in all coalfields, of leaving bodies in a mine'.[21] The dangerous conditions of a mine, however, sometimes prevented the recovery of all the bodies, denying those left behind the possibility of taking part in, or benefiting from, the funeral ritual, just as the nature of mechanized warfare meant that a local war memorial provided often the only outlet for public and private grief.[22]

The dominance of the mining industry was reflected in the commemoration process throughout the coalfield. At Mountain Ash the war memorial committee was organized and run entirely by men from the local Nixon's Navigation Colliery Workmen's Institute, and as early as January 1919 the committee had approved a model for the memorial.[23] The institute's committee consulted and co-operated with the local council, and the land on which the memorial would be sited had been granted by Lord Aberdare, but there is no doubt that the memorial was erected completely under the auspices of the local colliery.[24] The striking figurative memorial was designed by Professor J. Havard Thomas, and following his death it was completed by his son, George Thomas, who had served in the Great War and had been awarded the Military Cross.[25] At the unveiling ceremony in Mountain Ash in May 1922, the roll of honour was handed to a trustee of the institute and was to be kept in the institute itself rather than the local council offices. Part of the inscription on the memorial reads, 'Erected by the Workmen and Officials of Messrs Nixon's Workmen's Institute', reflecting both their efforts and also the very central position of the colliery within the local community.[26] On occasions, such centrality brought its own

---

[21] Lieven, *Senghennydd*, p. 236. An explosion at Gresford Colliery in 1934 claimed the lives of 261 miners, but due to the dangerous conditions it was not possible to retrieve all the bodies from the mine. See Roger Laidlaw, 'The Gresford disaster in popular memory', *Llafur*, VI, No. 4 (1995), pp. 123–46.

[22] Although attendance at funeral ceremonies was usually limited to men, it seems that after major tragedies such as Senghennydd, women did form part of funeral processions. See *Western Mail*, 20 October 1913, and *Caerphilly Journal*, 4 December 1913.

[23] *Western Mail*, 20 January 1919.

[24] Minute books of Mountain Ash Urban District Council: see esp. council meetings on 12 October 1919, 26 October 1920 and 11 January 1921.

[25] George Thomas subsequently worked on other war memorials in south Wales, including the Merthyr Vale and Aberfan memorial and at Abertillery. Both of these are figurative sculptures.

[26] For full details of the unveiling ceremony, see *Aberdare Leader*, 10 June 1922, and *Western Mail*, 6 June 1922.

problems, as the decision of the local mining work-force could enforce a change in a planned memorial. The original scheme at Caerphilly was to build a public hall and library as a war memorial, but this had to be abandoned once the miners opted to build their own institute and were unable to support a similar scheme for the town.[27]

At times, such dominance was questioned, as occurred at Aberbargoed, where the main employer was the Bargoed Colliery, owned by the Powell Duffryn Steam Coal Company. Eight hundred men enlisted from the district, of whom eighty did not return. At a managing committee meeting in August 1919 the company decided to erect memorial columns at Bargoed Colliery to commemorate their employees who fell in the war.[28] By June 1923, however, the company was investigating a more ambitious scheme in the shape of alterations and extensions to Aberbargoed Workmen's Cottage Hospital, at a total cost of £12,000, as a memorial to all their workmen who had fallen in the Great War.[29] This did not meet with universal approval in Aberbargoed, and in July 1923 a deputation from the local war memorial committee appeared before a meeting of the Bedwellty Urban District Council to put forward their own revised scheme for a memorial. The deputation made it clear that they represented 'the general public at Aberbargoed and the ex-service men'.[30] The original plan had been for a monument in the village, but the decision of the Powell Duffryn Company spurred the change of plan and the visit to the local council. The deputation's revised memorial was a gateway to the Workmen's Cottage Hospital, the pillars of which would be inscribed with the names of the eighty local men who had died in the war. It was made clear to the council that the revised plan had been necessitated by Powell Duffryn's decision to expand the hospital as a memorial

[27] *Merthyr Express*, 19 April 1924. A cenotaph was substituted as the local war memorial and was unveiled in August 1926.

[28] Powell Duffryn managing committee minute books, meeting, 21 August 1919. In the directors' report to the company's annual general meeting in March 1919, it was reported that: 'Up to the cessation of hostilities there had been 6407 or 40.38 per cent of the Company's officials and workmen serving with His Majesty's Forces. Of these 202 have fallen in service of their Country.' Directors' Annual Reports to Annual General Meetings, meeting, 4 March 1919.

[29] Powell Duffryn managing committee minute books, meeting, 12 June 1923.

[30] Minutes of Bedwellty Urban District Council, council meeting, 24 July 1923.

for their workmen but, as the *Merthyr Express* reported, 'that . . . would not be a memorial for Aberbargoed for other members of the community – such as shopkeepers and clerks – . . . who had fallen in the war'.[31] The extension to the hospital was opened in July 1925 with the addition of two new wings, a new operating theatre and X-ray equipment, at a total cost of £13,000, whilst the gates cost £1,000.[32] The dominance of Powell Duffryn is evident in that both the extension and the gates were designed by George Kenshole, architect to the company; the president of the Aberbargoed war memorial committee was Edmund L. Hann, general manager of the company, and a year later the name of the hospital was changed when it became the Powell Duffryn Workmen's Cottage Hospital.[33] In most mining communities, however, the local colliery assimilated easily with the commemoration process. A typical example is Abercynon, where 1,500 men had enlisted and 1,200 of these came from the local Dowlais-Cardiff Colliery: 143 men did not return. The memorial committee had been chosen by a meeting of the inhabitants of Abercynon, and a clock tower was the proposed memorial.[34] The £2,000 cost was raised by public subscriptions, half by the workmen of the Dowlais-Cardiff Colliery, a quarter by Guest, Keen and Nettlefolds Ltd. who owned the colliery, and the remainder by the general public.[35] The unveiling ceremony had been scheduled to take place on the morning of Thursday, 27 July 1922, but a meeting of workmen from the colliery decided to ask the memorial committee to change the date to a Sunday as otherwise 'work will be in "full swing" and miners could hardly appreciate the ceremony after coming home from work'.[36] The memorial committee decided to adhere to the original date,

---

[31] *Merthyr Express*, 28 July 1923.
[32] For details of opening ceremony, see *Merthyr Express*, 11 July 1925.
[33] In February 1926 the company decided to provide a cup worth £6 for competition among the local football teams to be known as the 'P.D. Workmen's Hospital Trophy Cup. ' Powell Duffryn managing committee minute books, meeting, 2 February 1926. The hospital is now known as Aberbargoed and District Hospital. Although the gates remain the focus of local commemoration ceremonies, they no longer provide direct access into the hospital.
[34] GKN also erected a memorial plaque at the Dowlais-Cardiff Colliery to their workmen who had fallen in the war.
[35] *Aberdare Leader*, 5 August 1922.
[36] *Rhondda Leader*, 2 June 1922.

although the timing was changed to the afternoon 'to make it easier for the workmen to attend'.[37] The memorial was unveiled by May Jones, the four-year-old daughter of a local soldier who had been killed in the war. Efforts had been made to obtain the services of Earl Haig, Lord French and the chairman of Guest, Keen and Nettlefolds. Only when these were unsuccessful was it decided to invite a child of one of the 'fallen heroes' to perform the unveiling.

Ambitious commemoration schemes inaugurated in the immediate post-war years were frequently overwhelmed by economic problems. Appeals for various distress funds appear with sad regularity in the pages of the press and the demands upon limited incomes often led to a memorial fund being downgraded in priority. By December 1924 the women's section of the Tonypandy branch of the British Legion had raised about £100 towards the Mid-Rhondda memorial and wrote to the Rhondda Urban District Council requesting a donation. The *Rhondda Leader* reported that the ladies

> were very anxious to make the movement a complete success but were handicapped by the great number of unemployed in the district and particularly at Clydach Vale. It was explained that similar movements were in progress in Trehafod, Porth and elsewhere and that the Council had no authority to make donations. With regret, therefore, they had to reply that they had no power to assist the fund.[38]

By the time a concert had been held at the Picturedrome in Tonypandy in April 1925, £112 had been raised and the MP for Rhondda West, Will John, appealed to the audience for wider co-operation from Mid-Rhondda 'for this very important object'.[39] Despite the extreme financial hardships that were

[37] *Rhondda Leader*, 23 June 1922. As a memorial to those from Abercynon who lost their lives in the Second World War, a local committee endeavoured to have the names inscribed on the clock tower and to provide a paddling pool in the welfare park. In his autobiography, *Abercynon to Flanders – and Back* (Risca, 1984), Wilf Bowden recounts the problems in raising money for these projects: see esp. pp. 58–69.

[38] *Rhondda Leader*, 19 December 1924. See also minutes of Rhondda Urban District Council, meeting, 10 December 1924. Rhondda UDC had encountered similar problems during the 1921 stoppage when, amongst other measures, work was suspended on all new projects. See Chris Williams, *Democratic Rhondda: Politics and Society, 1885–1951* (Cardiff, 1996), p. 132.

[39] *Rhondda Leader*, 17 April 1925. The memorial to the men of Mid-Rhondda who died in the war was unveiled in December 1929. *Rhondda Leader*, 14 December 1929.

common throughout the valleys, delays in erecting a memorial often invoked highly critical comment in the columns of the local press. A subscriber to the Pant war memorial asked in April 1925: 'It was understood by the subscribers to the above that it was to be completed by the last Armistice Day. Is it to be finished by the next, or are they waiting for another war?'[40]

As the effects of economic decline began to bite deeply into the coalfield, the early optimism evaporated. Increased industrial militancy appeared inevitable, with little room for compromise. The question of control remained high on the political agenda but in fact had perplexed the authorities for many years. In 1917, alarmed by reports of possible sedition throughout Britain, the government had set up a Commission of Industrial Unrest to look into labour relations. The commissioners painted a bleak picture in south Wales of mounting social tension, and commented in particular on the problems and nature of the community:

> The Rhondda has an abundance of cinemas and music halls, but not a single theatre. Owing to the absence of municipal centres and centralised institutions, the development of the civic spirit and the sense of social solidarity – what we may in short call the community sense – is seriously retarded.[41]

In the post-war years the commemoration process would provide at least a partial solution to this apparent problem. The existence of memorial halls and institutes in valley communities where both money and goodwill were in short supply was often due to the efforts of the Miners' Welfare Fund. The Coal

---

Ambitious schemes were not confined to the coalfield. In January 1920 it was announced that Newport's war memorial would take the form of a 'triumphal arch' costing between £40,000 and £50,000. By June 1920 this had increased to an estimated £66,000. In June 1923 a competition was held to design a memorial and the eventual 'winner' was a cenotaph, costing approximately £3,600. *Western Mail*, 10 and 16 January 1920, 8 June 1920 and 23 June 1922.

[40] *Merthyr Express*, 11 April 1925. The memorial was unveiled in July 1926. *Merthyr Express*, 10 July 1926. Economic problems were not, of course, limited to the south Wales coalfield. A similar pattern emerged in the slate industry of north Wales. See R. Merfyn Jones, *The North Wales Quarrymen, 1874–1922* (Cardiff, 1982), p. 310. Economic problems did not prevent the quarrymen from contributing financially to the building of the Festiniog and District Heroes' Hospital (now known as the Ffestiniog and District War Memorial Hospital), which opened in 1927.

[41] Commission of Enquiry into Industrial Unrest: No. 7 Division. Report of the Commissioners for Wales, including Monmouthshire, 1917 (Cd. 8668), p. 12.

Industry Commission of 1919 had recommended that a penny be collected on every ton of coal raised and applied to improve the indoor and outdoor recreational facilities in the British coalfield.[42] The fund itself was established under the auspices of the Mining Industry Act of 1920, with a central committee and joint district committees consisting of owners and workmen to administer the money.[43] Financial assistance provided by the fund appears to have given many communities the opportunity both to commemorate their fallen and to provide useful social facilities. This can be seen at Blackwood, where grandiose ideas had been put forward for a war memorial early in 1919. The *Western Mail* reported that a town hall was contemplated but a public meeting two weeks later resolved in favour of an institute, library and public hall. By mid-February this had reverted to a war memorial institute and library.[44] Silence descended on the plans until a letter appeared in the *Merthyr Express* in November 1924:

> We, ex-servicemen of the Blackwood Branch of the Legion, are wondering what the people of the town of Blackwood are going to do to commemorate the great sacrifice of those lads from this area who fell in the Great War. Pontllanfraith, as usual, are ahead of this town in this respect. We understand that a considerable sum of money was collected some years ago for war memorial purposes, and such being the case, we would like to know what has become of that fund and what the committee intend doing in the matter of a tangible memorial to the boys who 'went west'.[45]

This seems to have spurred the inhabitants of Blackwood into action and at a public meeting two months later it was admitted that the initial schemes had been 'of a rather ambitious character'. A subsequent meeting agreed that the war memorial should be erected and should take the form of a cenotaph.[46] In February 1925 the Miners' Welfare Fund voted a grant of £4,000 for the erection of an institute and public hall at

---

[42] The Coal Industry Commission Act, 1919. Interim Report (Cmd. 84).

[43] For further details, see Viscount Chelmsford, *The Miners' Welfare Fund* (London, 1927). See also Mining Industry Act, 1920, Section 20 (1). The *Mining Industry (Welfare Fund) Act*, 1925, extended the levy for a further five years.

[44] *Western Mail*, 10 and 27 January 1919; see also 26 February 1919.

[45] *Merthyr Express*, 29 November 1924.

[46] *Western Mail*, 14 and 28 January 1925.

Blackwood. The monument dedicated to the memory of 200 men from the district was unveiled in November 1926 and the institute was formally opened in August 1927, having received £7,000 from the Welfare Fund and £850 from miners' contributions.[47]

The Miners' Welfare Fund exercised great caution with its money and carefully checked applications for support. The memorial hall at Pontycymmer was delayed initially by the refusal of the Miners' Welfare Fund to fund the original scheme. At the eventual opening ceremony in March 1937, Finlay Gibson commented that

> The delay in building the hall was due to the fact that their committee was too ambitious. He believed the first scheme would have cost about £20,000. That was a sum which the Miners' Welfare Association considered not too much for the people of Pontycymmer, but too much for them to maintain afterwards and they thought it would be a millstone around their necks.[48]

Similarly, officials at the Welfare Fund had been approached for assistance with a scheme at Trehafod and intimated that they would be willing to help with it, although they stipulated that the inhabitants had to give 'real proof that they are striving to help themselves, for the Miners' Welfare Committee only help those who help themselves'.[49] The movement at Trehafod had not been initiated until September 1924, when the area was described as the

> Cinderella of the Rhondda . . . without an Institute, a recreation field, and even without a playground for children, apart from those attached to the schools. The residents, with characteristic thoroughness, are making a

---

[47] *Western Mail*, 15 November 1926 and 8 August 1927. At a meeting of the Coelbren Miners' Welfare Association in December 1922, it was decided to erect a memorial hall. A working committee was formed, the majority of its members being miners who represented collieries in the Dulais and Swansea valleys, including Seven Sisters, Dulais, Onllwyn Nos. 1 and 3, Cwmtawe, Abercrave and International. Other committee members included two teachers, two railwaymen, one shoemaker, three vicars from Onllwyn, Moriah and Coelbren and three women, whose status and/or occupations are not known. The Coelbren Miners' Welfare and Memorial Hall was opened in June 1925 after receiving a grant from the central welfare fund. Coelbren Miners' Welfare and Memorial Hall minute books, December 1922–June 1929.

[48] For a full report of the opening ceremony, see *Glamorgan Gazette*, 26 March 1937.

[49] *Rhondda Leader*, 26 September 1924.

splendid effort to meet these long and deeply-felt wants, and they have set
their hearts upon providing a War Memorial Institute.[50]

Local pride was very much in evidence at the ceremony to lay
the foundation stone for the memorial institute in February
1934. One speaker commented that 'he could not concur with
the views of some people that Trehafod was one of the ugliest
spots in the Rhondda. People were always loth to leave
Trehafod.'[51] At the opening ceremony of the institute itself in
December 1934, the chairman of the committee recalled that,
before approaching the Welfare Fund for a grant, the village had
raised in the region of £500 and, as he pointed out, this would
have been 'an impossibility in a little village like Trehafod
without assiduous endeavour on the part of a loyal band of
workers. Such a band made house to house collections of one or
two pennies a week'.[52] Even with such local enthusiasm it is
unlikely that Trehafod would have been able to finance a hall
seating 400 people with games rooms, library, kitchen and
administrative offices, without the substantial grant from the
Welfare Fund.

The opening ceremony at Trehafod was performed jointly by
Finlay Gibson, secretary of the Coal Owners' Association, and
Oliver Harris, secretary of the South Wales Miners' Federation,
in their capacities as joint secretaries of the South Wales Miners'
Welfare Committee. Finlay Gibson and Thomas Richards, the
first secretary of the South Wales Miners' Federation, performed
similar duties at Nant-y-moel and Bryncethin. The hall at Nant-
y-moel was part of a larger scheme prepared under the auspices
of the Welfare Fund and costing £5,000, of which £4,500 had
been granted by the Welfare Fund and the rest raised as a result
of local efforts. The commemorative aspect of the schemes was
not overlooked, for the ceremonies at both Nant-y-moel and
Bryncethin included the unveiling of memorial tablets bearing
the names of local men who had died in the war. Indeed, at
Nant-y-moel the local war memorial committee only joined in
with the common fund on condition that a memorial tablet was

[50] Ibid.
[51] *Rhondda Leader*, 17 February 1934.
[52] *Rhondda Leader*, 22 December 1934.

erected in or near the building.[53] At the opening ceremony at Trehafod, reference was made to the inception of the Miners' Welfare Fund and that this had coincided with plans to commemorate those who had died in the Great War. It was noted that Trehafod had 'resolved to set up a memorial that would be useful and at the same time do good for the future generations'.[54] It is interesting to note that in the coalfield communities studied which opted for a memorial hall, there is no extant evidence of the controversy that marked the provision of utilitarian memorials in other areas of Wales. By the mid-1930s it may be that sufficient time had elapsed to allow a totally utilitarian memorial to become more acceptable within communities, although it remains uncertain as to whether or not such schemes were simply capitalizing on commemoration. There seems little doubt, however, that the commemoration process and the Welfare Fund enabled many communities to obtain social and recreational facilities that would otherwise have been virtually impossible to realize in the inter-war years in south Wales.

Ceremonies held to unveil monuments or to open memorial halls were often described as the highlight of the local year and were comprehensively reported in the press. Memorials were usually unveiled either by members of the local élite or by others, often with local connections, who were imported specifically for the occasion. The lord lieutenant of the county, high-ranking military personnel, local landowners, industrialists and the local Member of Parliament were popular choices. The appearance of royalty or, even better in Wales, David Lloyd George was a rare but treasured occurrence. The public act of commemoration became a perfect occasion for people to create and express their coherence as a community but it also provided a useful propaganda opportunity. In June 1919 an eisteddfod was held at Oakdale to raise funds for the erection of a memorial hall for the village. The project received strong support from the Tredegar Iron and Coal Company and the gathering was addressed by the managing director. The *Merthyr Express* reported the speech in detail:

[53] For details, see *After Ten Years: A Report of Miners' Welfare Work in the South Wales Coalfield, 1921–1931* (Cardiff, 1932). For further details of the unveiling ceremony for Nant-y-moel, *Western Mail*, 21 April 1927; for Bryncethin, *Western Mail*, 30 March 1925.
[54] *Rhondda Leader*, 22 December 1934.

Speaking of the interest the Company had in the village, he observed that if the mines were taken over by the Government, promoters of these local efforts would have to apply for assistance to the Government but he did not think that they would be treated so generously as they were by the Tredegar Company.

Major W. C. Hepburn, who presided over the meeting, echoed these sentiments and declared that in the event of nationalization money for such local schemes would have to come out of their own pockets.[55] The eventual decision to return the mines to the coal owners and the subsequent lock-out in 1921 only served to harden attitudes, but the commemoration process continued to provide opportunities for the coal owners and their representatives to stress compromise and conciliation. In April 1922 Sir Shadforth Watts, chairman of the United National Collieries, performed the opening ceremony of the Wattstown Memorial Park. The guest list reads like a roll-call of the most powerful and influential men in the coalfield, and the speeches made at the ceremony placed heavy emphasis on co-operation and good relations at the colliery. The speakers included David Watts Morgan, miners' agent and MP for Rhondda East, who was elected unopposed in December 1918 whilst still on active service in France. He had been awarded the DSO and often appeared at unveiling ceremonies in military uniform. He spoke of his sincere hope that 'the employer and the workmen, especially the latter, would return to sanity, and sit around the table and hammer out their differences, as they used to do. It was only in that way that they could keep the wheels turning.'[56] Eloquent testimonies of co-operation mark the detailed report of the opening ceremony in the *Rhondda Leader*. There is only one reference to the men who had fought and died in the war, made by John Kane, the general manager of United National Collieries, but even this mentions the miners who remained in the coalfield:

The park which they were opening that day was a memorial to the men who went to the war, but it was also a memorial to the men who stayed at

[55] *Merthyr Express*, 14 June 1919.
[56] *Rhondda Leader*, 14 April 1922.

home . . . he thought it ought to be put on record that, during all those trying years, those men never overlooked their duty to the men who were at the Front.[57]

The real focus was on those empowered to make speeches at unveiling or opening ceremonies, where they were assured of a substantial and attentive audience. Twenty thousand people attended the unveiling of the Swansea war memorial in July 1923 and heard Admiral Sir F. C. Doveton Sturdee's views on the current political and economic problems:

> The war had been won by unity; men looked up to officers whom they knew they could rely on, and the officers knew they could rely on the men . . . Why should not the same spirit prevail in civic life? . . . They heard that class was against class. What for? The 2,700 Swansea men had not died for that.[58]

The local newspaper report of the Swansea ceremony was headed 'Admiral Sturdee and Class War', and the concept of class conflict occurs frequently in speeches made at unveiling ceremonies in south Wales. At the unveiling of the Cilfynydd war memorial in November 1925, General C. G. Bruce commented that:

> although the ceremony might appear a little belated it seemed to him to have come at a very opportune moment, because it recalled years when all classes were as one. There was a word that had come into the life of Britain lately; its origin was foreign, and distasteful – 'class warfare'. There was nothing that counteracted such words greater than ceremonies like the present, because on such occasions all such words were eliminated and

---

[57] For full details of the ceremony, see *Rhondda Leader*, 14 April 1922. John Kane was born in Lancashire and came to the Rhondda as a child. He started work as a door boy underground aged fifteen and rose to become general manager of the United National Colliery Company and president of the Colliery Managers' Association of Great Britain. I am grateful to Dr Chris Williams for this information. Colliery companies in south Wales played a major role in the provision of clubs for ex-servicemen. For example, in May 1919 the Mid-Rhondda Branch of the Welsh Federation of Discharged and Demobilised Men purchased the Old Brewery in Tonypandy as an ex-servicemen's institute. They were helped by the directors of the Cambrian Combine Company who donated £1,000, and in addition the Cambrian directors undertook to make up any deficiency in the purchase money after an appeal had been made: *Rhondda Leader*, 3 May 1919, and *Western Mail*, 5 September 1919.
[58] *South Wales Daily Post*, 23 July 1923.

unanimity reigned. It was a moment which commemorated mutual comradeship and sacrifice to everyone.[59]

The unveiling of memorials dedicated to those who died in the war prompted many of those who addressed the large crowds to espouse ideas of 'responsible citizenship', combined with the memory of war.[60] The speeches made at unveiling ceremonies remain as the main documentary evidence of those occasions and lacking are the reactions and thoughts of the many thousands of people who attended the ceremonies. Memorials can embody a multiplicity of meanings, and interpretation of these depends in turn on the outlook, sympathies and emotions of the observer.[61] Perception is selective, but it is perhaps more likely that people who attended unveiling ceremonies were more attentive to the names on the memorial and thoughts of relatives and friends who had died rather than to imbibing the words of men such as Admiral Doveton Sturdee and General Bruce.

Delineation of the commemoration process along strictly class lines may underestimate the complexity of the emotions and issues involved and it would be unwise to interpret the many hundreds of small local movements to commemorate the dead strictly in terms of class and control.[62] Local landowners or industrialists commonly had a prominent position in the commemoration process, through donating either money or land, or both. On occasion, it appears that a war memorial would not have been built without the intervention of a local 'pillar of the community'. The memorial movement at Ynys-hir in the Rhondda was inaugurated in November 1924 when a public meeting held at the Saron Chapel was informed that the proprietor of the local colliery, Sir William James Thomas, had

[59] *Rhondda Leader*, 6 November 1925.

[60] Alexander M. King, 'The politics of meaning in the commemoration of the First World War in Britain, 1914–1939' (unpublished Ph.D. thesis, University of London, 1993), see esp. p. 280.

[61] See Anthony P. Cohen, *The Symbolic Construction of Community* (London, 1993). David Kertzer makes a similar point by suggesting that it is the ambiguity of the symbols involved that can make ritual 'useful in fostering solidarity without consensus . . . Not only do the symbols mean different things to different people, but the same symbol often has diverse and conflicting meanings for the same individual.' David I. Kertzer, *Ritual, Politics, and Power* (New Haven, 1988), p. 69.

[62] See, e.g., N. Mansfield, 'Class conflict and village war memorials, 1914–24', *Rural History*, VI, No.1 (1995), pp. 67–87.

promised a donation of £250 to open the subscription list.[63] Sir William was duly appointed president of the war memorial committee and the chairman was to be John Kane, general manager of United National Collieries. Other officers appointed to the committee included Councillor George Dolling as vice-chairman, Evan Richards as treasurer and Emrys Harcombe as secretary.[64] Progress was slow and by 1930 a public meeting of subscribers and collectors sought additional sources of income. It was reported to the meeting that Sir William James Thomas 'was prepared to hand over to the fund a sum of £267 collected for a proposed testimonial to himself, provided the subscribers agreed to this course. This sum would be in addition to the sum of £250 already promised by Sir William and Lady Thomas.'[65] The memorial was finally unveiled in November 1936 by Sir William, and at the service in the local church he and his wife occupied the 'big seat'. The congregation was reminded that as well as being the major subscribers to the memorial, Sir William and Lady Thomas had endowed a bed in the local hospital at Porth with a gift of 1,000 guineas to be called the 'Bed of the Ynys-hir War Memorial'. During the service, Mr Dan Jones, vice-chairman of the war memorial committee, noted that 'We have just sung a hymn, "Onward Christian Soldiers". What if we had Christian soldiers like Sir William and Lady Thomas? Then there would be no need of war.'[66] Rather than interpreting this kind of involvement as overt examples of manipulation or patronage, it may be more appropriate to label this as a continuation of the Victorian philanthropic tradition. Whilst such interventions may indeed have reinforced their position within the local societal hierarchy, such men may also have had personal reasons for participation. Wealth and position offered

[63] *Rhondda Leader*, 14 November 1924.

[64] *Western Mail*, 18 February 1925. The appearance of George Dolling, in particular, is interesting. A member of the Independent Labour Party (ILP), who had maintained their unpopular anti-war stance, he was a co-author of *The Miners' Next Step* and had served on the Rhondda Federation of ILP branches; he was president of the local Plebs Club and had served for a period on the executive committee of the South Wales Miners' Federation. Opposition to the war does not seem to have precluded participating in commemorating those who had died: my thanks to Dr Chris Williams for the biographical information.

[65] *Rhondda Leader*, 5 July 1930.

[66] *Rhondda Leader*, 21 November 1936, and *Western Mail*, 16 November 1936. The war memorial committee had changed several times over the years. For example, the original chairman, John Kane, had resigned his post in 1926.

no protection against the ultimate impact of war. The loss of a close relative, often a son, suggests that the unveiling of war memorials may have been regarded as more than just another civic duty to perform. Lord Tredegar and Colonel Homfray each lost a son, whilst Sir Evan Jones lost a son, a son-in-law and a nephew in France and a son in Macedonia. Colonel Morgan Lindsay lost three sons in the war and probably the most difficult ceremony for him was in July 1932, when he unveiled the Ystrad Mynach and Hengoed memorial, on which are inscribed the names of his three sons.[67]

Commemoration of the Great War in the coalfields of south Wales witnessed co-operation and consensus between worker and employer to a surprising degree, given the bitter industrial climate of the 1920s. But rather than seeing the rituals surrounding commemoration as oases of conciliation, it is perhaps more appropriate to see such occasions as examples of what has been termed 'communitas', whereby everyday social hierarchies are temporarily put aside and individuals relate to each other as human beings.[68] The ceremonies surrounding the unveiling or opening of war memorials provided a suitable context for such spontaneous solidarities to re-form, albeit for a limited time. This temporary and fragile unity was highlighted in an incident in the Upper Afan Valley during the General Strike. The heightened atmosphere of 1926 provoked an attempt to disrupt the opening of the workmen's memorial hall at Glyncorrwg because of 'the scandal of glorifying the dead and starving the living'. The prime reason for the miners' action appears to have been the presence of the local coal owner, Robert Gibbs. Glyn Williams admitted that 'if Gibbs wasn't there nothing would have happened of course. Nothing.'[69] Of interest is the fact that Williams relates that it was the 'Legion boys' who thwarted the attempts to

---

[67] *Merthyr Express*, 23 July 1932. The fourth marquess of Bute, although a major landowner, does not appear to have played any role in the unveiling of local war memorials despite having lost his brother, Lord Ninian Crichton Stuart, who was killed in action in 1915. The marquess did contribute to the commemoration process in other ways, such as donations of land for the erection of war memorials and by providing finance for the purchase of huts for the use of local ex-servicemen. *Western Mail*, 31 March 1920 and 2 November 1923.

[68] V. Turner, *Dramas, Fields and Metaphors* (Ithaca, NY, 1974), and *The Ritual Process* (London, 1969).

[69] South Wales Miners' Library: interview with Glyn Williams (Glyncorrwg), 21 May 1974.

disrupt the ceremony and were angry with Williams and others for their efforts. Even though Williams himself had been born in 1908 and had not seen active service in the war, there must be a strong possibility that many members of the local British Legion branch were also out on strike at that time. It would appear that, on this occasion at least, the bonds of solidarity between ex-servicemen and their perceived duty to honour their dead comrades were stronger than allegiance to the strike. For a few hours, the public and private memory of war overcame contemporary concerns and loyalties. A more enduring legacy to the impact of the Great War remains today in the monuments, halls and other sites of memory in the valleys of south Wales.

VI

'MEMORIALS WITHIN GOD'S ACRE': CHURCH, CHAPEL AND COMMEMORATION

In the early days of war, controversy had occurred over the spiritual needs of the troops. In September 1914 a difference of opinion arose between Kitchener and Lloyd George over the sending of Nonconformist chaplains to the front. Kitchener apparently had treated the proposal with contempt and replied that it would be impossible. Lloyd George protested that Nonconformists only asked to be treated in the same way as the native Indian troops, the Sikhs and the Gurkhas, who were allowed to have priests of their own faith in their regiment. Lloyd George was also well aware of the importance of Nonconformist support in recruiting for the Welsh Army Corps: 'If you intend to send a Church of England Army to the front, say so! . . . but you cannot fight with half a nation.'[1] Four years later, religious differences were maintained even in victory as thanksgiving services for the end of hostilities were held throughout France. Major Wynn Wheldon of the 14th Battalion, Royal Welch Fusiliers, noted in his diary that Nonconformists held their service in the local village church whilst the Church of England congregation met in a nearby field.[2] Yet in the years after the war, both church and chapel co-operated and played an integral role in the commemoration process in Wales. Members of the

[1] Kitchener reluctantly agreed, asking Lloyd George to write down a list of denominations concerned. A. J. P. Taylor (ed.), *Lloyd George: A Diary by Frances Stevenson* (London, 1971), pp. 3–4. Lloyd George wrote home of the dispute: '28 September 1914 Row ofnadwy efo Kitchener heddyw ynghylch Noncon. Chaplains. Spoke out savagely. Carried Cabinet & got my way.' K. O. Morgan (ed.), *Lloyd George Family Letters, 1885–1936* (Cardiff and London, 1973); translation in text, 'Tremendous row with Kitchener today about Noncon. Chaplains', p. 173. The meetings of the Baptist Union of Wales in New Tredegar in October 1914 were quick to refute claims that Welsh Nonconformists had been slow to enlist (*Baptist Times*, 23 October 1914). See also K. W. Clements, 'Baptists and the outbreak of the First World War', *Baptist Quarterly* (April 1975), pp. 74–92. For general church attitudes in Britain, see Alan Wilkinson, *The Church of England and the First World War* (London, 1978), esp. pp. 13–31.
[2] War Diaries of Major Wynn Wheldon, DSO, 14th (Service) Battalion, Royal Welch Fusiliers, entry for 17 November 1918. Wynn Wheldon became registrar of the University College of North Wales, Bangor, and played a prominent role in the movement to erect the North Wales Heroes' Memorial.

clergy often participated in war memorial committees, and the unveiling ceremony, under the watchful supervision of the church, often took on the guise of a funeral service.[3] A strong religious element, usually in the form of prayers, blessings and dedications, was an intrinsic part of unveiling ceremonies, whether the memorial was sacred or utilitarian in nature. The rare omission of a spiritual element caused distress and consternation amongst members of a community.

The opening of the war memorial park in Rhymney in 1925, as already noted, had divided rather than united the local community, and one major problem had been the lack of any form of religious service at the opening of the park. Thomas Griffiths wrote to the *Merthyr Express* shortly after the war memorial park had been opened, and catalogued a number of grievances, which included the fact that every vestige of religiosity had been absent:

> Another injustice to those boys who gave their all was that at the opening ceremony no form of memorial service was held, no minister of religion took part, there was no hymn sung to comfort those who mourned, no silent tribute, no 'Last Post' played. But a great celebration, as if Wembley was being opened for the first time, with no thought of those 'heroes' who were gone, and no message of comfort to those who mourn.[4]

A further letter appeared in the paper a week later from members of the Rhymney and Pontlottyn Branch of the British Legion stating that 'the ceremony was void of all that appertained to the Christian idea of commemoration'.[5] Attempts by the local council to explain their action were interpreted as lame excuses and Thomas Griffiths, clearly not satisfied with their explanations, wrote a further letter in June 1925:

> No effort has been made to make the park worthy of such a memorial by arranging with the local ministers of religion to have the park dedicated in

---

[3] The church also played an influential role in some areas of Britain in the design of memorials, with some dioceses setting up special memorial committees to advise on proposed alterations and additions to churches and churchyards. See Catherine Moriarty, 'Christian iconography and First World War memorials', *Imperial War Museum Review*, VI (1992), pp. 63–75.

[4] *Merthyr Express*, 9 May 1925.

[5] *Merthyr Express*, 16 May 1925. A similar letter was published in the *Western Mail*, 14 May 1925.

honour of our fallen heroes who went forward with no fear of death and now lie in foreign lands in unconsecrated graves where they were laid by their comrades with greater reverence and sympathy than was granted them by the Rhymney Urban District Council on the occasion of the opening of the Rhymney War Memorial Park.[6]

A 'sacred' war memorial in the form of a Celtic cross was finally built and unveiled in 1929, four years after the war memorial park had been opened. On this occasion representatives from the various denominations were present, hymns were sung and the 'Last Post' was played.[7]

In November 1928, the Llanwrtyd Wells War Memorial Institute was formally opened and dedicated.[8] This was an impressive addition to the town and housed billiard and games rooms, together with large committee rooms. The porch of the building was regarded as the 'memorial' element to the building and a brass tablet listed the names of the fallen from the town itself and the surrounding area. The institute had been made possible by a good response to local appeals, but primarily because of a £1,000 gift from the local Calvinistic Methodist minister, the Revd Rees Evans, who unveiled the memorial tablet and also delivered an address. Dedication of the memorial tablet and prayers were delivered by other representatives of the clergy. The onset of heavy rain interrupted the proceedings, which were continued inside the Calvinistic Methodist chapel.[9] The fact that on this occasion the institute appeared to be largely in the gift of the minister of a local Nonconformist chapel may also have been influential, but in general the opening of memorial halls and institutes throughout Wales was accompanied by a religious service. In 1920 the directors and employees of the Port Talbot Steel Company presented Aberavon Hospital with electrical equipment in memory of the twenty-nine men connected with the steel works who had died in the war. A bronze roll of honour listing their names was also fixed in the entrance

---

[6] *Merthyr Express*, 20 June 1925.
[7] The vicar of Rhymney, Revd J. R. Dewi Williams, dedicated the memorial and was assisted by the Revds R. E. Peregrine and D. J. Davies. *Western Mail*, 28 October 1929.
[8] For details of the opening ceremony, see *Brecon and Radnor Express*, 15 November 1928.
[9] *Western Mail*, 13 November 1928.

hall of the hospital. The electrical equipment and roll of honour were dedicated at the same ceremony in November 1920 by the vicar of St Mary's church, Aberavon.[10] It is clear that even when the memorial was intended to fulfil the dual purpose of serving the living and honouring the dead, the religious element of what would otherwise appear a purely secular ceremony was deemed to be both integral and important.

At a public meeting in Carmarthen in 1922, the mayor spoke of the impossibility of a county memorial being built 'at the present time' as 'the churches and chapels in the borough had erected memorials and some people made this an excuse for not supporting the present movement'.[11] Yet fears that a prolifera-tion of memorials within churches and chapels would hinder the fund-raising and building of a single civic memorial appear not to have been borne out for the overwhelming impression is that chapels and churches co-operated in commemoration. On occasion, the various religious bodies in a community could also play an important role in mediating between competing com-memorative factions. Shortly after the Armistice, an open meet-ing in Prestatyn elected a representative town's committee to consider the question of a local war memorial. After twelve months of deliberation, the committee failed to reach unanimous agreement and submitted two reports: the 'Majority Report', signed by thirteen members of the committee, favoured a monu-ment, whilst a 'Minority Report', signed by one member, pre-ferred a utilitarian memorial. Both reports were put to a public meeting in February 1919, when a show of hands gave a majority of sixteen in favour of the 'Minority Report'.[12] This was not adopted, however, and led to the formation of a joint com-mittee representing the parish church and all the free churches of Prestatyn, 'supported by the unanimous resolution of a repre-sentative meeting convened by the chairman of the urban district council'. In May 1919 a public appeal was made for a 'Sacred Memorial to all the Men from Prestatyn who have fallen in the Great War', which made it clear that the memorial was to be erected 'within God's Acre' in Prestatyn. The appeal was signed

[10] *Western Mail*, 22 November 1920.
[11] *Carmarthen Journal*, 2 September 1921.
[12] *Prestatyn Weekly*, 22 February 1919.

by the vicar as chairman of the committee and by the president of the free church council acting as vice-chairman. The committee also hoped to provide 'for each church in which our fallen brothers were accustomed to worship, a plate, bearing their names and an engraving of the Sacred Memorial'.[13] The elaborate memorial was erected in the parish churchyard and unveiled in October 1920. The vicar 'recited some appropriate sentences' and the Revd Thomas Hughes (Wesleyan) read a lesson. The dedicatory prayers were offered by the dean of St Asaph. Approximately £1,000 had been subscribed to the memorial fund; the memorial itself cost £800 and the *Prestatyn Weekly* reported that £20 was voted to each church in the town 'belonging to which members had fallen, for the purpose of providing a brass tablet with names inscribed'.[14]

A cross, whether 'traditional' or Celtic in design, appears to be the most common form of war memorial in Britain, although this created problems in the south Wales community of Cefn-coed-y-cymer. A memorial was first discussed at a public meeting in September 1923, when the options considered were either a memorial hall or a cross. Poor attendances at public meetings ensured that a decision was constantly postponed until in June 1924 members of the local war memorial committee decided to go ahead with a memorial in the form of a cross and to issue an appeal to the public for subscriptions. The dispute that arose, however, was not about the type of memorial, even though much support had been expressed for a memorial hall, but rather over the choice of a cross. 'Cefnite' wrote to the *Merthyr Express* in July 1924:

> I quite agree, Mr Editor, that a memorial should be erected in our village in memory of the fallen, but what I and many others object to is that a few, who are decidedly fanatical about erecting a cross, should enforce their wishes upon the village when the majority, who are nonconformist, object to this particular form of memorial . . . I know many people who will not permit the names of their dead lost ones to appear upon a cross and many more will doubtlessly do the same . . . Such autocratic conduct drives decent people into the ranks of Socialism.[15]

[13] Papers re Prestatyn War Memorial.
[14] *Prestatyn Weekly*, 30 October 1920.
[15] *Merthyr Express*, 12 July 1924. For earlier correspondence on the proposed memorial at Cefn-coed-y-cymmer: *Merthyr Express*, 22 September, 3 November 1923 and 28 June 1924.

Despite these fears, a decorative cross was eventually unveiled in November 1930 and the inscription included the names of forty local men.[16] The memorial at Cefn-coed-y-cymmer records that it is dedicated to the men from Vaynor Parish who gave their lives in the Great War, although it is not situated in a churchyard. Memorials erected within church boundaries could record either the names of men who had worshipped at that particular church or the names of all the men from the district who had died, and this usually depended on the size and location of the community involved. In April 1926 Sir James German unveiled a memorial dedicated to sixty-six men from Ystrad Rhondda who lost their lives in the Great War. The memorial is situated within the churchyard at St Stephen's and was described as being 'somewhat unique, inasmuch as the church erected it to the proud memory of all those men from the district who paid the supreme sacrifice in the cause of freedom, and not merely to those of them who were Churchmen'.[17] A similar pattern emerged at Cwmbwrla in Swansea, where the war memorial committee of St Luke's church, chaired by the vicar, decided in January 1919 that a war memorial should be erected for the 'fallen members of St Luke's Church'. By September 1920, however, the committee recommended to a church meeting that the memorial should be built for 'all who had fallen in the Parish and not only the members of St Luke's Church.'[18] The memorial was sited within the church and consisted of a stained-glass window, an extension of the reredos and a marble tablet.

Early memorials often appeared in Nonconformist chapels. There was no geographical divide to this trend, even though it might be expected that north Wales, with its strong Nonconformist traditions, would lead the way.[19] Local newspapers regularly reported the unveiling of chapel memorials in south Wales during the 1920s, and it seems that congregations in the south were as keen to commemorate their dead as their counterparts in the north. Chapel memorials tended to be unveiled earlier, primarily because the numbers would often be smaller

[16] For full details of the unveiling ceremony, see *Merthyr Express*, 15 November 1930.
[17] *Rhondda Leader*, 9 April 1926.
[18] War Memorial Committee Minutes, St Luke's church, Cwmbwrla, Swansea, meetings held on 19 January 1919 and 14 September 1920.
[19] See, e.g., N. Mansfield, 'Class conflict and village war memorials, 1914–24', *Rural History*, VI, No. 1 (1995), pp. 67–87.

and the immediacy of the event lent an emotive edge to raising the necessary funds. Such memorials could take the form of either a monument outside the chapel, or memorials inside which tended to be marble or brass tablets or stained-glass windows. Slate was often used for memorials in north Wales and a particularly fine example exists at Nantlle, where the names of those who died are surrounded by a broad margin depicting slate mining juxtaposed with battlefield scenes.[20] Memorials in the form of tablets often included the names of all those who had served as well as those who had died, as on the roll of honour at the English Baptist church in Tredegar which includes the names of eight men who died and thirty men who had served, whilst the brass tablet at Bethesda Presbyterian church in Ebbw Vale listed twenty men who served and commemorated the death of one man.[21] There were exceptions to this, as occurred in July 1919 at Treherbert, where the ex-servicemen who worshipped at Bethany English Baptist church decided that the proposed war memorial should be confined to 'the fallen heroes of the church'.[22] The opportunity was sometimes taken to replace or refurbish existing fixtures and fittings within the chapel, such as the memorial pipe organ and tablet at the Ebenezer Baptist church, Cwmbran. The organ was unveiled by the sister of one of the men commemorated and the tablet unveiled by a wounded ex-serviceman.[23]

Inscriptions on memorials situated inside chapels and churches often contain biblical references, although verses or lines from local poets also featured quite prominently. Llwyn-yr-hwrdd chapel, outside the village of Tegryn, combined both traditional and local elements in its commemorative text. The memorial took the form of a monument with a Welsh inscription commemorating members of both Llwyn-yr-hwrdd and its sister chapel, Brynmynach, in the nearby village of Hermon. The inscription reads, 'Mewn angof ni chânt fod' (They shall not be forgotten) and a verse by a local poet:

[20] F. G. Aylott, 'The Nantlle Quarry war memorial, 1914–1918', *Bulletin of the Military Historical Society*, XXV, No. 100 (1975), pp. 128–30. The memorial remained in its original position at the quarry after closure but has now been moved to a central position in the village.

[21] *Merthyr Express*, 11 September 1920 and 5 March 1921.

[22] *Rhondda Leader*, 26 July 1919. The bronze tablet listing the fifteen men who had died was unveiled in March 1923. *Rhondda Leader*, 9 March 1923.

[23] *Western Mail*, 2 December 1927.

O sŵn corn ac adsain câd – huno maent,
Draw ymhell o'u mamwlad.
Gwlith calon ga' dewrion gwlad,
Wedi'r cur, – mwynder cariad.

(Away from the horn's sound and the battle's echo they are resting yonder, far away from their mother country. After the affliction hearts will bleed with gentle love for the country's heroes.)[24]

The most common arrangement would be for individuals to be commemorated on chapel memorials, with duplication of names on the civic, town or village memorial. The war memorial institute in Llanwrtyd Wells contained a memorial tablet listing the names of the fallen, but this was not the only site of remembrance in the town. The Zion Baptist chapel erected a white marble plaque listing the names of three men who had died in the war and these three names can also be found on the plaque inside the war memorial institute. Similarly, a plaque was erected in St James' church, on the east wall of the chancel: 'To the Glory of God And in Loving Memory of John Nicholas Lewis, Lieutenant 8th Welsh Regiment Killed in Action in the Dardanelles 8th August 1915 Aged 22 yrs. Dulce et Decorum Est Pro Patria Mori.' Lieutenant Lewis's name heads the list within the war memorial institute. Memorials to individual servicemen can often be found in places of worship. These usually commemorated members of local, wealthy families, who may also have provided the finance and land for the local war memorial. Invariably the name, or names, were included on the 'central' memorials. In smaller communities in Britain, particularly in rural areas, the parish church often served as the focus of a community and also became the focus of commemoration. The monument in the churchyard of St Cynfran's parish church in Llysfaen, north Wales, records the names of forty-five local men who died. The inscription records that it is 'the tribute of Llysfaen Parish to its fallen sons', while a memorial window

[24] I am grateful to Clydau Community Council for information on this memorial and to Professor J. Gwynfor Jones for the translation.

inside St Cynfran's is dedicated to the 'sons of the church' who died, including the rector's two sons.[25]

The role of chapels in Wales as focal centres of communities in the early decades of the twentieth century, especially in the urban and anglicized south, faced formidable opposition both from miners' institutes and lodges and increased leisure activity. Yet the image of chapels crumbling, physically and metaphorically, under the combined onslaught of secularism and socialism needs qualification. Although the miners' lodge became the dominant local institution in many communities by the end of the Great War, the chapels continued to play an important role in local life.[26] David Egan has urged caution in linking the rise of political and trade unions in the coalfield after the Great War to a breach with Nonconformist religion. His work on Maerdy in the Rhondda Valley illustrates the complex relationship that existed between the various religious denominations and the strong militant political tradition within the village and, indeed, the coalfield generally. Prominent political spokesmen often came from a religious background, a prime example being Arthur Horner, one of Maerdy's (and Britain's) leading communists, who had been a Baptist lay-preacher, and

the relationship was genuinely reciprocal, for when the Institute was destroyed by fire in November 1922, Carmel English Baptist Church allowed the Institute Committee . . . to use its facilities for their meetings . . . Ebenezer Chapel agreed to let its vestry be used as a reading room and Seion, Siloa and Bethania Chapels also offered their facilities.[27]

[25] I am grateful to Llysfaen Community Council for information on these memorials. See also W. G. Lloyd, *Roll of Honour* (Cwmbran, 1995). This book chronicles the role of the eastern valley of Monmouthshire during the Great War and includes a chapter on local war memorials (pp. 143–202). In Abersychan, the congregation of the High Street Baptist church unveiled a roll of honour and opened a memorial church library in November 1919; the English Congregational church unveiled a memorial tablet in January 1921, whilst a roll of honour was unveiled at the Noddfa Baptist church in November 1923. Many of the names on these chapel memorials can be found on the tablets surmounted on the memorial gates, which form the central joint memorial to men of Pontypool and Abersychan.

[26] See, e.g., David Gilbert, *Class, Community and Collective Action: Social Change in Two British Coalfields, 1850–1926* (Oxford, 1992). For a detailed study of Nonconformity in the Cynon Valley, including chapel membership figures, see D. Ben Rees, *Chapels in the Valley* (Upton, 1975), pp. 66–85.

[27] David Egan, '"Maerdy United Choir v The Spiritualists": popular culture and the use of Maerdy Workmen's Hall and Institute, 1918–1922', *South Wales Miners' Library Newsletter*, V (1993), pp. 4–7.

It appears that chapels were equally willing to allow their premises to be used for the holding of public and committee meetings to discuss a proposed local war memorial and not just a memorial for that particular chapel. The first meeting held at Ynys-hir to discuss the war memorial was held at the Saron Welsh Congregational church, described by the local press as playing 'a large part in the religious and social life of the District'.[28] In September 1919 a meeting of the Trelewis War Memorial Committee was held at the Ebenezer vestry, and a representative from the chapel was involved in the ceremony to unveil the memorial in May 1925.[29]

The ceremonies held to unveil local war memorials were very public occasions and as such provided a useful opportunity throughout Britain for the representatives of differing denominations to appear together in a demonstration of ecumenical unity. South Wales, whose industry and population made it the epicentre of the principality, witnessed many such displays. On Sunday, 14 December 1924 Lord Tredegar unveiled a memorial in Bedwellty Park in memory of 300 local men, and the ceremony provides a useful example of the demarcation of spiritual duties on such occasions. The local Baptist minister opened the proceedings with a scripture reading and the Calvinistic Methodist minister then led the assembled 'congregation' in prayers. After Lord Tredegar had unveiled the memorial and given a short address, the Congregational minister and the vicar of St George's church shared the consecration and dedication prayers. Finally, the benediction was given by the Wesleyan minister.[30] Clerical unity was demonstrated in west Wales at the unveiling of the Fishguard war memorial in April 1928 by Sir Evan Jones, who had lost two sons in the war. Prayers and blessings were given by the curate of St Mary's, the pastors of Pentower

[28] *Western Mail*, 18 February 1925, and *Rhondda Leader*, 14 November 1924. In February 1923, the inaugural meeting of the Nelson War Memorial Committee was held at the Penuel vestry under the chairmanship of the rector of Llanfabon. *Merthyr Express*, 3 February 1923. The vestry of the Tabernacle chapel was the site for a well-attended meeting of the Treharris War Memorial Committee in October 1928. *Merthyr Express*, 6 October 1928.

[29] *Western Mail*, 1 June 1925.

[30] *Western Mail*, 15 December 1924, and *Merthyr Express*, 20 December 1924. See also 'Programme for the Unveiling and Dedication Ceremony: Tredegar War Memorial Sunday, December 14th, 1924, at 2.30 p.m.' I am grateful to the National Inventory of War Memorials for a copy of this programme.

Calvinistic Methodist church and Tabernacle Congregational church, and the dedication prayer by the vicar of Fishguard.[31] The same pattern is demonstrated in north Wales, where the memorial at Trawsfynydd was unveiled in September 1921 by Lady Osmond Williams, wife of the lord lieutenant of Merioneth. It was dedicated by the rector of Trawsfynydd, who was assisted by the ministers of Moriah Calvinistic Methodist chapel and the Wesleyan chapel, Ffestiniog.[32]

A strong ecumenical presence was often evident at the opening of utilitarian memorials. At Llansilin in April 1924, Margaret Lloyd George opened the memorial hall commemorating thirty-one local men. On this occasion, local clergy and ministers seem to have vied for the honour of thanking their guest for her efforts. The prayers were led by the Congregational minister; a vote of thanks to Mrs Lloyd George was moved by the Baptist minister, swiftly followed by representatives of the Calvinistic Methodist and Wesleyan chapels, who seconded the vote of thanks. It was left to the vicar of Llansilin to pronounce the benediction. A trust was later created to administer and maintain the memorial hall and it was proposed that representatives of the different religious denominations 'who have places of worship in the parish' should be invited to act as trustees.[33] An unusual example of religious co-operation occurred at Llanddeiniolen in north Wales, where the memorial was unveiled by the 'four oldest men of the four religious bodies in the parish – all four are well over eighty'.[34]

The exception to these displays of unity would appear to be the Roman Catholic Church. Members of immigrant Spanish and Italian communities were numbered amongst Catholic congregations in Wales, but Roman Catholicism in Wales was firmly rooted amongst the Irish immigrant communities.[35] Whilst local

---

[31] *Western Mail*, 5 April 1928.

[32] The memorial was originally sited alongside the Seion chapel in the centre of the village before being moved to its present location.

[33] Papers *re* Llansilin Memorial Hall. For further details of the opening ceremony, see *Oswestry and Border Counties Advertiser*, 16 April 1924.

[34] *Holyhead Chronicle*, 27 May 1921. Programmes from unveiling ceremonies in Britain can be found in the War Memorial Ephemera Collection held at the Imperial War Museum. See, for example, the programmes for Barnstaple, Crieff, Leicester, Looe, Luton, Manchester, Norwich, Penrith, Sutton Coldfield and Taunton.

[35] For a comprehensive background to the Irish in Wales, see Paul O'Leary, 'Immigration and integration: a study of the Irish in Wales, 1798–1922' (unpublished Ph.D. thesis, University of Wales, 1989). For statistical information on the Roman Catholic community in the Cynon Valley, see Rees, *Chapels in the Valley*, pp. 85–6.

Catholic communities commemorated their fallen along 'traditional' lines, there were certain differences. At St Mary's Roman Catholic church in Newport, a war memorial church improvement fund was started in 1920 which successfully raised £7,000. This enabled the church to erect two memorial tablets listing 197 names, an altar within St Patrick's chapel, and an altar rail for the sanctuary, and to install a new organ. The tablets were unveiled in March 1922 by a local dignitary in the presence of the Most Revd Francis Joseph Mostyn, archbishop of Cardiff, who later blessed the tablets and sprinkled them with holy water and incense.[36] On Good Friday 1920, following the service of the Stations of the Cross in Our Lady and St Michael's church, Pen-y-pound, Abergavenny, a procession of the choir and congregation walked to the site of the war memorial cross. The cross itself had been in the possession of the church for some time but had deteriorated and the full cost of renovation and remounting was met by Lord Treowen, who was present at the ceremony.[37] Lord Treowen also took part in a very personal commemorative ceremony in June 1922. The 'settlement garden city' of Tre'elidyr near Llanover Park was conceived by him as a memorial to his son who had been killed in Palestine in 1917. A number of houses surrounded a village green, upon which a monument was built surmounted by a cross. Directly opposite is a stone recess with engraved brass tablets bearing inscriptions in Welsh and English and the names of those commemorated, all of whom were connected with the Llanover estate. The scheme was designed by a London architect, but the work was carried out by men from the estate. The monument was unveiled by Lord and Lady Treowen and the service was conducted by 'all ministers of all creeds in the neighbourhood'.[38] This included a Catholic priest, but generally priests played little or no part in the unveiling ceremonies of a town or village war memorial. Occasionally, the local priest would take part in the public discussion

---

[36] *Welsh Catholic Herald*, 1 April 1922; *South Wales Argus*, 31 March 1922, and *Western Mail*, 31 March 1922. Archbishop Mostyn was the fourth son of Sir Pyers Mostyn, the 8th baronet of Talacre, Flintshire.

[37] *Abergavenny Chronicle*, 9 April 1920.

[38] *Western Mail*, 17 June 1922. Lord Treowen also opened the Treforest Memorial Hall in October 1923 commemorating forty-six members of St Dyfrig's Roman Catholic church who lost their lives in the war. He was supported by Lord Pontypridd and a large number of Catholic clergy from south Wales. Archbishop Mostyn was also present. *Rhondda Leader*, 2 November 1923, and *Western Mail*, 23 October 1923.

over the type of memorial to be erected, but it appears to have been neither accepted nor indeed expected that Catholic clergy should take part in the unveiling ceremony. One reason for this may have been the interdict on Catholic clergy taking part in any public worship with clergy from other denominations. A public meeting in Mold in July 1919 discussed the forthcoming peace celebrations and accepted suggestions for the town's war memorial. The meeting was presided over by the chairman of the urban council, and the local Catholic priest, Dr Baron, was listed as being among the principal speakers. The *County Herald* reported that Dr Baron advocated a permanent memorial with the names inscribed of all local men who had fallen in the war, but he also wanted to see 'the most needy of the widows and children of those who had fallen comfortably housed free of rent'.[39] The memorial was unveiled in March 1926 and 'all the local ministers of religion' took part in the official procession, but no representative from the Catholic Church participated in the religious service. This was also the case at Bargoed, where the local Catholic priest, Father O'Donovan, was listed as being present at the ceremony to unveil the local war memorial but did not take part in the religious service.[40] Within Wales, Catholicism was very much a 'minority' religion associated primarily with Irish communities and, as these tended to be viewed with suspicion bordering at times on hostility, a reluctance either to invite or, conversely, to accept co-operation on local commemorative projects can be understood.[41] It remains true, of course, that individual local Catholics, in a private capacity, may well have been numbered amongst the large crowds attending civic unveiling ceremonies, whether the memorial was sited on sacred or on secular ground.[42]

In contrast, the Jewish population in south Wales appears to have participated fully in unveiling ceremonies. Although there

---

[39] *County Herald*, 11 July 1919.

[40] *Mold, Deeside and Buckley Leader*, 5 March 1926, and *Merthyr Express*, 9 June 1923.

[41] On anti-Irish hostility in Wales, see Paul O'Leary, 'Anti-Irish riots in Wales, 1826–1882', *Llafur*, V, No. 4 (1991), pp. 27–36. Adrian Gregory has suggested that arrangements for participation in Armistice Day ceremonies may well have been influenced by local attitudes towards the Irish war of independence and this may have been equally relevant in discussions over local war memorials. Adrian Gregory, *The Silence of Memory* (Oxford, 1994), pp. 198–9.

[42] I am grateful to Dr P. O'Leary and Professor J. Gwynfor Jones for their views on these points.

are no accurate figures for the number of Jewish immigrants who settled in south Wales, one estimate puts the number of Jews in Cardiff in 1914 at 2,000, and approximately 5,000 in south Wales, with synagogues at Merthyr, Tredegar, Pontypridd, Brynmawr, Aberdare, Ebbw Vale, Aberavon, Ystalyfera and Llanelli.[43] Brynmawr's Jewish population had its own cemetery as well as a synagogue, and the 'Hebrew Congregation' is listed as taking part in the procession to the war memorial at the unveiling ceremony in October 1927, although it did not take part in the religious service.[44] In July 1926 a tablet was unveiled in the synagogue in Windsor Place, Cardiff, in memory of the Jewish officers and men from Cardiff who had lost their lives in the war. It was unveiled by a local notable and an address was given by the vice-president of the Cardiff and District Council of the League of Nations. He spoke of the only hope for future peace and prosperity in the world being found in the League of Nations and 'called upon all the members of the congregation who believed in the ideals of the League to stand. There was a remarkable response, all the men and women rising to their feet and pledging themselves to support the League.'[45] Unveiling ceremonies and Armistice Day ceremonies with their obvious connotations of loss and sacrifice provided an opportunity for calls to be made to work for a better, peaceful future, thereby ensuring that the sacrifices enshrined in stone would not have been made in vain. A visit to the Rhondda by the bishop of St David's as president of the Welsh Council of the League of Nations in May 1925 appears to have elicited a good response. As a result of his address to a public meeting, thirteen local branches in connection with local chapels and churches were

[43] Information on the Jewish communities in south Wales is taken from Ursula R. Q. Henriques (ed.), *The Jews of South Wales: Historical Studies* (Cardiff, 1993). For the estimates on population numbers, see ibid., p. viii, and for information on the valley communities, see pp. 45–67.

[44] See the 'Programme of the Unveiling and Dedication of the Brynmawr War Memorial Sunday, October 30th,1927'. For a report of the ceremony, see *Western Mail*, 31 October 1927. Merthyr Tydfil's Jewish population erected a plaque at its synagogue to the memory of thirty-four men killed in the war. The inscription reads: 'To the glory of God. In honoured memory of the Jewish young men who served their country in the Great War. Merthyr Hebrew Congregation.' The synagogue was closed and sold in the early 1980s and the plaque is now stored at Cyfarthfa Castle Museum. I am grateful to Derek Phillips for this information.

[45] *Western Mail*, 5 July 1926. By 1918 there were two synagogues in Cardiff. For further details, see Henriques, *Jews of South Wales*, pp. 207–9.

formed.[46] The Welsh League of Nations Movement enjoyed wide support throughout the principality, and David Davies, one of the 'founders' of the Welsh League, was an active and enthusiastic proponent of the League's principles. As a Member of Parliament, landowner, industrialist and philanthropist, he was also a popular choice to unveil war memorials. In April 1927 Davies opened the memorial hall at Felin-fach in west Wales, built to commemorate fifteen local men who had died and to honour seventy-five men who survived, and he used the occasion to promote the League's cause. He hoped that

> the message of peace on earth was once more stirring the hearts of the people and that hall would ever be a reminder to the young people of the district of the great sacrifices made by those who died. He concluded with an earnest appeal to those present to support the cause of peace through the League of Nations so that war should cease in the world.[47]

Unveiling or opening ceremonies were not only useful occasions on which to espouse particular causes; they also provided a very public opportunity to proclaim the strength of organized religion in the face of declining church attendances. Ecumenical co-operation occurred throughout Wales, but to view this as an attempt to reaffirm the religious message and gain new recruits to the fold would be to underestimate the depths of sorrow and grief of individuals and communities. It would be equally misleading, however, to give the impression that religion was able to offer an effective panacea to the grief experienced by so many families; indeed, the apparent inability of orthodox religion to provide adequate comfort or explanation may have prompted many to seek alternative sources of consolation or to make attempts to contact their loved ones. Spiritualism witnessed an unprecedented growth in popularity during and after the war as the bereaved attempted to come to terms with their loss.[48] One of the most notable 'personalities' who toured and lectured

---

[46] *Rhondda Leader*, 29 May 1925. For detailed information on the Welsh League of Nations Union Movement, see Goronwy J. Jones, *Wales and the Quest for Peace* (Cardiff, 1969), pp. 97–124. The leading pacifist, George Maitland Lloyd Davies, used an Armistice Day service at Nant-y-moel in the 1930s to preach a message of peace: 'Armistice should mean penitence and repentance.' Papers of George M. Ll. Davies, National Library of Wales.

[47] *Western Mail*, 1 March 1927.

[48] A full account of this phenomenon is given by Jay Winter, *Sites of Memory, Sites of Mourning: The Great War in European Cultural History* (Cambridge, 1995), pp. 54–77.

extensively on spiritualism was Sir Arthur Conan Doyle, who lost his son, his brother and his brother-in-law in the war. In September 1919 Conan Doyle and his wife attended a seance at Portsmouth, where the medium was Evan Powell from Merthyr Tydfil. Conan Doyle had visited Merthyr Tydfil in February 1919 to address the Merthyr Spiritualist Society on 'Death and the Hereafter' and spoke to a 'packed Theatre Royal'. He was obviously deemed a success, as he returned in December the same year to deliver a lecture entitled 'The Evidence of Immortality'. On this occasion he also attended spiritualist meetings in the Rhondda Valleys and in Ebbw Vale and spoke on the subject of 'Spiritualism and the Churches'.[49] Throughout the early 1920s local papers in south Wales reported meetings of local spiritualist societies; for example, in October 1922 the *Aberdare Leader* reported on a meeting of the 'local Spiritualists' in Penrhiwceiber which was held at a local school: 'Mr David Jones gave clairvoyances and the circle was conducted by local people.'[50]

Congregations and individuals throughout Wales, whether 'established' or Nonconformist, sought to commemorate their dead in a way that would both honour the sacrifice and provide a degree of solace. The nature of the sculpture and inscriptions on British memorials, which are largely devoid of triumphal or aggressive images, reflected this desire to avoid the glorification of war. The messages were overwhelmingly of sadness, absence and loss, but also a determination to inscribe these sentiments on the nation's memory. Many inscriptions carry religious texts which emphasize both the sacrifice and also the importance of remembering that sacrifice.[51] Strong parallels were often drawn in the addresses made by clergy at unveiling ceremonies between the sacrifice of the soldier and that of Christ. At the unveiling of the war memorial cross at the church of Our Lady and St Michael in Abergavenny, the Revd Father Willson included the lines: 'Christ was obedient unto death, even unto the death of the Cross; so were these heroes of theirs obedient to the will of their

[49] *Merthyr Express*, 22 February 1919, and 6 December 1919.
[50] *Aberdare Leader*, 7 October 1922.
[51] For memorials as religious symbols, see Jon Davies, 'War memorials', in David Clark (ed.), *The Sociology of Death* (Oxford, 1993), pp. 116–19 (pp. 112–28).

King and country in giving up their lives for them all'.[52] It seems unlikely that many servicemen would have identified themselves in these terms, and such sentiments probably had more to do with attempts to comfort the bereaved.[53] The experience of war and bereavement certainly shaped individual responses and reactions to religious messages of consolation, but in the prolonged and painful process of coming to terms with personal loss, it is clear that the Christian message played an important role in the amelioration of grief for some, but proved insubstantial and inadequate for others.

[52] *Abergavenny Chronicle*, 9 April 1920.
[53] Moriarty, 'Christian iconography', pp. 63–75 (esp. p. 73).

VII

'GWELL ANGAU NA CHYWILYDD –
BETTER DEATH THAN DISHONOUR':
THE LANGUAGE OF COMMEMORATION

Disputes occurred in Wales over the type of memorial to be built and over the location, but it is clear that the use of the Welsh language was the least contentious feature of the commemoration process. In today's society this may appear surprising, given the place of the Welsh language as a component of Welsh identity, but in the decade after the Great War, debates over the place of the language in remembering the fallen were invariably consensual rather than confrontational. Three occasions are cited where the use of the Welsh language on war memorials was a source of disagreement within communities, but it appears that the issue was more a subject of debate during the war itself than in the post-war discussions over commemoration.

The attempted formation of a Welsh Army Corps in 1914 had been the subject of Cabinet debate and the use of the Welsh language formed part of the heated discussions between Lloyd George, then chancellor of the Exchequer, and Kitchener as secretary of state for war.[1] In May 1916 a letter of complaint was sent to the secretary of the Welsh Army Corps regarding an order issued by the officer commanding the 17th Battalion, Royal Welch Fusiliers, that

> anyone caught speaking the Welsh language will be severely punished: surely such a thing is an outrage in a Battalion, more than ¾ of whose officers and men are Welsh speaking Welshmen, and I am sure would not be tolerated were the whole facts known.[2]

In practice, the attitudes of individual officers towards the Welsh language determined its use, particularly on active service. Wyn

---

[1] For correspondence between Lloyd George and Kitchener on the language issue, see Creedy Papers, IWM 71/22/1.

[2] Welsh Army Corps Records, letter from Major Evan B. Jones, 20th Battalion, RWF, to secretary of the WAC, 11 May 1916.

Griffith was a native Welsh speaker and, as an officer in the 15th battalion of the Royal Welch Fusiliers, conversed in both languages with soldiers under his command. Griffith wrote later of his experiences in using his native language in the army:

> My regiment, the Royal Welch Fusiliers, consisted mostly of Welsh-speaking Welshmen whose background was similar to my own. In Welsh, we could talk freely, officers and men alike and with each other, without impinging in any way on matters of military protocol that seemed to belong exclusively to the world of English.[3]

Vivian de Sola Pinto did not speak Welsh but found this was not a problem when he became an officer in 2/6th Royal Welch Fusiliers in 1915:

> Our men were chiefly farm labourers and quarrymen from North Wales and Anglesey. A fair proportion of them only spoke Welsh and a very large number were called Jones. The Joneses were often distinguished by the names of the villages or districts where they lived and were known as Penmaenmawr Jones, Festiniog Jones and so forth . . . I was soon on excellent terms with the men in my platoon in spite of linguistic barriers; one of them even started to teach me Welsh.[4]

A problem for those officers not familiar with the Welsh language was raised by a fellow officer of Wyn Griffith during a rare lull in the fighting in Mametz Wood in 1916. Taylor, the brigade signalling officer, spoke of 'Evans the padre' who was 'going to do a bit of burying': 'I thought he looked queer . . . he was talking to himself, praying, may be, when I walked along with him. It was in North Wales Welsh, and I couldn't make much of it'. It transpired that the padre's son had been killed in action the previous day and the padre had attempted without success to find his grave. He was set to resume his own work: 'Going to bury other people's boys, he said, since he couldn't

---

[3] L. Wyn Griffith, 'The pattern of one man's remembering', in G. A. Panichas (ed.), *Promise of Greatness* (London, 1968), pp. 287–8.
[4] V. de Sola Pinto, *The City that Shone: An Autobiography (1895–1922)* (London, 1969), p.147.

find his own boy's grave to pray over . . . What could you say?
. . . You couldn't talk English to a man who had lost his boy'.[5]

As the war progressed, growing casualty lists posed new
problems for the administrative machinery. Communications
from the War Office were written in English and it was this
language that carried the official notification of death to the next-
of-kin. Whilst this did not present a linguistic problem for the
majority of the Welsh population, certain areas of the country
remained largely Welsh-speaking. The novelist Kate Roberts, a
staunch advocate of Welsh nationalism both in her life and works,
highlights this in her book, *Traed Mewn Cyffion* ('Feet in Chains').
The English language is depicted as a corrosive element within a
monoglot Welsh community and the effect is at its most painful
when the news of the death of a member of the family in the
Great War is brought by post. The central character of the novel,
Jane Gruffydd, awaits a letter from her son, Twm, who was
serving in France. The postman finally arrived:

> But it was not a letter from Twm, nor was it from any of the other
> children. It was a long envelope with an official stamp on it. 'Drat it,' she
> said to herself, 'another old form with questions to answer . . .' But when
> she opened it, she saw that it was not one of the usual forms. These were
> sheets of paper, written in English. She saw Twm's name, and his army
> number, and there was another sheet of thick white paper with only a few
> words on it in English. She ran with the letter to the shop. 'Some old letter
> in English has come here, Richard Hughes. Will you tell me what it is?
> Something to do with Twm, anyhow.' The shopkeeper read it, and held it
> in his hand for a while. 'Sit down, Jane Gruffydd,' he said gently.[6]

---

[5] Wyn Griffith, *Up to Mametz* (London, 1981), pp. 190–1. Interestingly, the identity of
'Evans the padre' became known many years later. G. D. Roberts, the author of *Witness
these Letters,* had been given a copy of *Up to Mametz* by Wyn Griffith. As he read this
section, he realized that 'Padre Evans' must have been his own father who served as a
chaplain and was attached to a line battalion of the 38th (Welsh) Division. In the course
of his duties he would have visited many different casualty clearing stations and this was
how he heard of the death in action of one of his sons, Glyn, during the early stages of the
battle of the Somme in July 1916. All four of his sons served in the Royal Welch Fusiliers
during the war. G. D. Roberts wrote to Wyn Griffith in 1931 who confirmed that 'Padre
Evans' was indeed Peter Jones Roberts, 'a better man never lived'. Griffith notes that had
the book been intended for publication he would have named him, 'but I wrote it
privately for my boys, and it was published more or less accidentally several years after it
was written'. See G. D. Roberts, *Witness these Letters* (Denbigh, 1983), pp. 104–5.
[6] *Feet in Chains: A Novel by Kate Roberts,* trans. Idwal Walters and John Idris Jones
(Cardiff, 1977), pp. 121–2. *Traed Mewn Cyffion* was first published in 1936.

For Kate Roberts it was the personal experience of the Great War with the death in action of her youngest brother, and its wider impact on Wales, that gave her the impetus to write. She recalled 'the terrible injustice I have felt personally, that a government took the children of monolingual Welsh smallholders to fight the battles of the Empire, and sent an official letter to say those children had been killed in a language that the parents couldn't understand'.[7] Though the writings of Kate Roberts undoubtedly set the war and its impact in Wales firmly within a Welsh nationalist context, this does not negate the very real anguish experienced by families who received such letters in a language they could not understand. The trauma continued for the bereaved with the official administration of commemoration which was carried out in English. The principle of equality of sacrifice and equality of treatment in death was paramount in the policy of the Imperial War Graves Commission (IWGC), but the officials involved were aware that the process ran the risk of appearing impersonal with little consideration for the feelings of the next-of-kin. The desire to avoid the memorials appearing 'institutional' prompted the commission early in 1918 to allow a personal inscription or text for the headstone.[8] The personal inscription was to be separate from the commission's official inscription of name and unit but could be in languages other than English, such as Welsh, Gaelic or Latin.[9]

---

[7] *The World of Kate Roberts: Selected Stories 1925–1981*, trans. Joseph P. Clancy (Philadelphia, 1991), p. xi.

[8] Minutes of the Second Meeting of the Imperial War Graves Commission, 18 February 1918. Initially a charge was to be made for each letter, but this became a matter of controversy, cases being reported of relatives being unable to pay the fee. At a meeting of the commission in October 1919 it was agreed that inscriptions should be proceeded with whether payment had been received or not, but that this should not be stated publicly. See minutes of the Sixteenth Meeting of Imperial War Graves Commission, 21 October 1919.

[9] The question of personal inscriptions in Welsh arose during the Second World War. Sir Henry Morris-Jones had raised the case in the House of Commons of a Welsh sergeant-pilot of the RAF who had been killed on flying duty; his widowed mother had submitted a Welsh-language inscription for his headstone which had been turned down by the IWGC. As vice-chairman of the IWGC, Major-General Sir Fabian Ware made it clear that that 'he was taking the same line that he took during the last war, and leaving the choice of the inscription entirely to the relatives concerned'. It transpired that the Welsh subscription submitted had been too long, and had been referred back to the relative. Unfortunately, she had misunderstood the commission's letter and had thought that they were objecting to the Welsh language itself. It was emphasized that it was the commission's practice to allow any language. Two Hundred and Sixty-Eighth Meeting of Imperial War Graves Commission, 19 April 1945. For the debate in the House of Commons, see *Hansard* 410 HC Deb. 5s.,17 April 1945. I am grateful to Alex King for advice on this point. The Honourable Society of Cymmrodorion assisted the IWGC

The inscription for Private E. H. Evans illustrates the policy of the commission towards both the personal inscription and the use of the Welsh language on headstones. Ellis Evans was a shepherd from Trawsfynydd, but is better known by his bardic name of Hedd Wyn. Evans was an established poet and had already won many honours at provincial eisteddfodau. The chief bardic prize had eluded him until the 1917 eisteddfod held in Birkenhead, where his poem, 'Yr Arwr' (The Hero), won the coveted chair, but the award was made posthumously as Evans had been killed in action shortly before the eisteddfod took place. A local movement was started in Trawsfynydd to commemorate Evans, but the posthumous prize and his existing high reputation as a poet appear to have spurred contemporaries to form a prestigious national memorial committee, chaired by Major David Davies with Sir Vincent Evans as treasurer.[10] The movement was instigated by R. Silyn Roberts, a preacher and a noted poet, who also entered into correspondence with the IWGC in 1920 over the question of a Welsh inscription on Evans's headstone:

> My Committee would be very much obliged if the Bardic name of E. H. Evans namely 'Hedd Wyn' could be inserted on the stone monument in brackets if necessary immediately after his name. Although a young man and a young peasant his name was a household word in Wales on account of the great distinction he had attained as a Poet. He was everywhere known in Wales as Hedd Wyn and comparatively few people outside his own parish knew that his name was E. H. Evans. Consequently the inscription of his Bardic name on the Head stone would assist Welsh visitors to find this grave.[11]

Over three years passed, but in September 1923 an official of the commission wrote to Ellis Evans's father asking his permission for the inscription, 'Y Prifardd Hedd Wyn' to be engraved on the headstone that was shortly to be erected over his son's

during and after the Second World War by studying and translating Welsh inscriptions. Papers of the Honorable Society of Cymmrodorion.

[10] *Welsh Outlook*, V (January 1918), p. 6, and (May 1918), p. 156.

[11] Letter from Silyn Roberts to the secretary, IWGC, 22 January 1920. In fact, Evans was so well known as 'Hedd Wyn' that he had submitted his winning poem in 1917 as 'Fleur de Lys'. The correspondence between Silyn Roberts and the Imperial War Graves Commission is taken from the Papers of R. Silyn Roberts, Bangor Ms.15291–15294 . See also 'E' File SL 10876 on Private E. H. Evans held at the Commonwealth War Graves Commission.

grave.[12] Seeking permission was necessary as the inscription had been submitted to the IWGC by the national memorial committee, but it was the commission's policy to engrave only inscriptions submitted by the next-of-kin. Evan Evans gave his consent in a short and moving letter:

> In reply to your letter dated 20.9.23 I have to inform you that Mr Silyn Roberts the Hon Sec. of my son's National Memorial Committee is acting with my knowledge and approval. My son was a peasant farmer like myself and only thirty years of age when he fell, but he had won a national reputation as a poet of great merit. The inscription suggested by the National Committee, namely, Y PRIFARDD HEDD WYN, is simple and most appropriate.[13]

The IWGC wrote to Silyn Roberts in April 1924 to inform him that 'a report was received on the 21st December 1923 from the Head Office of this Commission in France stating that the cross which marked the grave of Private E. Evans had been amended to read with his correct particulars'.[14] Welsh had been Ellis Evans's first language and it was through this medium that he lived, worked and wrote his poetry; his prominence as a leading poet certainly heightened his profile amongst contemporary literary intellectuals and prompted a very public campaign to ensure an appropriate Welsh inscription on his headstone.[15] Yet it is clear that the policy of the Imperial War Graves Commission on

---

[12] 'Y Prifardd' translates as Chief Poet or Bard.

[13] Letter from Evan Evans to the secretary, IWGC, 26 September 1923. Capitals in original document. Papers of R. Silyn Roberts.

[14] Letter from principal assistant secretary, IWGC, to R. S. Roberts, 16 April 1924. Papers of R. Silyn Roberts.

[15] Ellis Evans was not the only inhabitant of Trawsfynydd to lose his life in the Great War. The village war memorial to the memory of thirty-three local men was unveiled in September 1921 by Lady Osmond Williams, the wife of the lord lieutenant of Merionethshire. It was originally sited in the centre of the village, but the combination of a narrow road and a rise in the volume of traffic led to the memorial being moved in the early 1930s. It is now in a peaceful location overlooking Trawsfynydd Lake. The names are listed in alphabetical order and Evans is listed as Ellis Evans (Hedd Wyn). The Hedd Wyn memorial was designed by L. S. Merrifield (who would later design the Merthyr Tydfil war memorial). It takes the form of a bronze statue of Hedd Wyn dressed in the clothing 'typical' of a shepherd or farm worker at the time, although there was debate over choosing the most appropriate form of dress. The memorial cost £600; the remaining £378 in the fund was used to establish a scholarship at the University College of North Wales at Bangor. The statue was unveiled by Ellis Evans's mother in August 1923. I am grateful to Mr M. S. Roberts of Trawsfynydd for information on the Hedd Wyn memorial and other war memorials in this area.

the use of Welsh and other languages on headstones in their cemeteries was both flexible and pragmatic, and that this approach was reflected at a local level throughout Wales. The rare examples found to date where the language did become a focus of controversy appear exceptions in the post-war debates over commemoration in Wales.

By December 1924 the site for the war memorial in Nelson, Glamorgan, had been decided upon and in the same month a letter was published in the *Merthyr Express* signed by 'Respect for the Fallen' calling for a Welsh language-inscription:

> it is to be hoped that when the design and the inscription to be placed thereon have been arranged, that a place will be given to a Welsh inscription – the native and home language of a large number of the fallen. It is a source of regret and implies a certain amount of disrespect that in the towns and villages of Wales many of the memorials have no Welsh inscription. The English people resident in Wales would certainly have cause for complaint if the war inscriptions were all in Welsh, and the Welsh people have equal, if not more cause for complaint when the inscriptions are all in English. Let Justice be done.[16]

Successive meetings of the local war memorial committee discussed many different inscriptions and in February 1926 decided on the words 'Erected by the people of Nelson in proud and loving memory of the men of this village who died as a result of the Great War 1914–1918', but no mention was made of either a Welsh translation of these words or a separate Welsh inscription.[17] This point was picked up by 'One of the Subscribers' in a letter to the *Merthyr Express* a week after the committee meeting:

> the report did not state whether the inscription is to be in the Welsh or English language or both. If in Welsh only, it would be an insult to the memory of the men of English nationality, whose names are recorded. On the other hand if the inscription is to be in the English language only, it will be an insult to the families and friends and to the memory of the men of Welsh nationality who fell in the war that a monument erected on their native heath should ignore the native language. In Nelson, Lancashire, one would not expect to find an inscription other than in English, but in

---

[16] *Merthyr Express*, 6 December 1924.
[17] *Merthyr Express*, 20 February 1926.

Nelson, Glamorgan, an inscription in English only would be very inappropriate and against the wishes of many of the subscribers.[18]

The committee bowed to the wishes of the subscribers and it was decided to add the Welsh 'motto', 'Gwell Angau Na Chywilydd' ('Better Death than Dishonour' or 'Death rather than Dishonour') to the inscription.[19] 'Gwell Angau Na Chywilydd' is probably the most common Welsh-language phrase found on Great War memorials, with examples at Bala, Blackmill, Caerphilly, Kidwelly, Llanbradach, Llangefni, Llanidloes, Llansadwrn, Pencarreg, Pontlottyn, Tonyrefail and Trelewis.[20] The phrase had been used on monuments commemorating Welsh involvement in earlier conflicts, such as the memorial to the men of Llanelli who had died as a result of the South African War, unveiled in August 1905 by Earl Roberts. On the front face of the memorial is 'Gwell Angau Na Chywilydd', followed by a lengthier message in English: 'This Memorial was erected by public subscription in honour of the Men of Llanelly and District who, at the Empire's call, laid down their lives during the War in South Africa, 1899–1902'.[21]

Newport in south Wales in the 1920s would appear to be an unlikely location for a dispute over the use of the Welsh language. Newport was prosperous, ambitious and anglicized; indeed, in 1921 the numbers of Welsh-only speakers were recorded as 0.0 per cent whilst the total number of Welsh speakers was 2.1 per cent; yet just such an argument occurred over the omission of a Welsh inscription from the cenotaph.[22] The movement to commemorate the 1,476 men and women of Newport who had lost their lives in the Great War was organized under

---

[18] *Merthyr Express*, 27 February 1926.

[19] Ibid. The memorial committee made their final decision on the inscription in April 1926: 'To commemorate the end of the Great War, 1914–1918, and to the memory of the fallen sons of Nelson', followed by the names and 'Gwell Angau Na Chywilydd'. The memorial was unveiled in August 1926. *Merthyr Express*, 28 August 1926, and *Western Mail*, 20 August 1926.

[20] The phrase has a strong link with the military in Wales as a regimental motto and in 1895 it was reported to be inscribed on the headgear of soldiers from Welsh regiments. *Western Mail*, 5 August 1895. It has also been described as the motto of various Welsh families.

[21] J. Gildea, *For Remembrance and in Honour of Those who Lost their Lives in the South African War, 1899–1902* (London, 1911), p. 259. My thanks to Catherine Moriarty for this reference.

[22] John Williams, *Digest of Welsh Historical Statistics*, vol. 1 (Cardiff, 1985), p.86.

the auspices of the town council, with the war memorial committee composed of councillors. The sum of £3,000 had been
raised by public subscriptions and the design of the memorial
had been the subject of a competition, twenty-three designs
being submitted from throughout Britain. Two local architects
were successful and gained the commission to design the
memorial as well as the £100 prize offered by the war memorial
committee. The memorial, which took the form of a cenotaph,
was unveiled by Lord Tredegar in June 1923, with the war
memorial committee and, in particular, the chairman of the
committee, Alderman Fred Phillips, playing a prominent role in
the proceedings.[23] The inscription on the cenotaph was in
English only, with 'To Our Heroic Dead' on one panel and
'Their Memory Endureth For Ever' on another, and this had
been decided on by the war memorial committee two months
before the unveiling ceremony.[24] A subsequent request from a
member of the public direct to the war memorial committee that
the inscription should be in Welsh was, if not ignored, then
politely brushed aside.[25]

However, the council found themselves facing a more
formidable opponent one month after the cenotaph was unveiled
and on this occasion was forced to confront the issue of a Welsh-
language inscription. A full council meeting in July 1923 received
an 'influential deputation' which pressed the case for the
addition of a Welsh inscription to the cenotaph. The deputation
was headed by Sir Garrod Thomas, a doctor by training who
had been Liberal MP for South Monmouth during the war.[26]
Ecumenical support was evident with the presence of the
archdeacon of Monmouth, the rural dean of Newport and
clerical representatives from England, Ireland and Scotland,
whilst Lords Tredegar and Treowen lent their written support.
Sir Garrod Thomas spoke for the deputation and seems to have
gone to great lengths to further his cause. He told the assembled
members of the council that he had 'felt the pulse of

[23] For details of the unveiling ceremony, see *South Wales Argus*, 4 June 1923, and *Western Mail*, 4 June 1923.

[24] Newport Town Council, meeting of war memorial committee, 16 April 1923.

[25] The members of the war memorial committee resolved 'that Mrs N. Llewellyn be informed, in reply to her letter suggesting that the inscription on the war memorial should be in Welsh, that the words to be inscribed have already been chosen'. Newport Town Council, meeting of war memorial committee, 31 May 1923.

[26] See *Who's Who in Wales (1st edition) 1920* (Cardiff, 1921), p. 453.

representative Welshmen, and I feel justified in saying that the desire among the Welsh is universal and warm that you should concede to our request'.[27] He emphasized that the deputation consisted of representatives of England, Ireland, Scotland and Wales and cited as a precedent for their request the inscription on the monument of Sir Charles Morgan, the great-grandfather of Lord Tredegar, in Park Square, which had both English and Welsh inscriptions. The proposed inscription was 'I'n Dewrion, Eu henwau'n perarogli sydd' ('To our Heroes, Their names are ever fragrant'), but it was not the form of words that caused problems for the council but whether to accept that a Welsh inscription was necessary.[28] The fear was voiced that if the request were to be granted, it would 'set up a precedent and have other people in the town – such as the Irish – coming forward and making a similar request'. The proposal was eventually agreed to with four dissentients including, significantly, Alderman Fred Phillips, who had been chairman of the war memorial committee. He demanded to know how many Welshmen could actually read Welsh and suggested that as the cenotaph had been accepted by the mayor on behalf of the town it would be wrong to alter the inscription or add anything to it.[29] Alderman Phillips could not let the matter rest and notified the council and the press of his intention at the next full meeting to ask the council to revoke their decision. This heralded immediate cries of protest in the columns of the local press, with the *South Wales Argus* printing an editorial strongly in favour of the proposed Welsh inscription

[27] Newport Town Council, minutes of Council Meeting, 10 July 1923; report of meeting in *South Wales Argus*, 10 July 1923, and *Western Mail*, 11 July 1923. The motivation behind the original deputation to the council is unclear; the *South Wales Argus* had published a letter from 'N.L.' on 13 July 1923 after the council had agreed to the inscription. The letter expresses thanks both to the council for agreeing to the inscription and to the deputation for their efforts. It is probable that 'N.L.' was the 'Mrs N. Llewellyn' who had written to the war memorial committee in May 1923 in an unsuccessful attempt to gain a Welsh inscription before the memorial was unveiled. The letter mentions an earlier publication in the *South Wales Argus* and it may be that Mrs Llewellyn wrote to the local paper after the war memorial committee had turned down her request and that Sir Garrod Thomas and other members of the deputation decided to act after seeing the letter.

[28] The same inscription can be found on the memorial erected at Coedpoeth in memory of men from the parish of Bersham in north Wales and also on the war memorial for men from the parish of Waen in north Wales.

[29] Newport Town Council, minutes of Council Meeting, 10 July 1923; report of meeting in *South Wales Argus*, 10 July 1923, and *Western Mail*, 11 July 1923.The war memorial committee had disbanded once the memorial was unveiled but its members, as councillors, would have attended subsequent council meetings.

and a separate column of letters which, predictably, were also in favour. The editorial appealed to emotion and dismissed questions of expense or whether Newport was in England or Wales. The issue, as far as the paper was concerned, was more straightforward:

> The call for volunteers was made to the Welsh as well as to the English, Scottish or Irish . . . During the war, Newport was included in the Welsh military area. Many of those who served were attached to Welsh units, whose regimental mottoes are expressed in Welsh. Some of the fallen were Welshmen by birth. Surely there can be no real objection to their sacrifices being recorded in the Welsh language? We would suggest that if the placing of a Welsh inscription on the Cenotaph gives pleasure to only one bereaved mother, widow, sweetheart, or any other relative, the adoption of that course should be regarded as a town's duty.[30]

The day before the crucial meeting, the paper reported a meeting of Newport Trades Council, which had passed a resolution urging the council not to revoke its decision to place a Welsh inscription on the cenotaph. The same edition also published several other letters on the subject, all of which were in favour of the Welsh inscription, leading the paper to comment that 'the case for a Welsh inscription seems unanswerable'.[31] Alderman Fred Phillips attempted to argue the opposite at the council meeting the following day. He stated that he was presenting his resolution on behalf of the Newport branch of the British Legion, which felt that, as the memorial had been dedicated and consecrated, no additional inscriptions should be permitted. This may well have been a valid reason and Alderman Phillips gained sympathy by describing how he had been 'abused most shamefully in anonymous letters and postcards'. However, his subsequent statement that since the 'mother tongue of the vast majority of the men of the town who served and fell being English, no other language was necessary to commemorate their part in the Great War' infuriated many of those present and led to statistics on the numbers of Welsh speakers in relation to English speakers in Newport being flung

[30] *South Wales Argus*, 11 August 1923.
[31] *South Wales Argus*, 13 August 1923.

around the council chamber. Major I. C. Vincent, who had been against the Welsh inscription from the start, declared that as only three persons out of every thousand in Newport could read Welsh, they might just as well have the inscription in Yiddish. Alderman Phillips protested that the original war memorial committee had not been given the slightest indication that such an inscription was desired by any section, although this is not borne out by the minutes of the committee which had received just such a request in May 1923.[32] The point was also made that an argument probably would not have taken place if they were discussing a Latin inscription, which still fewer people could read. The beleaguered Alderman Phillips did receive support from the architects of the memorial who felt that any further inscription would detract from the spirit of the memorial. This was to no avail and the resolution was heavily defeated.[33] The cenotaph received its Welsh-language inscription, although the letters are considerably smaller than those in English and as a whole the Welsh inscription appears indistinct. The small numbers of Welsh speakers in Newport and the arguments put forward both by the group promoting the inscription and in the columns of the local press suggest that it was a movement motivated by idealized romantic sentiments of Welsh involvement in the war rather than by a burning desire for linguistic equality. It was the intervention of a small, articulate, educated group that had prompted the movement and, without this intervention, it is a matter of conjecture whether the issue would have been raised at all, especially as language does not seem to have been a problem in other Great War memorials in Newport.[34] This is confirmed by the fact that the war memorial committee had not considered a dual inscription in its original deliberations and had dismissed an appeal from a member of the public. It is also clear that the original objections to the Welsh inscription, before it became a statistical debate over the numbers of Welsh speakers

[32] See n. 25.
[33] Newport Town Council, minutes of Council Meeting, 14 August 1923; *South Wales Argus*, 14 August 1923, and *Western Mail*, 15 August 1923.
[34] E.g. see 'Some Newport war memorials', *The Newport Christmas Annual* (Newport, 1925). This lists twenty-one war memorials, apart from the cenotaph in Clarence Place, within the county borough of Newport. Welsh and English inscriptions exist on memorials in churches, chapels and places of work and recreation including the post office, Newport Athletic Club and John Lysaght Limited.

in the area, did not emanate from cultural or political considerations but from the opinion held by the British Legion that it was inappropriate to add a further inscription once the memorial had been dedicated. The point should also be made that the war memorial committee had received only one letter requesting a Welsh-language inscription and the subsequent cries of protest had been strangely silent in the months leading up to the unveiling. Language had simply not been an issue in commemoration discussions at Newport.

The small village of Llanbadarn Fawr in mid-Wales, with a much higher proportion of Welsh speakers, appears a more likely location for a dispute over the use of the language. The parishes of Vaynor Ucha, Issa'n dre and Ucha'n dre combined to commemorate their fallen in a single memorial at Llanbadarn Fawr, and by December 1920 the memorial was ready for unveiling.[35] The fund-raising process and discussion over the location of the memorial had passed off smoothly until it was noted that the inscription on the memorial was to be in English and Latin. An open meeting was held in the village on 8 December and the results conveyed to the secretary of the war memorial committee:

> At a Public Meeting (which included Exservice men) . . . I was instructed to inform your Committee that it is the unanimous wish of the public that an inscription in Welsh should be inserted by some means or other on the Memorial Cross before it is unveiled, and until this has been complied with the Exservicemen of Llanbadarn Fawr do not feel inclined to discuss any arrangements with regard to their attendance at the Unveiling Ceremony.[36]

The letter was acknowledged, but as it became clear that the committee intended to take no action, a further meeting was held just a few days before the unveiling ceremony, resulting in a very public rebuke to the officers of the war memorial committee.[37]

---

[35] See E. G. Bowen, *A History of Llanbadarn Fawr* (Llandysul, 1979), pp. 183–5.

[36] Letter from A. Griffiths to R. J. Greer, Secretary of Llanbadarn Fawr War Memorial Committee, 9 December 1920. Llanbadarn Fawr Parish War Memorial Papers.

[37] Letter from Evan Jones to R. J. Greer, 7 January 1921. 'At a Public Meeting held 5th I was instructed to inform your committee that that meeting strongly disapproved of the way in which your committee . . . had delayed the reply to resolution passed at the meeting held on the 8th Dec. last, the meeting felt that had this resolution received proper consideration all differences would have been removed long ago.' Ibid.

The memorial was unveiled on 8 January 1921 by Lieutenant Colonel Lewis Pugh Evans, VC, but, as the *Cambrian News* reported, the ex-servicemen of the parish made their displeasure known:

> In connection with the memorial a meeting of ex-servicemen, held the previous week, expressed strong views because the inscription upon the memorial was in Latin and English with not a word of Welsh, and because a protest to this effect had not been dealt with in the way they wished, they decided to take no part in the ceremony, and although a large number was present they held aloof. During the proceedings no untoward incident occurred, but afterwards opinions were very freely expressed and some heated remarks were passed between some of the parties.[38]

By February 1921 the committee had agreed funds to allow the addition of another plinth to the memorial cross and to place an inscription in the Welsh language on the front panel. In December 1921 the secretary received a letter from G. T. Bassett, architect and surveyor, which sums up the controversy engendered by the inscription: 'I suppose there is nothing to prevent my writing for a price for the work in connection with the Memorial Cross, but if it becomes known I fear there would be much unpleasantness and you have had a great deal already.'[39]

The inhabitants of Llanbadarn Fawr were successful in their campaign to gain a Welsh inscription, and the combination of English, Latin and Welsh can also be found on memorials as far apart as Prestatyn and Ystrad Mynach. A month after the unveiling of the Swansea war memorial, which has a Latin inscription, a letter appeared in the local paper appealing for the addition of a Welsh inscription. There had not been a dispute over the inscription before the unveiling ceremony and this letter did not elicit any public or press support. No action was taken and the memorial retains its English and Latin inscriptions.[40] The most prominent example can be found in Cardiff on the Welsh

---

[38] *Cambrian News*, 14 January 1921. See also *Welsh Gazette*, 13 January 1921.

[39] Letter from G. T. Bassett to R. Greer, 8 December 1921. Llanbadarn Fawr Parish War Memorial Papers. The Welsh inscription added to the Llanbadarn Fawr memorial was suggested by John Ballinger, a committee member who was also at that time librarian at the National Library of Wales in Aberystwyth. The name of his son, Lieutenant Henry John Ballinger, is inscribed on the memorial.

[40] *South Wales Daily Post*, 25 August 1923.

National War Memorial, where the major inscriptions are in Welsh and English. Early photographs of the model of the memorial reveal that, in the planning stages, the English inscription is on the outside and the Welsh inside although this was reversed on the completed memorial.[41] The English and Welsh inscriptions on this occasion do not mirror each other. The English verse was composed by Sir Henry Newbolt: 'Remember here in peace those who in tumult of War by sea, on land, in air, for us and for our victory endured unto death.' The Welsh inscription read as 'I Feibion Cymru a roddes eu Bywyd dros eu Gwlad yn Rhyfel MCMXIV–MCMXVIII' ('To the sons of Wales who gave their lives for their country in the war 1914–1918'). Quotations from Welsh literature were chosen as inscriptions over the three entrances to the interior spaces of the memorial.

The practice in choosing an inscription in smaller communities was generally the same throughout Wales; the local war memorial committee chose a form of words and usually this would be put to a public meeting for approval. It appears that a similar pattern was followed in Scotland, although the language used was overwhelmingly English, with the sentiments following those found on memorials in other areas of Britain. The exceptions are the West Highlands and the Hebridean Islands, where memorials have either a whole or a partly Gaelic inscription and these usually mirror the English inscription.[42] In general, Welsh-language inscriptions largely reflect those that can be found on war memorials throughout Britain. For example, 'Eu henwau byth a gofir' ('Their names will be remembered forever') or a variation on the same theme, 'Eu henw a bery byth' ('Their names will last forever'), or 'Yn Anghof Ni Chânt Fod' or 'Mewn Anghof Ni Chânt Fod' ('They will not be forgotten'). The two exceptions are 'Gwell angau na chywilydd' ('Better death than dishonour'), as previously noted, and the less common 'Dros ryddid collasant eu gwa'd' ('For freedom they gave their blood'), a line from the Welsh national anthem, which can be found on

---

[41] The photographs are held in the library of the National Museum & Gallery, Cardiff.
[42] A study of Scottish Great War memorials dismisses such inscriptions: 'One suspects that the Celtic fringe had as much a dearth of originality of ideas and expressions as the rest of the nation but merely had the benefit of a different language in which to say it.' Gilbert T. Bell, 'Monuments to the fallen: Scottish war memorials of the Great War' (unpublished Ph.D. thesis, University of Strathclyde, 1993), pp. 318–19.

memorials in Caerswŝ, Clocaenog, Port Dinorwic and Ruthin. The single words 'Teyrnged' ('Tribute'), 'Aberth' ('Sacrifice') and 'Rhyddid' ('Freedom') also appear regularly. Lines from Welsh poetry were a popular choice for inscriptions and particular lines by Hedd Wyn also appear to have been favourites for use on memorials.[43] There is no clear geographical demarcation area for Welsh-only or English-only inscriptions and this was no doubt due to the spontaneous nature of commemoration and the plethora of memorials often within the same community. Such memorials may have had very different inscriptions depending on the wishes of those involved, and it appears that the use of both Welsh and English was the popular choice.[44] Bilingual memorial inscriptions are by far the most common in Wales but even these could occasionally give rise to problems. The cenotaph unveiled in Barry in November 1930 bore the following inscription which would appear to demonstrate complete equality of languages: 'In Proud Memory of the Men of Barry who Fell in the Great War, 1914–1918: Er Cof Annwyl am Feibion y Barri a Syrthiodd yn y Rhyfel, 1914–1918; For Freedom, Dros Ryddid.' The following month, however, the *Barry and District News* published a letter from an ex-serviceman criticizing the inscription:

> As a Welsh Legionaire I am not satisfied with it. For example, the English version 'In Proud Memory' – that is as it should be, but in Welsh it is Er Cof Annwyl ('In Dear Memory'). Why the 'Dear Memory' in comparison with the 'In Proud Memory'. The one sounds so much more glorifying

---

[43] E.g.: 'Ei aberth nid a heibio – ei wyneb, / Annwyl nid a'n ango, / Er i'r Almaen ystaenio, / Ei dwrn dur yn ei waed o.' (His sacrifice will not be forgotten, His countenance so dear will ever be remembered Tho' Germany's Iron Fist by his blood is stained.) This verse was composed by Hedd Wyn in memory of a friend who had been killed earlier in the war and appears on a plaque in front of Hedd Wyn's statue in Trawsfynydd. The verse was also printed in the *Welsh Outlook* on the news of Hedd Wyn's death in battle. *Welsh Outlook*, IV (October 1917), p. 331.

[44] Words taken from the 'Next of Kin Memorial Scroll' appear on a number of war memorials. For example, the Pembrokeshire County War Memorial in Haverfordwest reads: 'In remembrance of the men of the county of Pembroke who at the call of King and Country, left all that was dear to them, endured hardness, faced danger and finally passed out of the sight of men by the path of duty and self-sacrifice giving up their own lives that others might live in freedom. Let those who come after see to it that their names be not forgotten.' See Malcolm Brown, *The Imperial War Museum Book of The First World War* (London, 1991), p. 281. See also Philip Dutton, ' "The dead man's penny": a history of the next of kin memorial plaque', *Imperial War Museum Review*, III (1988), pp. 60–8.

than the other. Surely a better Welsh word could have been put in than 'annwyl'.[45]

The inscription was unchanged and this appears to have been the only public voice of dissent raised against it.

This duality extends to the place of the Welsh language in the ceremonies to unveil war memorials. Ceremonies were usually conducted in English with prayers and hymns offered in both languages. The published programmes for unveiling ceremonies reveal the same tendency to use English and Welsh, and this appears to have been common practice in north and south Wales. Extant programmes using both Welsh and English were printed for the unveiling ceremonies at Caernarfon, Denbigh, Gwyddelwern, Kidwelly, Llanbadarn Fawr, Llanwrda, Mountain Ash, Nevin, Penmaenmawr, Pwllheli and Senghennydd. It is much more unusual to come across an unveiling programme printed entirely in either Welsh or English.[46] The controversies over the use of the language during the war and in the official commemoration process emanated from outside Wales, yet at a local level the use of the Welsh language was not a problem. This is because the language itself was not a controversial issue in Wales in the post-war years. English was the language of administration at that time, as is confirmed by the minute books for 138 local authorities throughout Wales in mid-1919; all but three were written in English.[47] Similarly, extant proceedings of war memorial committees are usually in English. At a meeting of the Lampeter War Memorial Committee in February 1919 the secretary specifically noted in the minutes that two speakers addressed the meeting in Welsh.[48]

[45] *Barry and District News*, 19 December 1930.

[46] Examples of English programmes can be found at Abertillery, Briton Ferry, Brynmawr, Connah's Quay and Shotton, Llandrindod Wells, Overton and Tredegar. Purely Welsh-language programmes seem to have been less common. Bethesda did produce a Welsh-language programme, although even this had one line of English on the front page ('This Memorial was designed by Mr R. J. Hughes, A.R.I.B.A., Llanfairfechan, and erected by Mr Richard Williams, Contractor, Llanfairfechan, and is of Anglesey Limestone').

[47] By 1911 92 per cent of the population could speak English and 84 per cent of the Welsh-speaking Welsh aged between fifteen and sixty-five were bilingual: 'Henceforth, over extensive areas of Welsh-speaking Wales, those with no knowledge of Welsh were more numerous than those with no knowledge of English, a justification for giving priority to English in local activities.' John Davies, *A History of Wales* (London, 1994), p. 497.

[48] Minutes of Lampeter War Memorial Committee, 25 February 1919.

It has been suggested that 'the most obvious impact of the First World War upon the Welsh language was the carnage it caused among young, Welsh-speaking Welshmen. There was a lost generation of Welsh-speakers, perhaps twenty thousand in all', but it is unclear how these figures can be substantiated, particularly as the question as to whether a recruit could speak Welsh was not asked on attestation forms.[49] Similar problems are encountered in a recent study of the experiences of the Welsh soldier in the British Army in the Great War; a sample was constructed by choosing service files of Welsh recruits on the basis of 'typically Welsh surnames', and with confirmation of nationality provided by place of birth or county of residence, and those without 'typically Welsh surnames' excluded from the study. Although the problems with sources are acknowledged, the author does suggest that

> the sample can be used effectively when considering the voluntary enlist-
> ment of Welsh speakers. Although the records themselves do not record
> whether a man was Welsh-speaking or not, the likelihood of this can be
> determined by noting his county of origin and the percentage of the
> population of that county that spoke Welsh . . . It would seem that men in
> predominantly Welsh speaking counties were no less likely to enlist than in
> counties where the English language predominated.[50]

Attempting to analyse by statistics the element of 'Welshness' in the British Army appears problematic, if not impossible. An estimated 280,000 men from the principality volunteered or were conscripted into the British Army, yet they cannot automatically be labelled as 'Welsh', whether Welsh-speaking or not. This is particularly true in the industrialized areas of south Wales which in the late nineteenth century had acted as a magnet to thousands of young men not only from north and west Wales but also from other parts of the British Isles, particularly south-west England. The difficulties of commemorating these men became apparent to the local war memorial committee at Bargoed. It

---

[49] Janet Davies, *The Welsh Language* (Cardiff, 1993), p. 58. I am grateful to Clive Hughes and Peter Simkins for advice on this point.

[50] Gervase Phillips, 'The Welsh soldier in the First World War' (unpublished M.Phil. thesis, University of Wales, 1991). The main arguments are contained in his article, 'Dai Bach Y Soldiwr: Welsh soldiers in the British Army 1914–1918', *Llafur*, VI, No. 2 (1993), pp. 94–105.

decided on a 'comprehensive inscription only' and opted against putting individual names on the memorial as 'a number of young men who made the supreme sacrifice were only in lodgings in the district'.[51] Even the statistic of 35,000 Welsh lives lost must be treated with caution, as this does not mean that all the casualties were Welsh; the Welsh Roll of Honour lists 'men and women of Welsh birth and parentage and of all the men belonging to the regiments of Wales who gave their lives in the war'.[52] Welsh regiments, however, attracted many recruits from outside the principality. In 1915 Emlyn Davies was posted to the 17th Battalion, Royal Welch Fusiliers, stationed at Llandudno, and recalled that the battalion contained a number of 'Lancashire lads' who chose to enlist as 'the North Wales resorts formed their favourite holiday spots' and they were also attracted by the prospect of 'a few months training by the sea'.[53] Men from Wales served in British and colonial regiments as the soaring casualties necessitated men being sent to wherever there was the greatest need for manpower and this was not based on nationality. For example, in April 1917 Vivian de Sola Pinto was posted to the 19th Battalion, Royal Welch Fusiliers, and found that his platoon 'consisted mainly of Lancashire and Staffordshire men with three Londoners and only one Welshman', whilst the 7th Royal Berkshires 'included a platoon of Welsh miners as well as a large number of men from the Midlands'.[54] A glance at the lists of names on most war memorials in Wales confirms that the conflict itself and the people commemorating local losses paid no heed to socio-linguistic considerations. It was a natural reaction to include both Welsh- and English-language inscriptions on Great War memorials. As individuals and communities struggled to come to terms with their losses, the priority was to ensure that those who had lost their lives were remembered appropriately and the choice of inscription was just one of many decisions and compromises that had to be made.

[51] *Merthyr Express*, 21 April 1923. This uncertainty was shared by other areas in Britain. The programme for the unveiling ceremony at Larne states that the memorial was to the '147 men – sailors and soldiers – who were natives, lived in, or left from Larne Urban District, and who fell in the Great War, 1914–1918.' Order of Proceedings at the Unveiling of the Larne War Memorial, March 1922. IWM War Memorial Ephemera Collection.

[52] *Western Mail*, 12 June 1928.

[53] Emlyn Davies, *Taffy Went to War* (Knutsford, 1976), p.3.

[54] V. de Sola Pinto, *The City that Shone*, p.192; Peter Simkins, *Kitchener's Army: The Raising of the New Armies, 1914–16* (Manchester, 1988), p. 70.

VIII

WELSH WAR MEMORIALS:
CELTIC PRIDE OR IMPERIAL PROPAGANDA?

In 1919 an account of Welsh participation in the Great War was published, and the preface by Sir E. Vincent Evans, high sheriff of Merioneth, set the tone for the rest of the book:

> There must be many Welshmen and others who would like to know what Wales did to help in the colossal struggle now so triumphantly concluded. How our sister-nations in the United Kingdom wrought and suffered, their sons have not been slow to tell; but Wales, never eager to advertise herself, has up to now been silent as to the part she played.[1]

A chapter in the book includes a section on 'Recruiting in Wales' and comments on the speech made in the House of Commons in January 1918 by Sir Auckland Geddes, minister of national service, in which he attempted to sum up the recruiting within the United Kingdom in terms of manpower contribution from the four nations. At 280,000 men, Wales was deemed to have contributed 3.7 per cent towards the overall total from the 'British nations'.[2] However, this was not accepted as a fair method of calculation by the authors, who suggested that 'If comparisons are to be instituted between the manpower contribution of the four nations it would perhaps have been fairer to estimate the percentage on a population basis.' By using this method of calculation, it appears that at 13.82 per cent Wales's record is easily ahead that of England, Scotland and Ireland. Having put the record straight, the authors conclude that 'These

[1] The preface concluded: 'One may be forgiven a little national pride when he remembers that the Welsh archers were the real victors of Cressy and Agincourt.' Ivor Nicholson and Trevor Lloyd-Williams (eds.), *Wales: Its Part in the War* (London, 1919), p. xi.

[2] 'The effort which the British nations have made under the one item of provision of men for the Armed Forces of the Crown amounts to not less than seven and a half million men. Of these 4,530,000, or 60.4 per cent have been contributed by England, 620,000, or 8.3 per cent by Scotland, 280,000, or 3.7 per cent by Wales,170,000, or 2.3 per cent by Ireland, and 900,000, or 12 per cent have been contributed by the Dominions and Colonies.' 4 January 1918. *Hansard* 101 HC Deb. 5s.

figures speak for themselves and show how eagerly the men of Wales came forward to do battle for the cause of freedom and liberty.'[3] These extracts epitomize the difficulties encountered when looking at the question of national identity in Wales in the post-war years. Expressions of pride in the contribution to the empire's cause are matched by the desire to maintain and articulate an independent Welsh spirit and identity. This point, however, illustrates a dichotomy in modern Welsh history: the need, or perhaps the desire, to assert a distinctively Welsh voice or identity while recognizing that this identity was undoubtedly nurtured, shaped and influenced by the British state. This point was made by Professor Gwyn Williams, who has written of the 'massive growth of an industrial Wales of British-Imperial character' and how this has shaped and influenced Wales.[4] He cited two cultural symbols of simultaneously Welsh-populist and British-imperial identity, namely, David Lloyd George and Welsh rugby; but it appears that the commemoration of the Great War in Wales could also be listed as an example of the symbiotic relationship that shaped the modern Welsh nation.[5]

Even before the war was over, the strong links with the empire were utilized as a useful component in the struggle to raise funds for war memorials. In April 1917 the organizing committee of the North Wales Heroes' Memorial managed to combine images of empire with a degree of xenophobia in early appeals for new science buildings at the University College of North Wales, Bangor:

> If the Empire is to prove worthy of the heroic sacrifices made by the flower of its youth in this war, and to continue to play a leading part in the world, and in the advancement of civilisation, the Mother-country must take her full share in the after-war development of Imperial resources. Her great contribution to this task should be a fresh army of vigorous young men and

---

[3] Nicholson and Lloyd-Williams, *Wales*, pp. 25–6.
[4] Gwyn A. Williams, *The Welsh in their History* (London, 1982), p. 182.
[5] 'There was David Lloyd George, leaping like a Magic Goat from the aggressive middle class of north Wales now on the offensive against Anglican landlords and creating a Welsh nation in its own image, into Downing Street and to the pinnacle of British imperialism at its moment of peril. And there was and is, Welsh rugby which, after an initial struggle, became the Welsh "national game" . . . and where Wales, safely lodged as a major directive element within imperial Britain, could express its now self-confident identity in a continuous eisteddfod of Grand Slams and a continuous rugby-dinner chorus of God Bless the Prince of Wales.' Ibid., p. 185. For further reading on 'Imperial Wales', see Gwyn A. Williams, *When Was Wales?* (London, 1991), especially pp. 220–51.

women, thoroughly trained in science and business methods . . . They
would replace the Germans and other foreigners who have hitherto filled
so many of these posts both at home and in the rest of the Empire.[6]

In similar vein, an editorial appeared in the *Penarth News* in May
1922 chiding local residents for their 'apparent apathy' over the
lack of a war memorial, and the empire was enlisted as part of
the public reminder of the debt to be paid:

It is to be hoped, too, that the higher object will not be lost sight of. After
all, the people were proud of the fact that our boys went gladly to the
assistance of the Empire in the hour of need . . . Are we the same Britons
who declared that we should never be German slaves? Or, HAVE WE
FORGOTTEN?[7]

As war memorials appeared throughout Wales, certain
similarities emerged, whether the memorial was situated in city,
town or village, church or chapel, in civic, secular, urban or rural
location. Row upon row of names appear on most war memorials;
some give rank and regiment, others include age, date and place of
death, and on occasion, usually in small rural communities, the
home address is also inscribed. Minor details may vary but there is
little doubt that the predominant language of remembrance,
whether Welsh or English, is that of loyalty: loyalty to the
monarch, to Britain and to the empire. In the small village of
Llanbradach 800 men enlisted and the inscription on the
memorial pays tribute to the 'Immortal Memory of the 122 gallant
men of Llanbradach who laid down their lives for the Empire in
the Great War'. At Llangollen the inscription reads 'Live Thou for
Britain, We for Britain Died', and virtually the same inscription,
'Live ye for Britain as we for Britain died', can be found on the
memorial at Kenfig Hill.[8] The inscription on the memorial at
Connah's Quay in north-east Wales includes the words, 'What
stands if freedom fall, Who Dies if England Live', whilst a panel on
the Pembroke memorial in west Wales includes the verse,

---

[6] Appeal dated 10 April 1917. UCNW Heroes Memorial File.

[7] *Penarth News*, 11 May 1922 (capitals in text).

[8] This is included on the programme printed for the unveiling of the Kenfig Hill
memorial. The cover of the programme for the unveiling of the war memorial in Overton
carries the words, 'Live thou for England: we for England died'.

Forget us not, O land, for which we fell.
May it go well with England, still go well.
Keep her bright banners without spot or stain.
Lest we should dream that we had died in vain.[9]

The overwhelming majority of inscriptions on Great War memorials in Wales include references to God, King and Country, and the sentiments expressed were often reflected and reiterated in speeches made at the unveiling ceremonies. The speeches regularly articulated expressions of loyalty to the empire and this was a common theme that appeared in ceremonies throughout Britain. In Swansea, Admiral Sir Doveton Sturdee prefaced his speech at the unveiling ceremony by stating that 'they were there to recognize the great services rendered by the men of Swansea to the Empire', and similar sentiments were expressed by General Sir Francis Lloyd as he unveiled the Pembroke memorial in 1924. He told the assembled crowd that

It was the unselfishness of the British soldier led by the dauntless British officer that won the war. When the bugle call of war was sounded, it was answered by the men of the Empire and of the Great Dominions, who all came to the help of the Motherland. They went and faced death and their only idea was to do everything possible for the Motherland.[10]

Four months later, at the unveiling of the Tonyrefail war memorial, Colonel H. R. Homfray suggested that the 'memorial depicted in glowing terms actions of courage, of endurance, of every energy that went to make a Britisher what he was and what he would continue to be', whilst the archdeacon of Cardigan drew on a military metaphor in his address at the unveiling of the memorial at Llanbadarn Fawr in January 1921: 'The battle before them at present was the battle to obtain peace. There was also the work of uplifting and reconstructing and making the

[9] The words on the Connah's Quay memorial are from Rudyard Kipling's poem, 'For All We Have and Are'. I am grateful to Graham Farthing for information on the Pembroke memorial.
[10] *South Wales Daily Post*, 23 July 1923, and *Pembroke County Guardian*, 4 July 1924. After unveiling the Llandrindod Wells memorial in July 1922, 'Lord Ormathwaite said that eight summers ago the honour of England and the safety of Europe were at stake, and Britain without hesitation flung herself into the fearful struggle. Men responded to the call from every rank and place. The men of Radnorshire had no unit of their own to go to, but they ranged themselves along with the soldiers of the King.' *South Wales News*, 3 July 1922.

British Empire the best, holiest, and most flourishing in the world.'[11] Field Marshal Allenby unveiled the Abertillery memorial in December 1926 and commented:

> Such memorials were to be found wherever the Imperial flag was flying; they were erected not in a spirit of boastfulness but of humble gratitude and in commemoration of those who died for their Empire, their country, and their countrymen. The Empire for which those lads paid the price was not a selfish organisation; it was unselfish, altruistic; it existed for others, but it jealously watched the Imperial rights and was always ready to uphold them, even to death, through the sons of the Empire.[12]

Unveiling the Bridgend war memorial in November 1921, Colonel J. I. Nicholl suggested that those gathered at the ceremony did so 'in common with every town and village in the Empire' and it seems that sentiments of belonging to the empire were shared by certain Welsh emigrants to Australia.[13] In 1923, in response to an appeal by the local war memorial committee in Tamworth, New South Wales, the lord mayor of Cardiff had sent 'a fine Red Dragon flag' to be unfurled as a memento from the Welsh people at the unveiling ceremony 'in that distant part of the British Empire'. The committee had also asked for messages of greetings from Wales, and Mr Lewis Davies of Merthyr Vale, 'the well-known contributor to the *Western Mail*, sent some specially composed verses and he has now received the following acknowledgment':

> Hearty greetings from Tamworth, New South Wales to the Welsh National Poet, Lewis Davies. Your wonderfully kind letter and poem came to hand, and the committee desire to express their sincere appreciation of your goodness and thoughtfulness in sending a poem for our ceremony. It has already been read to the public school children, and will be published with all the other patriotic messages. It is so encouraging for us to know that you so gladly respond to us away out here. We are not forgotten by our fellow-Britons at home. I am so sorry I can't call on you to express our sense of your patriotic feelings, so charmingly expressed in your poem. We send our hearty greetings, and desire again and again to earnestly thank you.
>   Your faithful fellow-Briton, T. G. Adamson, Honorary Secretary.[14]

[11] *Rhondda Leader*, 21 November 1924; *Cambrian News*, 14 January 1921.
[12] *Western Mail*, 2 December 1926.
[13] *Glamorgan Gazette*, 18 November 1921.
[14] *Western Mail*, 1 January 1924.

It may seem that British national unity reached its zenith in its response to the war, but Keith Robbins has also suggested that 'It is more difficult, in national terms, to decide what Englishmen, Scotsmen, and Welshmen thought they were fighting for. Was it "England", "Scotland", or "Wales", or was it "Britain", or even, just conceivably, "the United Kingdom"?'[15] A poignant example exists in the pages of the *Abergavenny Chronicle*, which regularly published letters from local men serving in the war. On 14 May 1915 a letter was published from Private H. Roach of the 3rd Monmouthshire Regiment, describing his first period of duty in the trenches in March 1915: 'Their artillery was deadly . . . I thought every minute my number was up . . . It was an interesting day, because you mustn't forget it was our baptismal day, and the dear old boys of Aber. behaved like Britons.'[16] It is clear that the project to raise a Welsh Army Corps, even if not successfully completed, was at the time of its inauguration clearly viewed as the Welsh contribution to the imperial effort:

> No project was ever launched in more promising circumstances. Realising the righteousness of the cause for which the British Empire was fighting, the delegates at the Conference expressed their readiness to work wholeheartedly in raising this great Cymric Army to supplement the large contribution which Wales had already made to the British Forces since mobilisation began.[17]

But in the towns and villages of the principality it has been suggested that: 'People joined up as Welshmen, or as members of local communities rather than as British citizens . . . The combined influence of Wales and the locality was crucial; the British Empire was remote and intangible and did not have this immediate appeal.'[18] 'Local communities' may well have acted

[15] Keith Robbins, *Nineteenth Century Britain: Integration and Diversity* (Oxford, 1995), p. 180.
[16] *Abergavenny Chronicle*, 14 May 1915. Private Roach was wounded in action on 5 May 1915 and died the following day. The details of his death are taken from Janet Dixon and John Dixon, *With Rifle and Pick* (Cardiff, 1991), p. 172.
[17] *Welsh Army Corps, Report of the Executive Committee, 1914–1919* (Newport, 1989; originally published Cardiff, 1921), p. 6–7. See also *Western Mail*, 30 September 1914, for full coverage of the conference.
[18] Neil Evans, 'Gogs, Cardis and Hwntws: regions, nation and state in Wales, 1840–1940', in Neil Evans (ed.), *National Identity in the British Isles*, (Coleg Harlech, 1989), p. 68.

as the foundation of the identities which assisted mobilization but whatever came after that is less certain. Whereas for some 'the British Empire was remote and intangible', for others perhaps it was any meaningful notion of 'Wales' that was lacking in relevance. It is clear that the idea of empire would have been instilled in the schoolroom and purveyed through a variety of images such as advertising and popular literature so that it became possible to believe in the empire as a noble cause to defend and, often, to die for.[19] It was also crucial for those left behind to believe that the cause for which their loved ones had died was worthy and that the sacrifices had not been in vain. At the laying of the foundation stone for the Cricieth Memorial Hall in June 1922, Lloyd George, as prime minister, spoke of the moral sacrifice made by those who had died: 'They fought for one of the attributes, the everlasting attributes, of the divine justice. That is what makes the action of millions of young men in Britain one of the most glorious episodes in the history of this glorious country.' Two years later, Lloyd George returned to open the memorial hall, although no longer prime minister, and the tone and content of his address reflected his earlier speech. The *Western Mail* headed its report of the occasion with 'The Sacrifices of Great Britain', as Lloyd George spoke again of Britain's young men: 'Supposing Britain had not put millions of her best in the field, what terms do you think they would have been discussing now, not in London, but in Berlin?'[20] The sentiments of loyalty to King and Country on many war memorials, both in the inscriptions and expressed in speeches at unveiling ceremonies, provided a panacea for the bereaved and also perhaps acted as a reassurance for those who had fought and survived. The ex-servicemen of mid-Rhondda were also ready to take up arms again on behalf of the empire. In June 1922 Sir Henry Wilson was murdered by two IRA men as he returned home from unveiling a memorial at Liverpool Street Station to

---

[19] See John M. MacKenzie, *Propaganda and Empire: The Manipulation of British Public Opinion, 1880–1960* (Manchester, 1984), pp. 2–3. Alvin Jackson has suggested that positive images of the British Empire helped consolidate patriotism amongst Irish Protestants in the nineteenth and early twentieth centuries. Alvin Jackson, 'Irish Unionist imagery, 1850–1920', in Eve Patten (ed.), *Returning to Ourselves* (vol. 2 of papers from the John Hewitt International Summer School, Belfast, 1995), pp. 344–59.
[20] *Western Mail*, 5 June 1922 and 21 July 1924. See also *Carnarvon and Denbigh Herald*, 25 July 1924.

employees of the Great Eastern Railway Company killed in the war. Late in June the *Rhondda Leader* reported a meeting of ex-servicemen in Tonypandy, who had sent a message to the King:

> Sire, it has been unanimously decided by the Mid Rhondda members of the British Legion that we tender your Majesty our deepest sympathy in the loss sustained by yourself, the Empire, and the Army in the dastardly assassination of Field Marshal Sir Henry Wilson. We further ask your Majesty to accept our loyal assurance of our readiness to volunteer at any time in the service of your Majesty and the Empire.[21]

On occasion, the speeches referred to sacrifices made specifically for England rather than Britain or empire. Even before the war was over, parishioners of St Saviour's church in Roath, Cardiff, unveiled a memorial in memory of the forty-four men attached to the parish who had lost their lives in the war or, as Bishop Crossley put it, 'They had laid down their lives for England and God'.[22] In Cosheston, General Sir Ivor Philipps spoke of the qualities of the British armed forces: 'The British soldier and sailor, in hundreds and thousands, officers, non-commissioned officers and men, willingly gave their lives that England might live', whilst a local press account of the unveiling of the Kidwelly memorial reported that the local community were 'especially proud of the lads of Kidwelly, they had the spirit which made England great'.[23] In November 1921, Edward Loveluck, chairman of Bridgend Urban District Council and also chairman of the war memorial committee, addressed the crowds gathered for the unveiling of the local war memorial:

> Throughout this afternoon's ceremony many thoughts have crowded through my mind, and many memories have been stirred. Name after name on the roll of honour has brought back to me recollections of men, dear friends of mine, whom I have known as schoolboys or comrades in this dear old town of ours. Today they sleep in peace in some corner of a foreign field that is for ever England.[24]

[21] *Rhondda Leader*, 30 June 1922.
[22] *South Wales Daily News*, 9 July 1918.
[23] *Pembroke County Guardian*, 14 January 1921; *Carmarthen Journal*, 1 August 1924.
[24] *Glamorgan Gazette*, 18 November 1921.

The utilization of England, Britain and the empire may sound a discordant note to those listening for evidence of the birth, or re-birth, of Welsh nationhood in the wake of the Great War.[25] Yet to regard such evidence as imperial propaganda would be to misunderstand the historical perspective and underestimate the symbiotic relationship that existed between Wales and the British state. Gwyn A. Williams succeeded in getting to the heart of this complex and emotive issue:

> Our survival has been a kind of miracle. What is immediately clear from even a cursory survey of our broken-backed history, is that the tiny Welsh people, for we were always very thin on the ground, have survived by being British. Welsh identity has constantly renewed itself by anchoring itself in variant forms of Britishness.[26]

Of course, attempts to define 'Britishness' are no easier than those to define Welshness and it remains true that to many commentators 'Britain' was interpreted as 'England', but in the years following the Great War it is clear that there was no contradiction in the use and interchangeability of such terms.[27] Few commentators, however, would be quite as effusive in their comments as Lord Glanusk at a ceremony in Crickhowell in September 1919 to mark the return of local demobilized men:

> It made one proud to be an Englishman, a happy-go-lucky Englishman, the Englishman who is never prepared for emergency but generally comes out top in the end, the Englishman who puts politics before necessaries but who dropped it all to combine against a common foe, the Englishman who made no display of patriotism, or very little of it, until it was wanted and . who then was a solid lump of it . . . England would survive.[28]

---

[25] At the unveiling ceremony of the 'National' War Memorial in 1928, the *Western Mail* was particularly effusive on the subject of nationhood. See *Western Mail*, 13 June 1928.

[26] Gwyn A. Williams, *When Was Wales?*, p.195.

[27] 'Britain was neither a clear identity nor an exclusive loyalty . . . The British polity, of which England was the head and core, refrained from major internal enterprises, did not press definitions of identity. Yet the consciousness of Britain was predominantly English . . . In the matter of Britain the consciousness of England dominated even among the Welsh and the Scots. Yet this dominance was neither designed nor imposed. It was just that to historians England was overwhelmingly there.' J. H. Grainger, *Patriotisms: Britain, 1900–1939* (London, 1986), pp. 49–53.

Lloyd George, that most ambivalent of Welshmen, moved between his two 'identities' with consummate ease. At the eisteddfod held in Bangor in August 1915, the minister of munitions or, as he described himself, 'a bit of a Welshman in an office in London', spoke of his pride in Wales's contribution to the war effort:

> I am proud to know Wales has flung its whole strength into the struggle for humanity . . . We have a greater army from Wales alone than Wellington commanded at Waterloo . . . Our Welsh martial spirit was not dead. It was not even slumbering. It was simply hiding in its caves amongst the hills until the call came from above.[29]

By the time Lloyd George unveiled the Pwllheli war memorial in June 1924, his thoughts on the Welsh military tradition had softened somewhat. He spoke of the need to have fought the war and then turned to the contribution from Wales:

> We as a whole are a pacific nation. It had been so for centuries. We had turned our swords into ploughshares for generations. We did not teach war to our sons, and yet, when the call came, there was a larger proportion of volunteers from Wales than from any other country inside the whole of the British Empire.[30]

Sentiments of loyalty to empire expressed in the speeches made at unveiling ceremonies were accompanied by a plethora of imperial iconography in the form of flags and anthems, and occasionally by the sculpture of the memorial itself. By 1914, 'Hen Wlad Fy Nhadau' ('The Land of My Fathers') was widely accepted as the Welsh national anthem, but Wales still had no representation in the Union flag.[31] The outbreak of war and the need for a distinctive badge for the recruits of the fledgling Welsh Army Corps provided a convenient stimulus, as the Welsh

---

[28] *Abergavenny Chronicle*, 12 September 1919.

[29] *Western Mail*, 6 August 1915.

[30] *Carnarvon and Denbigh Herald*, 13 June 1924; *Western Mail*, 13 June 1924. Lloyd George had used an alternative image of 'ploughshares' in the Bangor speech in August 1915: 'The fields of Europe are being rent by the ploughshares of war. The verdure of the old civilisation is vanishing in the desolating upheaval of the conflict. Let us see to it that wheat and not tares are sown in the bleeding soil, and in due season we shall reap if we faint not.' *Western Mail*, 6 August 1915.

[31] Robbins, *Nineteenth Century Britain*, p. 170.

Dragon increasingly became recognized as the official symbol of Wales both on and off the battlefield.[32] Despite its obvious connotations of 'Welshness', the Welsh flag was seldom used to cover local war memorials prior to the unveiling ceremony. The memorial itself was the focal point of the entire ceremony and draping the structure in the flag of the country might have conveyed a powerful message of identity to the onlookers, yet at every ceremony studied to date the Union flag appears. Extant film of the unveiling ceremonies at Aberystwyth in September 1923 and Ystalyfera in December 1922 clearly shows both memorials draped with the Union flag, and at the unveiling of the Welsh National War Memorial in Cardiff in June 1928, the three entrances to the 'shrine' were draped with the Union Jack, the White Ensign and the flag of the Royal Air Force.[33] On the rare occasions when the Welsh Dragon did make an appearance it was always in conjunction with the Union flag. The small village of Trawsfynydd in north Wales was the home of Hedd Wyn and thirty-two other men who lost their lives in the war. The war memorial was unveiled in September 1921 by Lady Osmond Williams, wife of the lord lieutenant of Merioneth, and an extant photograph clearly shows the memorial draped in the Union flag. Similarly, the small community of Gwyddelwern in north Wales chose to drape its memorial, which has a Welsh-only inscription, with the Union flag. The inhabitants of Dolgellau covered their memorial with the Union flag, although duality was maintained with the carving of two leeks on one panel of the memorial and a crown on the other.[34] Even the memorial in Lloyd George's own constituency of Caernarfon was draped with both the Welsh and Union flags and both

[32] For the background to this and details of an interesting clash between dragons and lions, see Clive Hughes, 'The Welsh Army Corps, 1914–15: shortages of khaki and basic equipment promote a "national" uniform', *Imperial War Museum Review*, I (1986), pp. 91–100; see especially pp. 95–7.

[33] *Western Mail*, 13 June 1928. The films of the unveiling ceremonies at Aberystwyth and Ystalyfera are stored at the National Library of Wales and the Imperial War Museum respectively.

[34] The memorial was initially situated in the centre of Dolgellau but has since been relocated in the park.

national anthems were sung at the ceremony.[35] Welsh-language newspaper reports of unveiling ceremonies did not stress a specifically Welsh contribution to the conflict, and emphasis was placed on the impact of war on the locality.[36] The unveiling of the Dolgellau memorial in October 1921 was reported by *Y Dydd*; the comprehensive report contains the usual details and notes that some of the speeches and hymns were delivered in English. A much smaller English-language report of the ceremony appeared in the *Carnarvon and Denbigh Herald*.[37] *Y Seren* covered the unveiling of the Bala memorial in April 1922, although the reports of the ceremony, and publicity in the days preceding it, were printed in English.[38]

The memorial at Caernarfon boasts a dragon, but this most potent symbol of the Welsh nation is represented in sculptural form on very few memorials in Wales, and the designs used in most Welsh memorials can be found in villages and towns throughout Britain.[39] Similarly, the popular visual embodiment of empire in the form of Britannia is rarely seen as a British war memorial and the National Inventory of War Memorials has

[35] The memorial at Caernarfon was unveiled in November 1922 by the mayor, who was also chairman of the war memorial committee. Lloyd George had been due to perform the unveiling but backed out two days before the ceremony on 'medical advice'. *Carnarvon and Denbigh Herald*, 17 November 1922. Lloyd George had also been due to unveil the memorial at Llandudno in November 1922 but withdrew from this ceremony as well. The memorial was unveiled on Armistice Day by the chairman of the council instead. *Holyhead Chronicle*, 17 November 1922. The collapse of Lloyd George's government and premiership in the previous month may well have contributed to his absence.

[36] For details of the Welsh-language press, see Aled Jones, *Press, Politics and Society: A History of Journalism in Wales* (Cardiff, 1993), pp. 177–201. Welsh-language newspapers were in a minority compared with the English press, but it appears that both Welsh- and English-language titles declined in Wales after the Great War.

[37] *Y Dydd*, 7 October 1921. See also *Carnarvon and Denbigh Herald*, 7 October 1921.

[38] *Y Seren*, 8 April 1922, and *Cambrian News*, 7 April 1922. The unveiling programme for the Bala ceremony was printed mostly in Welsh, although 'O God, our help in ages past' and 'Abide with me' were printed in full and in English, and both national anthems were sung.

[39] There remains an element of doubt as to whether the sculpture on the Pembrokeshire County War Memorial represents a dragon or a griffin. However, newspaper reports of the unveiling ceremony refer to the sculpture as a 'Welsh dragon'. See *Pembrokeshire Herald and General Advertiser*, 2 and 9 September 1921, and *Pembrokeshire Telegraph*, 7 September 1921. Anglesey does seem to have more than its fair share of clock towers as war memorials, with examples at Llanfairpwllgwyngyll, Rhos-y-bol, Llanfechell, Gwalchmai and Rhosneigr. Such a concentration of clock towers may be attributable to the 'domino' effect, but the Boer War may have provided a precedent with a clock tower erected in Llangefni in memory of one man.

recorded only ten major figurative depictions.[40] Images of Britannia, however, often appeared in Welsh newspapers on Armistice Day; in November 1921 the *Cambria Daily Leader* portrayed Britannia placing poppies on a war grave, and the image was chosen as a memorial to the memory of 144 men in Bridgend.[41] The design was chosen without apparent dissent and the only major criticism occurred because of the perceived delay in erecting the memorial. Shortly before the monument was unveiled, it was described in the local press as

> a singularly appropriate expression of the idealistic sentiments and emotions – national and individual – thus embodied in perpetuity. The conception is at once bold, striking, and original. When erected it will greatly beautify the Town Hall Square as the civic centre of the town, and for all time it will be a worthy memento of the great war, and serve, too, as a moving and stimulating inspiration.[42]

The visual symbol epitomizing 'Englishness' in the form of St George is more common as a war memorial in Britain and is often found in stained-glass windows. A figurative example can be found in Wales at Johnstown but unusually, given the symbolism involved, St George is in the process of slaying a dragon. The design for the memorial was chosen by local ex-servicemen and the successful design and tender had been submitted by a London firm. After discussion, it was decided to place the contract for the work locally, although the original design and choice of the ex-servicemen were adhered to.[43] The memorial at Johnstown was covered with the Union flag, but the unveiling ceremony itself was held on 1 March, St David's Day, 1926, although Armistice Day had been the original choice of date.[44] It appears that only a small number of memorials in Wales were unveiled on St David's Day, including Mold in 1926 and Senghennydd in 1921. The emotive impact of unveiling a

---

[40] I am grateful for information from the National Inventory of War Memorials.

[41] *Cambria Daily Leader*, 11 November 1921.

[42] *Glamorgan Gazette*, 15 April 1921. The memorial as a whole stands 24 ft high and Britannia herself measures 7′ 6″. She remains an impressive sight at a busy junction in the town.

[43] *Wrexham Advertiser*, 19 September 1925.

[44] For details of the unveiling ceremony on 1 March 1926, see *Rhos Herald*, 6 March 1926, and *Wrexham Advertiser*, 6 March 1926.

war memorial on Armistice Day must have prompted some committees to aim for 11 November, but surprisingly few Welsh memorials appear to have been unveiled on Armistice Day itself: Bagillt, Blackmill, Bridgend, Colwyn Bay, Kenfig Hill and Llandudno are exceptions. The actual day and date of unveiling may have been affected by various external factors, such as the availability of personnel as well as delays in completing the memorial. Ceremonies that took place at the weekend obviously made it easier for people to attend, particularly ex-servicemen. Both Colwyn Bay and Llandudno memorials were unveiled on Armistice Day 1922 which fell on a Saturday, whilst Bagillt held its ceremony in 1923 on a Sunday.[45] The inhabitants of Bangor-is-y-coed in north-east Wales made the interesting choice of Empire Day to unveil their memorial. Indeed, it was suggested during the ceremony that a 'more suitable day they could not have had for the ceremony, for had not Mr Paterson Moran in his address reminded all those gathered there that it was Empire Day'.[46]

In the early days of the war, popular images of empire combined with the 'righteousness of the cause' were powerful components in the recruitment campaign. In September 1914 Lloyd George had also successfully utilized the image of Wales as one of the 'little five-feet-high nations' fighting in defiance of the 'road hog' of Europe.[47] The experience of war ensured that the 'rights of small nations' moved up the political agenda. This theme would, on occasion, appear in unveiling ceremonies. In April 1923 the archbishop of Wales dedicated the memorial erected by the borough of Welshpool. In the course of his address, the archbishop stated that 'probably in no war had the rights of small nations been more unselfishly upheld, and a Welshman, speaking to Welshmen, could not forget that throughout the history of the Empire the valour of the people of

---

[45] The inter-war years witnessed a subtle change to commemorating the war on the nearest Sunday to Armistice Day and it was in 1946 that the nation started to commemorate its war dead on Remembrance Sunday. See A. Gregory, *The Silence of Memory* (Oxford, 1994), pp. 188–91.

[46] *Wrexham Leader*, 29 May 1925.

[47] A section of the speech contained various references to small nations, e.g.: 'God has chosen little nations as the vessels by which he carries the choicest wines to the lips of humanity' and 'The world owes much to little nations (cheers) and to little men.' *The Times*, 21 September 1914.

Wales had been again and again recognised'.[48] The report of the executive committee of the Welsh Army Corps had earlier suggested that the war had 'proved beyond question the inalienable right of a small nation to recognition of its own separate entity, as one of the sister nations that entered the lists in defence of the liberties and freedom of other small nations on the Continent of Europe'.[49] The widespread portrayal of the Great War as a struggle on behalf of small nations provided additional ammunition for those keen to ignite the home rule campaign in Wales. As early as July 1919, Major David Davies, Liberal MP for Montgomery, put forward a persuasive argument for the establishment of a Welsh legislature:

> The War has ostensibly been fought for the rights of small nations . . . Is Wales to be the only small nation who is not prepared to assert her individuality, or to claim that, in matters affecting her own people, she is not to be allowed to have a separate administration and a separate legislature to meet her needs and requirements?[50]

A series of conferences in the immediate post-war years made little progress and this 'served only to convince a small band of young nationalists of the need for an entirely separate political movement, owing no allegiance to any British party and declaring Welsh national identity as its fundamental *raison d'être*'.[51] Yet any links between the formation of the Welsh Nationalist Party in 1925 and the experience of war are tenuous, even though both Saunders Lewis and Lewis Valentine saw active service on the Western Front.[52] Many thousands of men returned to Wales having served from Flanders to Gallipoli with myriad memories of the war, and the memoirs and writings of

---

[48] *Western Mail*, 25 April 1923.

[49] *Welsh Army Corps, Report 1914–1919*, p. 5.

[50] *Welsh Outlook*, VI (July 1919), p. 176.

[51] D. Hywel Davies, *The Welsh Nationalist Party 1925–1945: A Call to Nationhood* (Cardiff, 1983), p. 3. For details of the conferences, see ibid., pp. 20–2.

[52] In his letters to Margaret Gilcriest whilst serving on the Western Front, Lewis makes reference both to himself and to his companions in arms as 'English soldiers'. See letters dated 3 June 1916, 7 June 1916 and 21 June 1916. Returning to France after a period of home leave in April 1917, he wrote: 'Of course, I was glad of the leave, glad to get away, very happy to be able to say every five minutes as the train sped north from London "This is England, this is England".' *Saunders Lewis: Letters to Margaret Gilcriest*, ed. Mair Saunders Jones, Ned Thomas and Harri Pritchard Jones (Cardiff, 1993), pp. 208–11 and p. 247.

ex-servicemen frequently refer to their lives having been altered by the experience of war. John Davies has written that

> for half a century after 1918 there were in every community in Wales men who remembered the war as their only exciting experience . . . It is possible also to over-emphasize the anti-English feeling aroused by the arrogance of English officers. By suffering alongside Geordies and Brummies, Cockneys and Scousers, Micks, Jocks and Aussies, the Taffs became part of a new brotherhood; to become a soldier was to assume a new nationality.[53]

David Jones reflected on the experience of the trenches for nearly twenty years before writing *In Parenthesis,* and in the preface he speaks of the Londoners and Welshmen who were his 'companions in the war':

> Both speak in parables, the wit of both is quick, both are natural poets; yet no two groups could well be more dissimilar . . . to see them shape together to the remains of an antique regimental tradition, to see them react to the few things that united us – the same jargon, the same prejudice against 'other arms' and against the Staff, the same discomforts, the same grievances, the same aims, the same deep fears, the same pathetic jokes; to watch them, oneself part of them, respond to the war landscape; for I think the day by day in the Waste Land, the sudden violences and the long stillnesses, the sharp contours and unformed voids of that mysterious existence, profoundly affected the imaginations of those who suffered it.[54]

The experiences of serving in the Great War obviously left deep impressions on many participants, but it is questionable whether national identity was a cause of great concern to those who fought on behalf of the empire. Disillusionment with the war and difficulties with reintegration into civilian life may have

[53] Davies, *History of Wales,* p. 514.

[54] David Jones, *In Parenthesis* (London, 1975; 1st published 1937), preface p. x. Jon Stallworthy has suggested that the opening words of the Dedication 'proclaim it part of the work – THIS WRITING IS FOR ALL MY FRIENDS. Printed in capital letters and without punctuation, it looks like a war memorial and sounds like a poem. The dedication states the theme, which is the commemoration of the dead – friends and enemies who shared the same pains.' Jon Stallworthy, *Survivors' Songs in Welsh Poetry* (Cardiff, 1982), p. 11. David Jones enlisted in the 15th (London Welsh) Battalion of the Royal Welch Fusiliers in January 1915 and served throughout the war as a private on the Western Front. See *David Jones: A Fusilier at the Front,* ed. Anthony Hyne (Bridgend, 1995). See also William Blissett, 'The Welsh thing in here', in Paul Hills (ed.), *David Jones, Artist and Poet* (Aldershot, 1997), pp. 101–21.

been widespread, but it appears that this did not transmogrify into a burning desire for Welsh home rule on demobilization.[55] The commemoration process in Wales emphasized in an unprecedented manner the importance of locality over nationality. Neil Evans has noted that 'the people of Llanbedr refused to contribute to the Rhuthun memorial and insisted on their own, as did several small communities in the area. It was local worlds that had to be mobilised for the war effort, and to commemorate it too.'[56] The immediacy and importance of local commemoration have been noted, and it was normal practice for communities throughout Wales, large and small, to insist upon their own memorials. Indeed, Llanbedr was not the only community to withdraw from the Ruthin scheme.[57] It is also undoubtedly true that 'local worlds had to be mobilised' for both enlistment and commemoration, yet the ironic result of so much determination to have local memorials was a proliferation of stone testaments proclaiming pride in the part local men had played in an imperial war. It is clear that an individual may have enlisted, fought and died as a Welshman, but he was commemorated as a British citizen.

The commemoration process provided a perfect opportunity for the population of Wales to express its coherence and identity as a nation; the fact that this was not used to articulate burgeoning Celtic identity should not be interpreted as indifference to Wales or 'Welshness'. Rather it can be seen as a desire to communicate pride in the Welsh contribution to the empire's cause and in doing so to provide tangible evidence of a nation at ease with its own position within the British state and the empire. This attitude allowed Wales to commemorate its part in the Great War whilst maintaining that it was very much a 'Welsh' contribution. The desire to publicize the Welsh contribution to

---

[55] Writing of the period between the Armistice and signing the peace treaties, Robert Graves recalled: 'We now half hoped that there would be a general rising of ex-service men against the Coalition Government, but it was not to be. Once back in England the men were content to have a roof over their heads, civilian food, beer that was at least better than French beer, and enough blankets at night. They might find over-crowding in their homes, but this could be nothing to what they had been accustomed to; in France a derelict four-roomed cottage would provide billets for sixty men. They had won the war and they were satisfied. They left the rest to Lloyd George.' Robert Graves, *Goodbye to All That: An Autobiography*, ed. Richard Perceval Graves (Oxford, 1995), p. 255.

[56] Evans, 'Gogs, Cardis and Hwntws', p. 68.

[57] Ruthin war memorial is discussed in more detail in ch. 3.

the imperial effort lay behind the decision to publish the report of the executive committee of the Welsh Army Corps:

> This Report has been drafted in the hope and expectation that it will be supplemented by a full and faithful record of the movements and doings of the men of the Welsh Army Corps on the battlefields, and that the whole story, from the inception of the Corps to the demobilisation or dispersal of its last unit, will be put in the form of a permanent record of the greatest military contribution ever made to the British and Imperial Forces by the Principality of Wales.[58]

The empire provided a sense of British identity which was accentuated by imperial and world wars, but this did not preclude or erode existing identities, whether regional or national. This is particularly noticeable in Wales, where the interactions and contradictions between Welsh and British identities are apparent, and provides a useful note of caution to those who may attempt interpretations of national identity based solely on socio-political or linguistic considerations. Loyalty to Britain and the empire did not preclude loyalty to Wales and this was acknowledged and accepted at the time. As the *Western Mail* pointed out in its report of the unveiling of the 'National' War Memorial in 1928, the Welsh people were 'conscious of their nationhood, but equally conscious of their partnership in Empire'.[59]

---

[58] *Welsh Army Corps, Report 1914–1919*, p. 44.

[59] Similar sentiments were expressed at small, local ceremonies. At the unveiling of the Llanddeiniolen memorial in north Wales, the Revd W. Morgan Jones spoke of 'Welshmen as members of the great and mighty British Empire'. The memorial itself was draped with the Union flag. *Holyhead Chronicle*, 27 May 1921. For details of the ceremony in Cardiff, see *Western Mail*, 12 June 1928.

CONCLUSION

On Wednesday 1 December 1926 Field Marshal Lord Allenby unveiled the Abertillery war memorial in south Wales to the memory of 400 men from the district who had lost their lives in the Great War. A photograph of the ceremony captures the moment just after the monument had been unveiled: the flag lies at its base and a representative of the clergy addresses the gathering, whilst a young man attempts to copy down the speech, possibly for a newspaper report.[1] The unveiling of a war memorial was undoubtedly an important event in a community, and local newspapers throughout Wales contained many accounts and photographs of similar ceremonies in the decade after the Great War as communities sought public acknowledgement and private consolation for their pride and grief.

The photograph of the Abertillery ceremony demonstrates the inclusion and exclusion of individuals, for those who played a prominent role in their community saw it as a natural progression to extend that role to the commemoration process. The space immediately surrounding the memorial was deemed the 'Memorial enclosure' and only the holders of 'white tickets' were permitted to enter; these privileged few included representatives of the local urban district council and officers of the war memorial committee. The relatives 'of those whose names are inscribed on the Memorial and who have previously obtained blue tickets' were admitted to a space reserved for them on 'the Queen Street side of the Memorial'. Yet people deemed 'outsiders' were determined not be excluded from the ceremony; men, women and children fill every possible vantage point, packed together leaning over walls, young men, perhaps ex-servicemen, perched precariously on rooftops, or faces crowding around a window to gain a better view of the ceremony. All are anxious to be part of the occasion. A local war memorial was a

---

[1] Details on the unveiling of the Abertillery memorial are taken from *Western Mail*, 2 December 1926, and from the programme, 'Proceedings of the Unveiling and Dedication of the Abertillery War Memorial, 1st December 1926'.

very public affirmation of community, with the memorial itself acting as a 'marker' by signifying its exclusivity and uniqueness.[2] It proclaimed a local contribution to the war not only by mourning the loss of its young men but by making a clear statement that these were 'our' young men.[3] The location of a memorial was therefore crucial; unlike regional and national memorials, local commemoration was relevant, accessible and provided a permanent, daily reminder of collective and individual loss. Themes of community and local identity were important elements in the commemoration process. The photograph of the Abertillery ceremony leaves no doubt that this ceremony took place in Wales but also succeeds in displaying the ambiguities inherent in any definition of Welsh national identity. The Welsh dragon, enlisted as a recruiting symbol during the war and adopted as the unofficial Welsh flag, is very much in evidence in the photograph, yet it is attached to a wall behind the memorial; the monument itself, focus of the occasion and centre of attention, had been draped in the Union flag.[4]

Unveiling ceremonies throughout Wales witnessed repeated examples of spiritual solidarity, and Abertillery was no exception. The local vicar dedicated the memorial and spoke of those who died 'in defence of freedom, mercy, and good faith among the nations . . . Accept their sacrifice: let it not be in vain', and suggested that those who were left behind should look upon the memorial and prove themselves worthy of those who had died. Ecumenical co-operation continued with addresses from Ensign T. Greaves of the Salvation Army; the Revd D. Glanmor Jenkins, chairman of the Abertillery Free Church Ministers' Fraternal, and by the Revd A. Snadow of the Jewish synagogue.

---

[2] In June 1919 Abertillery Urban District Council had opted not to support the proposed regimental memorial to men of the 3rd Battalion Monmouthshire Regiment to be erected in Abergavenny; at the same meeting they took no action over the invitation from Cardiff City Council to attend a conference to discuss a Welsh National War Memorial. This is discussed in more detail in ch. 3.

[3] This echoes Edna Longley's comment that 'Commemorations are as selective as sympathies. They honour *our* dead, not your dead.' 'The Rising, the Somme and Irish memory', in Mairin Ni Dhonnchadha and Theo Dorgan (eds.), *Revising the Rising* (Londonderry, 1991), p. 29 (italics in text).

[4] The lingering effects of empire and imperialism in Welsh culture in the inter-war years would appear to warrant further investigation especially because, as John MacKenzie has pointed out, 'The war has acted as a convenient climax to most studies, and the inter-war years have not been blessed with the close examination the earlier period has enjoyed.' *Propaganda and Empire: The Manipulation of British Public Opinion, 1880–1960* (Manchester, 1984), p. 9.

The plethora of unveiling ceremonies in the decade following the Great War witnessed representatives of church and chapel preaching messages of good citizenship, but such ceremonies also perhaps provided a useful public platform to reassure those who doubted the churches' ability to comfort and guide after the experiences of war.

The need and desire to remember the dead were never in question. A lone figure sits in front of the war memorial. The *Western Mail* report of the ceremony states that she is Miss Williams from Blaina.[5] She sits alone, wearing the military decorations awarded to her three brothers who were killed in the war. Her position was gained not by individual loss but because, prior to the ceremony, she had been introduced to Allenby. She sits with her back to the memorial, physically and mentally detached from those around her. They in turn appear lost in their own thoughts; none appears to look directly at her, whilst she in turn gazes straight ahead, listening to but perhaps not really hearing the words of the speaker directly beside her. Those standing closest to her look upwards towards the memorial and this only serves to increase her isolation; she is overlooked, both by the participants in the ceremony and by society. The photograph of the Abertillery ceremony serves as a permanent reminder of the contemporary importance of war memorials as markers of local identity and civic pride, yet it also reveals the individual pain of bereavement.[6]

Questions of site, size, cost and form of war memorials stimulated much debate and, on occasion, controversy, but it appears that the need for commemoration itself was not a matter for public debate. The ultimate choice of memorial was usually governed by financial considerations rather than by the scale of loss. Communities sought to commemorate 'their' dead and the

[5] It should perhaps be pointed out that on a different page of the same edition, in a caption under a photograph of the ceremony, the woman is described as 'Mrs Fisher'. Other local newspaper reports of the Abertillery ceremony do not mention her at all.

[6] 'How healing occurs, and what quietens embitterment and alleviates despair can never be fully known. But not to ask the question, not to try to place the history of war memorials within the history of bereavement, a history we all share in our private lives, is both to impoverish the study of history and to evade our responsibility as historians. For we must attend to the faces and feelings of those who were bereft, and who made the pilgrimages to these sites of memory, large and small, in order to begin to understand how men and women tried to cope with one of the signal catastrophes of our century.' Jay Winter, *Sites of Memory, Sites of Mourning: The Great War in European Cultural History* (Cambridge, 1995), p. 116.

loss of seven men or seven hundred was equally devastating to those left behind. Comparison of commemorative processes in Wales and the rest of Britain reveals more similarities than differences. The use of the Welsh language on memorials remains the most notable difference yet language was the least contested issue of commemoration in Wales. The use of the Welsh flag, the singing of Welsh hymns and the Welsh national anthem at unveiling ceremonies and Welsh-language inscriptions on memorials all proclaimed the Welsh contribution to the war. The position of Wales within the wider British polity was not challenged either by the experience of war or in commemorating the fallen.

The major cause for controversy in the commemoration process was the location of a memorial. Pierre Nora has suggested that 'Statues or monuments to the dead . . . owe their meaning to their intrinsic existence; even though their location is far from arbitrary, one could justify relocating them without altering their meaning'.[7] Analysis of the commemoration process in Wales, however, suggests that location was crucial to the meaning of a memorial. The Welsh National Memorial provides a useful example, for it was the initial suggestion that the memorial should be located in Cardiff that prompted so much resentment from other parts of the principality. The predominant reason for rejecting the national scheme was the proliferation of local schemes, and the resulting memorials are testament to the strength of local affiliations, loyalties and identity. The location invested a memorial with meaning for those who had fought and survived and demanded adequate tribute to their fallen comrades; for those who sought to make a public statement on civic pride and dignity in the community's sacrifice; for the representatives of church and clergy seeking to reaffirm the consolatory and healing power of a God whose credibility had for some been severely tested and found wanting by the experience of war; above all, the location was crucial for the bereaved as a site of individual and collective mourning. Commemoration of the dead became a flourishing business in the decade after the war and as such provided useful commercial

---

[7] Pierre Nora, 'Between memory and history: les lieux de mémoire', *Representations*, XXVI (1989), pp. 7–25 (p. 22).

opportunities for some, while others sought to put forward individual or collective statements on how the war should be remembered. Inscriptions on war memorials often invoked notions of honour, sacrifice and loyalty, and memorials in Wales were no exception, whether the sentiments were expressed in Welsh or English. Those left behind were given a clear message both to honour those who had died and to display the same qualities of selflessness and citizenship in life as had those who had died. The debate about the most appropriate way to remember the fallen in Wales became part of a wider debate on social, political and national identity in the post-war years.[8] Above all, however, the study of war memorials in Wales has revealed the human price of participation in the Great War and illustrated the complexities involved in remembering the dead and the myriad influences that shaped the way society chose to remember them.

[8] There is a case for comparative work on commemoration in Britain, particularly with regard to the question of national identity. Commemoration was clearly contested in Ireland, and it would be interesting to know if expressions of Celtic independence were more prominent in Scotland·than appears to have been the case in Wales.

BIBLIOGRAPHY

1. Archival Sources
2. War Memorial Programmes
3. Contemporary Works: Books and Articles
4. Secondary Works: Books and Articles
5. Theses and Dissertations

1. Archival Sources

Aberdare Library, Aberdare:
Aberdare Leader

Anglesey Record Office, Anglesey:
File of miscellaneous documents relating to Rhosybol War Memorial
File on Llanfairpwllgwyngyll Memorial Institute
Llandegfan War Memorial Minute Book
Menai Bridge War Memorial File

Local Authority Minute Books:
Aethwy Rural District Council (RDC)   Llangefni UDC
Amlwch Urban District Council (UDC)   Menai Bridge UDC
Anglesey County Council   Twrcelyn RDC
Dwyran RDC   Valley RDC
Holyhead UDC

Arts and Social Studies Library, University of Wales Cardiff:
Welsh Outlook

Barry Public Library, Barry:
Barry Dock News (from November 1925 *Barry and District News*)
Barry Herald

British Library: Newspaper Library, London:
Baptist Times

Cardiff Central Library, Cardiff:
Local Authority Minute Books:
Cardiff City Council

Newspapers:
Cardiff Times   *South Wales Echo*
Evening Express   *The Times*
Glamorgan Gazette   *Western Mail*
South Wales Daily News

Carmarthen Public Library, Carmarthen:
Carmarthen Journal

Carmarthenshire Record Office, Carmarthen:
Carmarthen Borough Council: correspondence *re* County War Memorial

Local Authority Minute Books:
Carmarthen Borough Council	Llandilo Fawr RDC
Carmarthen RDC	Llandilo UDC
Carmarthenshire County Council	Llandovery Borough Council
Cwmamman UDC	Newcastle-in-Emlyn RDC

Ceredigion Archives, Aberystwyth:
Lampeter War Memorial Book
Minute Books of Lampeter War Memorial Committee

Local Authority Minute Books:
Aberaeron RDC	Lampeter Borough Council
Aberystwyth RDC	Lampeter RDC
Ammanford UDC	Llandyssul RDC
Cardigan Borough Council	New Quay UDC
Cardiganshire County Council	

Commonwealth War Graves Commission, Maidenhead:
File on Private E. H. Evans (CWGC) 'E' File SL 10876
Minutes of meetings of Imperial War Graves Commission

Denbighshire Record Office, Ruthin:
Ruthin War Memorial – town clerk's papers

Local Authority Minute Books:
Abergele and Pensarn UDC	Llansilin RDC
Chirk RDC	Ruthin Borough Council
Colwyn Bay and Colwyn UDC	Ruthin RDC
Denbigh Borough Council	Uwchaled RDC
Edeyrnion RDC	Wrexham Borough Council
Llangollen RDC	Wrexham RDC
Llanrwst RDC	

Newspapers:
Denbighshire Free Press

Department of Manuscripts, University of Wales, Bangor:
Documents related to memorial to 38th (Welsh) Division at Mametz Wood
Handbook produced by British Legion for the Llanfairpwllgwyngyll memorial
Papers of R. Silyn Roberts
University College of North Wales Heroes' Memorial File
University of Wales, Bangor, Ms. 5056 (10-30)
War Diaries of Major Wynn Wheldon, DSO, 14th (Service) Battalion, Royal Welch Fusiliers

Dolgellau Record Office, Dolgellau:
Bangor Heroes' Memorial Book

Festiniog Roll of honour
File on Llanbedr War Memorial Fund

Local Authority Minute Books:
Deudraeth RDC   Merioneth County Council
Dolgellau UDC   Mallwyd UDC
Dolgellau RDC   Penllyn RDC

Flintshire Record Office, Hawarden:
County of Flint War Memorial
Papers *re* Prestatyn War Memorial

Local Authority Minute Books:
Buckley UDC   Mold UDC
Connah's Quay UDC   Overton RDC
Hawarden RDC   Prestatyn UDC
Holywell RDC   Rhyl UDC
Holywell UDC   St Asaph RDC

Glamorgan Record Office, Cardiff:
Cardiff Royal Infirmary: Board of Management Minute Books
Letter Books of S. O. Davies
Llanharan Strike Duty Journal
Minute Books of Rhymney Iron Company Board
Minutes of Maesteg War Memorial Committee
Powell Duffryn Steam Coal Company Limited: Minutes of Directors' Meetings and
    Managing Committee; Directors' Annual Reports to Annual General Meetings

Local Authority Minute Books:
Barry UDC   Maesteg UDC
Bridgend UDC   Merthyr Tydfil Borough Council
Caerphilly UDC   Mountain Ash UDC
Cowbridge Borough Council   Ogmore and Garw UDC
Cowbridge RDC   Penarth UDC
Gelligaer UDC   Penybont RDC
Glamorgan County Council   Pontypridd UDC
Llancarfan Parish Council   Porthcawl UDC
Llantrisant and Llantwit Fardre RDC   Rhondda UDC

Gwent Record Office, Cwmbran:
Local Authority Minute Books:
Abercarn UDC   Llantarnam UDC
Abergavenny Borough Council   Monmouth RDC
Abergavenny RDC   Monmouth UDC
Abertillery UDC   Mynyddislwyn UDC
Bedwas and Machen UDC   Nantyglo and Blaina UDC
Bedwellty UDC   Newport Borough Council
Brynmawr UDC   Pontypool RDC
Caerleon UDC   Risca UDC
Chepstow RDC   Rhymney UDC
Chepstow UDC   Tredegar UDC
Ebbw Vale UDC   Usk RDC
Llanfrechfa UDC

Gwynedd Archives, Caernarfon:
Documents of Caernarvon War Memorial Committee
Minutes of Bettwsycoed War Memorial Committee

Local Authority Minute Books:
Caernarvonshire County Council   Glaslyn RDC
Caernarvon Borough Council   Penmaenmawr UDC
Criccieth UDC

Imperial War Museum, London:
Film of unveiling of Ystalyfera War Memorial
Interviews from sound archives: Jane Cox, Eleanor Cain, Kitty Eckersley and Catherine Hambleton
National Inventory of War Memorials
Programme for visit of Earl Haig to Swansea to lay foundation stone for war memorial, July 1922
Sir Herbert Creedy Papers
War Memorials Ephemera Collection

Law Library, University of Wales, Cardiff:
Coal Industry Commission Act, 1919, Interim Report, Cmd. 84
Commission of Enquiry into Industrial Unrest, No. 7 Division, Report of the
    Commissioners for Wales, including Monmouthshire, 1917 (Cd. 8668)
Hansard Parliamentary Debates
Mining Industry Act, 1920, Section 20
Mining Industry (Welfare Fund) Act, 1925
War Memorials (Local Authorities' Powers) Act, 1923

Library, National Museum & Gallery, Cardiff:
Annual Reports of the National Museum of Wales

Liddle Collection, Brotherton Library, University of Leeds:
Diary of Private W. D. Jones, 10th Battalion, Royal Welch Fusiliers
Diary of L/Cpl. D. G. Gregory, 13th Battalion, Royal Welch Fusiliers
Napier family papers
Papers of 2nd Lt. D. A. Addams-Williams, 4th Battalion, South Wales Borderers

National Library of Wales, Aberystwyth:
Film of the unveiling of Aberystwyth War Memorial
General Minute Books of Monmouthshire and South Wales Coal Owners Association
MS Solva Roads of Remembrance
Papers of George M. Ll. Davies
Papers of the Honourable Society of Cymmrodorion
Papers re Aberystwyth War Memorial Fund
Papers re Llansilin Memorial Hall
Papers re Tabernacl Chapel War Memorial, Aberystwyth
Report of the Executive of the East Denbighshire Parliamentary Recruiting Committee
Welsh Army Corps Papers

Newspapers:
Abergavenny Chronicle   *Caerphilly Journal*
Brecon and Radnor Express   *Cambria Daily Leader*
Carnarvon and Denbigh Herald   *Cambrian News*

County Herald
Free Press of Monmouthshire
Holyhead Chronicle
Merthyr Express
Mold, Deeside and Buckley Leader
North Wales Chronicle
Oswestry and Border Counties Advertiser
Pembroke County Guardian
Pembrokeshire Herald and General Advertiser
Pembrokeshire Telegraph

Prestatyn Weekly
Rhos Herald
Rhyl Journal
Welsh Catholic Herald
Welsh Gazette
Wrexham Advertiser
Wrexham Leader
Y Dydd
Y Seren

Newport Central Library, Newport:
South Wales Argus

Pembrokeshire Record Office, Haverfordwest:
Local Authority Minute Books:
Fishguard UDC
Haverfordwest RDC
Haverfordwest Borough Council
Llanfyrnach RDC
Milford Haven UDC
Narberth RDC

Narberth UDC
Neyland UDC
Pembroke Borough Council
Pembrokeshire County Council
Pembroke RDC
Tregaron RDC

Penarth Library, Penarth:
Penarth News

Penarth Times

Powys County Archives Office, Llandrindod Wells:
Llandrindod Wells War Memorial File

Local Authority Minute Books:
Brecknock RDC
Brecon Borough Council
Brecon UDC
Breconshire County Council
Builth RDC
Builth Wells UDC
Colwyn RDC
Crickhowell Parish Council
Crickhowell RDC
Hay RDC

Hay UDC
Knighton RDC
Llandrindod Wells UDC
Llanwrtyd Wells UDC
Montgomeryshire County Council
New Radnor RDC
Painscastle RDC
Radnorshire County Council
Rhayader RDC

Sound Archive, Museum of Welsh Life, Cardiff:
Interview with Agnes Greatorex
Interview with O. M. Roberts
Interview with Rupert Rees
Taped interviews from BBC Wales series 'All Our Lives'

South Wales Coalfield Archive, University of Wales Swansea:
Blackwood Miners' Welfare Institute and Library Committee Minutes
Coelbren Miners' Welfare and Memorial Hall Minute Books
Coelbren Miners' Welfare and Memorial Hall Account Book
Fund-raising leaflet and order of service for Ferndale Miners' Memorial
Minute Books of Mineworkers' Federation of Great Britain

Minute Book of Annual and General Meetings of Ferndale Lodge
Minutes of Afan Valley District Miners' Association
Minutes of the South Wales Miners' Federation Executive Council and Annual and
    Special Conferences
Oakdale Navigation Lodge Minute Books
Pontyberem Memorial Hall and Institute Minute Books

South Wales Miners' Library, University of Wales Swansea:
Interview with Glyn Williams (Glyncorrwg) 21 May 1974

Swansea Central Library, Swansea:
South Wales Daily Post

Treorchy Library, Treorchy:
Rhondda Leader

University of Wales Registry, Cardiff:
Annual Reports of the Council, University College of South Wales and Monmouthshire,
    Cardiff

West Glamorgan Archive Service, Swansea:
Minute Books of Seven Sisters Lodge
War Memorial Committee Minutes. St Luke's church, Cwmbwrla, Swansea

Local Authority Minute Books:

Aberavon Borough Council	Neath UDC
Briton Ferry UDC	Pontardarwe RDC
Margam UDC	Swansea Borough Council
Neath Borough Council	Swansea RDC

2. War Memorial Programmes

Held at: Carmarthenshire, Dolgellau, Flintshire and Gwynedd Archives; Personal
Collection; War Memorials Ephemera Collection and National Inventory of War
Memorials, Imperial War Museum, London

Abertillery	December 1926
Bala	April 1922
Bethesda	June 1924
Briton Ferry	November 1921
Brynmawr	October 1927
Carmarthen	September 1924
Carnarvon	November 1922
Colwyn Bay	November 1922
Connah's Quay	May 1927
Denbigh	November 1922
Gwyddelwern	October 1921
Holyhead	September 1923
Kenfig Hill and Pyle	November 1925
Kidwelly	July 1924
Larne	March 1922
Llanbadarn Fawr	January 1921

Llandrindod Wells	July 1922
Llandudno	November 1922
Llantilio Pertholey	October 1921
Llanwrda	April 1923
Mountain Ash	June 1922
Neath	May 1925
Nevin	February 1923
Overton	November 1921
Pant	July 1926
Penmaen-mawr	May 1925
Port Talbot	June 1925
Pwllheli	June 1924
Senghennydd	March 1921
Swansea	July 1923
Tredegar	December 1924
Walsall	February 1920
Welsh National War Memorial	June 1928
Ystalyfera	December 1922

In addition, 700 town and community councils in Wales were contacted for details of local war memorials: 259 replies have been received to date.

3. Contemporary Works: Books and Articles

After Ten Years: A Report of Miners' Welfare Work in the South Wales Coalfield, 1921–1931 (Cardiff, 1932)

Annual Reports of Miners' Welfare Fund (London, 1923)

Astle, John G. E., *Merthyr Tydfil Incorporation 1897 and 1903: Proceedings on Inquiries* (Merthyr Tydfil, *c.*1903)

Bard, Albert S., 'What sort of war memorial', *Community Buildings as War Memorials Bulletin*, I, Bureau of Memorial Buildings and War Camp Community Service, (New York, 1919), pp. 1–16.

Cardiff Directory (Cardiff, 1919)

Chelmsford, Viscount, *The Miners' Welfare Fund* (London, 1927)

Hall, Hubert, 'A National War Museum and a Public Record Office for Wales', *Y Cymmrodor: The Magazine of the Honourable Society of Cymmrodorion*, XXVII (1917), pp. 206–29

Harcourt Smith, C. (ed.), *Inscriptions Suggested for War Memorials* (London, 1919)

Lethaby, W. R. 'Memorials of the fallen: service or sacrifice?', *The Hibbert Journal*, XVII (1918–19), pp.621–5.

Morgan, Revd J. Vyrnwy, *The War and Wales* (London, 1916)

Nicholson, Ivor and Trevor Lloyd-Williams (eds.), *Wales: Its Part in the War* (London, 1919)

'Some Newport war memorials', *The Newport Christmas Annual* (Newport, 1925)

Report of the Executive Committee, Welsh Army Corps, 1914–1919 (Newport, 1989; originally published Cardiff, 1921)

The Land of my Fathers: A Welsh Gift Book (London, 1915)

The Register of the Names Inscribed on the Thiepval Memorial, France (London, Imperial War Graves Commission, 1931)

The War Graves of the British Empire: France (London, Imperial War Graves Commission, 1928)

The War Graves of the British Empire: Gallipoli (London, Imperial War Graves Commission, 1928)

Who's Who in Wales, 1st edn. 1920 (Cardiff, 1921)

Williams, Oakley, *A War Memorial: Cardiff's Debt to Dead Heroes* (Cardiff, 1917)

4. SECONDARY WORKS: BOOKS AND ARTICLES

Adams, Bernard, *Nothing of Importance: A Record of Eight Months at the Front with a Welsh Battalion* (Stevenage, 1988)

Aldis, Arnold S., *Cardiff Royal Infirmary, 1883-1983* (Cardiff, 1984)

Arnot, R. Page, *South Wales Miners: A History of the South Wales Miners' Federation*, vol. 2: *1914–1926* (Cardiff, 1975)

Aylott, F. G., 'The Nantlle Quarry war memorial 1914–1918', *Bulletin of the Military Historical Society*, XXV, No. 100 (1975), pp. 128–30

Barber, Bernard, 'Place, symbol and utilitarian function in war memorials', *Social Forces*, XXVIII (1949), pp. 64-8

Beddoe, Deidre, 'Munitionettes, maids and mams: women in Wales, 1914–1939', in Angela V. John (ed.), *Our Mothers' Land: Chapters in Welsh Women's History, 1830–1939* (Cardiff, 1991)

Bodnar, John, *Remaking America: Public Memory, Commemoration and Patriotism in the Twentieth Century* (Princeton, 1992)

Boorman, Derek, *At the Going Down of the Sun: British First World War Memorials* (York, 1988)

Booth, Allyson, *Postcards from the Trenches* (Oxford, 1996)

Borg, Alan, *War Memorials from Antiquity to the Present* (London, 1991)

Bourne, J. M., *Britain and the Great War, 1914–1918* (London, 1989)

Bowden, W. G., *Abercynon to Flanders – and Back* (Risca, 1984)

Bowen, E. G., *A History of Llanbadarn Fawr* (Llandysul, 1979)

Boyns, Trevor, 'Work and death in the South Wales coalfield, 1874–1914', *Welsh History Review*, XII, No. 4 (1985), pp. 514–37

Braybon, G., 'Women and the war', in S. Constantine, M. W. Kirby and M. B. Rose (eds.), *The First World War in British History* (London, 1995), pp. 141–67

Brittain, Vera, *Testament of Youth* (London, 1980)

Brown, J. H., *The Valley of the Shadow* (Port Talbot, 1981)

Brown, Malcolm, *The Imperial War Museum Book of the First World War* (London, 1991)

Bruce, Alex, *Monuments, Memorials and the Local Historian* (London, Historical Association, 1997)

Burke, Peter, *History and Social Theory* (Cambridge, 1992)

Bushaway, Bob, 'Name upon name: the Great War and remembrance', in Roy Porter (ed.), *Myths of the English* (Cambridge, 1992), pp. 136–67

Cannadine, David, 'War and death, grief and mourning in modern Britain', in J. Whaley (ed.), *Mirrors of Mortality: Studies in the Social History of Death* (London, 1981), pp. 187–242

Capps, L. M., 'The memorial as symbol and agent of healing', in W. Capps (ed.), *The Vietnam Reader* (London, 1991)

Cardiff 1889–1974: The Story of the County Borough (Cardiff, 1974)

Chapman, Guy, *A Kind of Survivor* (London, 1975)

——, *A Passionate Prodigality* (Leatherhead, 1993)

Chappell, Edgar L., *Cardiff's Civic Centre – A Historical Guide* (Cardiff, 1946)

Chrimes, S. B. (ed.), 'University College, Cardiff: A Centenary History, 1883–1983' (unpublished)

Clayton, C. P., *The Hungry One* (Llandysul, 1978)

Clements, K. W., 'Baptists and the outbreak of the First World War', *Baptist Quarterly* (April 1975), pp. 74–92

Cohen, Anthony P., *The Symbolic Construction of Community* (London, 1993)

Curl, James Stevens, *A Celebration of Death* (London, 1980)

Curtis, Penelope, 'The Whitehall Cenotaph: an accidental monument', *Imperial War Museum Review*, IX (1994), pp. 31–41

David, Edward (ed.), *Inside Asquith's Cabinet: From the Diaries of Charles Hobhouse* (London, 1977)

Davies, David Wyn, *A Welshman in Mesopotamia* (Aberystwyth, 1986)

Davies, Emlyn, *Taffy Went to War* (Knutsford, 1976)

Davies, Janet, *The Welsh Language* (Cardiff, 1993)

Davies, John, *Cardiff and the Marquesses of Bute* (Cardiff, 1981)

——, *A History of Wales* (London, 1994)

Davies, Jon, 'War memorials', in David Clark (ed.), T*he Sociology of Death* (Oxford, 1993), pp. 112–28

Davies, Russell, *Secret Sins: Sex, Violence and Society in Carmarthenshire, 1870–1920* (Cardiff, 1996)

Davies, D. Hywel, *The Welsh Nationalist Party, 1925–1945: A Call to Nationhood* (Cardiff, 1983)

Dixon, Janet, and John Dixon, *With Rifle and Pick* (Cardiff, 1991)

Douglas, R., 'Voluntary enlistment in the First World War and the work of the Parliamentary Recruiting Committee', *Journal of Modern History*, XLII, No. 4 (1970), pp. 564–85

Duckham, Helen, and Baron Duckham, *Great Pit Disasters: Great Britain, 1700 to the Present Day* (Newton Abbot, 1973)

Dunn, Captain J. C., *The War the Infantry Knew, 1914–1919* (London, 1991)

Dutton, Philip, ' "The dead man's penny": a history of the next of kin memorial plaque', *Imperial War Museum Review*, III (1988), pp. 60–8

——, 'Moving images? The Parliamentary Recruiting Committee's poster campaign, 1914–1916', *Imperial War Museum Review*, IV (1989), pp. 43–58

Egan, David, 'The Swansea Conference of the British Council of Soldiers' and Workers' Delegates, July 1917', *Llafur*, I, No. 4 (1975), pp. 162–87

——, ' "Maerdy United Choir *v* The Spiritualists": popular culture and the use of Maerdy Workmen's Hall and Institute 1918–1922', *South Wales Miners' Library Newsletter*, V (1993), pp. 4–7

Eurig, Aled, 'Agweddau ar y Gwrthwynebiad i'r Rhyel Byd Cyntaf yng Nghymru' (Aspects of the opposition to the First World War in Wales), *Llafur*, IV, No. 4 (1987), pp. 58–68

Evans, Gwynfor, *Land of my Fathers* (Swansea, 1974)

Evans, Neil, ' "The first charity in Wales": Cardiff Infirmary and South Wales Society, 1837–1914', *Welsh History Review*, IX, No. 3 (1979), pp. 319–46

——, 'The Welsh Victorian city: The middle class and civic and national consciousness in Cardiff, 1850–1914', *Welsh History Review*, XII, No. 3 (1985), pp. 350–87

——, 'Gogs, Cardis and Hwntws: regions, nation and state in Wales, 1840–1940', in Neil Evans (ed.), *National Identity in the British Isles* (Coleg Harlech, 1989)

Firth, Raymond, *Elements of Social Organization* (London, 1951)

Francis, Hywel, and David Smith, *The Fed: A History of the South Wales Miners in the Twentieth Century* (Cardiff, 1998)

Freud, Sigmund, 'Thoughts for the times on war and death', in J. Strachey and A. Freud (eds.), *The Standard Edition of the Complete Psychological Works of Sigmund Freud*, vol. 14 (1914–1916) (London, 1957)

Gilbert, David, *Class, Community and Collective Action: Social Change in Two British Coalfields, 1850-1926* (Oxford, 1992)

Gilbert, Martin, *Winston S. Churchill*, vol. 3 (London, 1972)

Gildea, James, *For Remembrance and in Honour of Those who Lost their Lives in the South African War, 1899–1902* (London, 1911)

Goodman, Alice, *The Street Memorials of St Albans Abbey Parish* (St Albans, 1987)

Gough, Paul, 'Conifers and commemoration: the politics and protocol of planting', *Landscape Research*, XXI, No. 1 (1996), pp. 73–87

Grainger, J. H., *Patriotisms: Britain, 1900–1939* (London, 1986)

Graves, Robert, *Goodbye to All That: An Autobiography*, ed. Richard Perceval Graves (Oxford, 1995)

Greenberg, Allan, 'Lutyens' Cenotaph', *Journal of the Society of Architectural Historians*, XLVIII, No. 1 (1989), pp. 5–23

Gregory, Adrian, *The Silence of Memory* (Oxford, 1994)

Griffith, Wyn, *Up to Mametz* (London, 1981)

——, 'The pattern of one man's remembering', in G. A. Panichas (ed.), *Promise of Greatness* (London, 1968), pp. 286–94

Griffiths, Bruce, *Saunders Lewis* (Cardiff, 1989)

Hausen, Karin, 'The German nation's obligations to the heroes' widows of World War I', in Margaret Randolph Higonnet et al. (eds.), *Behind The Lines: Gender and the Two World Wars* (New Haven, 1987), pp. 126–40

Heffernan, Michael, 'For ever England: the Western Front and the politics of remembrance in Britain', *Ecumene*, II, No. 3 (1995), pp. 293–323

Henriques, Ursula R. Q. (ed.), *The Jews of South Wales: Historical Studies* (Cardiff, 1993)

Herbert, Trevor and Gareth Elwyn Jones (eds.), *Wales, 1880–1914* (Cardiff, 1988)

——, *Wales between the Wars* (Cardiff, 1990)

Homberger, E., 'The story of the Cenotaph', *Times Literary Supplement* (12 November 1976), pp. 1429–30

Hopkin, Deian, 'Patriots and pacifists in Wales, 1914–1918: the case of Capt. Lionel Lindsay and the Rev. T. E. Nicholas', *Llafur*, I, No. 3 (1974), pp. 132–46

Hughes, Clive, 'The new armies', in Ian F. W. Beckett and Keith Simpson (eds.), *A Nation in Arms* (Manchester, 1985), pp. 99–125

——, 'The Welsh Army Corps, 1914–15: shortages of khaki and basic equipment promote a "national" uniform', *Imperial War Museum Review*, I (1986), pp. 91–100

Hughes, Colin, *Mametz: Lloyd George's 'Welsh Army' at the Battle of the Somme* (Norwich, 1990)

Hughes, Les and John Dixon, *'Surrender Be Damned': A History of the 1/1st Battalion the Monmouthshire Regiment, 1914–18* (Caerphilly, 1995)

Huppauf, Bernd, 'War and death: the experience of the First World War', in M. Crouch and B. Huppauf (eds.), *Essays on Mortality* (Sydney, 1985), pp. 65–87

Hurst, Sidney, *The Silent Cities* (London, 1993)

Hyne, Anthony (ed.), *David Jones: A Fusilier at the Front* (Bridgend, 1995)

Ignatieff, Michael, 'Soviet war memorials', *History Workshop Journal*, XVII (1984), pp. 157–63

Inglis, K.S., 'Memorials of the Great War', *Australian Cultural History*, VI (1987), pp. 5–17

——, 'The homecoming: the war memorial movement in Cambridge, England', *Journal of Contemporary History*, XXVII, No. 4 (1992), pp. 583–605

——, 'Men, women and war memorials: Anzac Australia', *Daedalus*, CXVI, No. 4 (1989), pp. 35–59

——, 'War memorials: ten questions for historians', *Guerres mondiales et conflits contemporains*, CLXVII (1992), pp. 5–21

——, 'World War One memorials in Australia', *Guerres mondiales et conflits contemporains*, CLXVII (1992), pp. 51–8

——, and Jock Phillips, 'War memorials in Australia and New Zealand: a comparative survey', in J. Rickard and P. Spearritt (eds.), *Packaging the Past? Public Histories*, special issue of *Australian Historical Studies*, XXIV, No. 96 (1991), pp. 179–91

Jackson, Alvin, 'Irish Unionist imagery, 1850–1920', in Eve Patten (ed.), *Returning to Ourselves* (Vol.2 of papers from the John Hewitt International Summer School, (Belfast, 1995), pp. 344–59)

Jones, Aled, *Press, Politics and Society: A History of Journalism in Wales* (Cardiff, 1993)

Jones, David, *In Parenthesis* (London, 1975)

Jones, Goronwy J., *Wales and the Quest for Peace* (Cardiff, 1969)

Jones, R. Merfyn, *The North Wales Quarrymen, 1874–1922* (Cardiff, 1982)

Kertzer, David I., *Ritual, Politics, and Power* (New Haven, 1988)

Kingsley Kent, Susan, *Making Peace: The Reconstruction of Gender in Interwar Britain* (Princeton, 1993)

——, 'Love and death: war and gender in Britain, 1914–1918', in Frans Coetzee and Marilyn Shevin-Coetzee (eds.), *Authority, Identity and the Social History of the Great War* (Oxford, 1995), pp. 153–74

Koss, Stephen, *Nonconformity in British Politics* (Hamden, Conn., 1975)

Laidlaw, Roger, 'The Gresford disaster in popular memory', *Llafur*, VI, No. 4 (1995), pp.123-46

Leed, Eric J., *No Man's Land: Combat and Identity in World War I* (Cambridge, 1979)

Lieven, Michael, *Senghennydd: The Universal Pit Village, 1890–1930* (Llandysul, 1994)

Lloyd, Tecwyn, 'Welsh public opinion and the First World War', *Planet*, X (February/March 1972), pp. 25–37

——, 'Welsh literature and the First World War', *Planet*, XI (May 1972), pp. 17–23

Lloyd, W. G., *Roll of Honour* (Cwmbran, 1995)

Longley, Edna, 'The Rising, the Somme and Irish memory', in Mairin Ni Dhonnchadha and Theo Morgan (eds.), *Revising the Rising* (Londonderry, 1991)

Longworth, Philip, *The Unending Vigil: A History of the Commonwealth War Graves Commission, 1917–1984* (London, 1985)

MacCannell, D., 'The Vietnam Memorial in Washington, DC', in *Empty Meeting Grounds* (London, 1992), pp. 280–2

McCarthy, Chris, *The Somme: The Day by Day Account* (London, 1993)

McIntyre, Colin, *Monuments of War: How to Read a War Memorial* (London, 1990)

MacKenzie, John M., *Propaganda and Empire: The Manipulation of British Public Opinion, 1880–1960* (Manchester, 1984)

Maclean, C., and J. Phillips, *The Sorrow and the Pride: New Zealand War Memorials* (Wellington, NZ, 1990)

Mansfield, N., 'Class conflict and village war memorials, 1914–24', *Rural History*, VI, No. 1 (1995), pp. 67–87

Marden, Major-General Sir Thomas, *The History of the Welch Regiment*, vol. 2: *1914–1918* (Cardiff, 1932)

Marwick, Arthur, *The Deluge* (London, 1991)

May, Edward, 'Charles Stanton and the limits to "Patriotic" Labour', *Welsh History Review*, XVIII, No. 3 (June 1997), pp. 483–508

Mayo, J. M., *War Memorials as Political Landscape: The American Experience and Beyond* (New York, 1988)

Morgan, Dennis, *The Cardiff Story* (Cowbridge, 1991)

Morgan, Kenneth O. (ed.), *Lloyd George Family Letters, 1885–1936* (Cardiff and London, 1973)

——, 'The New Liberalism and the challenge of Labour: the Welsh experience, 1885–1929', *Welsh History Review*, VI, No. 3 (1973), pp. 288–312

——, 'Peace movements in Wales, 1899–1945', *Welsh History Review*, X, No. 3 (1981), pp. 398–430

——, 'Post-war reconstruction in Wales, 1918 and 1945', in J. M. Winter (ed.), *The Working Class in Modern British History: Essays in Honour of Henry Pelling* (Cambridge, 1983), pp. 82–98

——, *Rebirth of a Nation: Wales 1880–1980* (Oxford, 1990)

——, *Wales in British Politics, 1868–1922* (Cardiff, 1991)

Morgan, Prys, and David Thomas, *Wales: The Shaping of a Nation* (Newton Abbot, 1984)

Moriarty, Catherine, 'Christian iconography and First World War memorials', *Imperial War Museum Review*, VI (1992), pp. 63–75

——, 'The absent dead and figurative First World War memorials', *Transactions of the Ancient Monuments Society*, XXXIX (1995), pp. 7–40

——, 'Private grief and public remembrance: British First World War memorials' in

Martin Evans and Ken Lunn (eds.), *War and Memory in the Twentieth Century* (Oxford, 1997), pp. 125–42

Mosse, George L., *The Nationalization of the Masses* (New York, 1975)

——, *Fallen Soldiers. Reshaping the Memory of the World Wars* (New York, 1990)

Nora, Pierre, 'Between memory and history: les lieux de mémoire', *Representations*, XXVI (1989), pp. 7–25

Officers Died in the Great War, 1914–1919 (Polsted, 1988 edn)

O'Leary, Paul, 'Anti-Irish riots in Wales, 1826–1882', *Llafur*, V, No. 4 (1991), pp. 27–36

Phillips, Gervase, 'Dai Bach Y Soldiwr: Welsh soldiers in the British Army 1914–1918', *Llafur*, VI, No. 2 (1993), pp. 94–105

Prost, Antoine, 'Mémoires locales et mémoires nationales: les monuments de 1914–1918 en France', *Guerres mondiales et conflits contemporains*, CLXVII (Paris, 1992), pp. 41–50

Rees, D. Ben, *Chapels in the Valley* (Upton, 1975)

Richards, Frank, *Old Soldiers Never Die* (Sleaford, 1994)

Richards, John (ed.), *Wales on the Western Front* (Cardiff, 1994)

Robbins, Keith, *Nineteenth Century Britain: Integration and Diversity* (Oxford, 1995)

Roberts, G. D., *Witness these Letters* (Denbigh, 1983)

Roberts, Kate, *Feet in Chains: a novel by Kate Roberts*. Trans. Idwal Walters and John Idris Jones (Cardiff, 1977)

——, *The World of Kate Roberts: Selected Stories 1925–1981*. Trans. Joseph P. Clancy (Philadelphia, 1991)

Robin, Ron, ' "Footholds in Europe": the aesthetics and politics of American war cemeteries in western Europe', *Journal of American Studies*, XXIX, No. 1 (1995), pp. 55–72

Roderick, Alan, *The Newport Kaleidoscope* (Newport, 1994)

Saunders Jones, Mair, Ned Thomas and Harri Pritchard Jones (eds.), *Saunders Lewis: Letters to Margaret Gilcriest* (Cardiff, 1993)

Shipley, R., *To Mark Our Place: A History of Canadian War Memorials* (Toronto, 1987)

Silsoe, Lord, *Sixty Years a Welsh Territorial* (Llandysul, 1976)

Simkins, Peter, *Kitchener's Army: The Raising of the New Armies, 1914–16* (Manchester, 1988)

Smith, Dai, *Aneurin Bevan and the World of South Wales* (Cardiff, 1993)

Sola Pinto, V. de, *The City that Shone: An Autobiography (1985–1922)* (London, 1969)

Soldiers Died in the Great War, 1914–1919: The Welch Regiment (Polsted, 1988)

Stallworthy, Jon, *Survivors' Songs in Welsh Poetry* (Cardiff, 1982)

Stamp, Gavin, *Silent Cities* (London, 1977)

Stead, Peter, 'Working-class leadership in south Wales, 1900–1920', *Welsh History Review*, VI, No. 3 (1973), pp. 329–53

——, 'The town that had come of age: Barry, 1918–1939', in Donald Moore (ed.), *Barry: The Centenary Book* (Barry, 1984)

Stonelake, Edmund, *The Autobiography of Edmund Stonelake*, ed. A. Mor-O'Brien (Mid Glamorgan Education Committee, 1981)

Strange, Keith, *Wales and the First World War* (Mid Glamorgan County Supplies Department, n.d.)

——, 'Welsh images of the Great War: a documentary history of the Great War' (unpublished)

Taylor, A. J. P. (ed.), *Lloyd George: A Diary by Frances Stevenson* (London, 1971)

Taylor, Margaret S., *County Borough of Merthyr Tydfil: Fifty Years a Borough, 1905–1955* (Merthyr Tydfil, 1956)

Thomas, Myfanwy, *One of these Fine Days* (Manchester, 1982)

Thomas, R. G., *Edward Thomas: A Portrait* (Oxford, 1985)

Trow, A. H. and D. J. A. Brown, *A Short History of the University College of South Wales and Monmouthshire* (Cardiff, 1933)

Turner, V., *The Ritual Process* (London, 1969)

——, *Dramas, Fields and Metaphors* (Ithaca, NY, 1974)

Wagner-Pacifini, R., and B. Schwartz, 'The Vietnam Veterans Memorial: commemorating a difficult past', *American Journal of Sociology*, XCVII (1991), pp. 376–420

Waites, Bernard, 'The effect of the First World War on class and status in England, 1919–20', *Journal of Contemporary History*, XI, No. 1 (1976), pp. 27–48

——, *A Class Society at War: England, 1914–1918* (Oxford, 1987)

Walter, T., 'War grave pilgrimage', in I. Reader and T. Walter (eds.), *Pilgrimage in Popular Culture* (London, 1993), pp. 63–91

Ward, Stephen R., 'Great Britain: land fit for heroes lost', in S. R. Ward (ed.), *The War Generation: Veterans of the First World War* (New York, 1975)

Warner, W. L., *The Living and the Dead* (Hamden, Conn., 1975)

Whittick, Arnold, *War Memorials* (London, 1946)

Wilkinson, Alan, *The Church of England and the First World War* (London, 1978)

Williams, Chris, *Democratic Rhondda: Politics and Society, 1885–1951* (Cardiff, 1996)

Williams, Gerwyn, *Tir Neb: Rhyddiaith Gymraeg a'r Rhyfel Byd Cyntaf* (Cardiff, 1996)

Williams, Gwyn A., *The Welsh in their History* (London, 1982)

——, *When Was Wales?* (London, 1991)

Williams, J. Gwynn, *The University College of North Wales: Foundations, 1884–1927* (Cardiff, 1985)

Williams, John, *Digest of Welsh Historical Statistics*, Vol. 1 (Cardiff, 1985)

Williams, R., and D. Jones, *The Cruel Inheritance: Life and Death in the Coalfields of Glamorgan* (Pontypool, 1990)

Williamson, Henry, *The Wet Flanders Plain* (Norwich, 1987)

Winter, Denis, *Death's Men* (London, 1979)

Winter, Jay, *The Great War and the British People* (London, 1986)

——, 'Catastrophe and culture: recent trends in the historiography of the First World War', *Journal of Modern History*, LXIV (1992), pp. 525–32

——, *The Experience of World War One* (London, 1994)

——, *Sites of Memory, Sites of Mourning. The Great War in European Cultural History* (Cambridge, 1995)

——, 'Communities in mourning', in Frans Coetzee and Marilyn Shevin-Coetzee (eds.), *Authority, Identity and the Social History of the Great War* (Oxford, 1995), pp. 325–55.

Wootton, Graham, *The Official History of the British Legion* (London, 1956)

——, *The Politics of Influence* (London, 1963)

5. THESES AND DISSERTATIONS

Barr, Niall J. A., 'Service not self: the British Legion 1921–1939' (Ph.D., University of St Andrews, 1994)

Bell, Gilbert T., 'Monuments to the fallen: Scottish war memorials of the Great War' (Ph.D., University of Strathclyde, 1993)

Cayford, J. M., 'The Western Mail 1869–1914: a study in the politics and management of a provincial newspaper' (Ph.D., University of Wales, 1992)

Connelly, M. L., 'The commemoration of the Great War in the City and East London, 1916–1939' (Ph.D., University of London, 1995)

Croll, Andrew J., 'Civilising the urban: popular culture, public space and urban meaning, Merthyr, c.1870–1914' (Ph.D., University of Wales, 1997)

Hughes, Clive, 'Army recruitment in Gwynedd, 1914–1916' (M.A., University of Wales, 1983)

King, Alexander M., 'The politics of meaning in the commemoration of the First World War in Britain, 1914–1939' (Ph.D., University of London, 1993)

Lloyd, David, 'Tourism, pilgrimage and the commemoration of the Great War in Great Britain, Australia and Canada, 1919–1939' (Ph.D., University of Cambridge, 1994)

May, Edward Charles, 'A question of control: social and industrial relations in the south Wales coalfield and the crisis of post-war reconstruction, 1914–1922' (Ph.D., University of Wales, 1995)

Moriarty, Catherine, 'Narrative and the absent body: mechanisms of meaning in First World War Memorials' (Ph.D., University of Sussex, 1995)

O'Leary, Paul, 'Immigration and integration: a study of the Irish in Wales, 1798–1922' (Ph.D., University of Wales, 1989)

Phillips, Gervase, 'The Welsh soldier in the First World War' (M.Phil., University of Wales, 1991)

Quinn, Desmond F., 'Voluntary recruitment in Glamorgan, 1914–1916' (M.A., University of Wales, 1994)

Stryker, Laurinda S., 'Languages of sacrifice and suffering in England in the First World War' (Ph.D., University of Cambridge, 1992)

INDEX

INDEX